Contents

EIGHTH EDITION

STANDARDS OF PRACTICE HANDBOOK

1999

Association for
Investment Management
and Research

To obtain the AIMR *Product Catalog*, contact:
AIMR, P.O. Box 3668, Charlottesville, Virginia 22903, U.S.A.
Phone 434-951-5499; Fax 434-951-5262; E-mail info@aimr.org or
visit AIMR's World Wide Web site at
www.aimr.org
to view the AIMR publications list.

ISBN 0-935015-39-6
Printed in the United States of America
August 1999

Preface

The purpose of this *Handbook* is to provide up-to-date guidance to the people who grapple with real ethical problems in the investment profession, where theory meets practice and ethics gain meaning. This *Handbook* is intended for a diverse and increasingly global audience: AIMR members and compliance officers navigating ambiguous ethical situations, supervisors and subordinates determining the nature of their responsibilities to one another and to the investing public, and candidates preparing for the Chartered Financial Analyst examinations.

Ethics in the Investment Profession

Years ago, before a true investment profession existed, capable, honest practitioners had no easy way to distinguish themselves from the fly-by-night charlatans who left unsavory schemes and scandals in their wake. Finance was stuck at the margins of public acceptability. Several early practitioners recognized the benefits that self-organization could have in gaining public trust. With the recognition that ethical integrity is strongest when it is voluntarily embraced, not imposed from outside, the early practitioners laid the foundations for turning the investment business into the investment profession. AIMR is firmly committed to this tradition, and for nearly forty years, the CFA® designation has set apart those investment professionals who have mastered the arts of the investment profession and committed themselves to the highest ethical standards.

Good ethics will always be a work in progress, as reflected in the fact that this publication represents the eighth edition of the *Handbook*. Since first taking shape in the 1960s, the Code of Ethics and Standards of Professional Conduct have been regularly refined and updated to promote ethical conduct and address new public concerns. As the investment profession evolves, the list of ethical issues lengthens, from personal investing and soft dollars to misleading advice and the need to separate objective analysis from company advocacy. And new challenges are always emerging. As economies become more sophisticated and interconnected, new investment opportunities are constantly being created, along with new financial instruments to make the most of those opportunities for clients. But although the investment world has become a far more complex place since this handbook was first published, distinguishing right from wrong remains the paramount principle of the Code of Ethics and Standards of Professional Conduct.

Ethics Is Good Business

Ethics is a necessary component of professional knowledge. Investment professionals, like doctors, lawyers, and teachers, are in a position of trust. People entrust their physical health to doctors and their financial well-being to investment professionals. In any profession, there must be public confidence that its practitioners are using their knowledge and expertise to benefit clients. Conduct that suggests otherwise can erode public trust and cause great harm to the profession.

Investment professionals with solid ethical credentials not only save money on the problems they avoid but also gain from the competitive advantage a reputation for integrity brings. This "reputational capital" accrues at a very high compounded rate of return. Relationships with existing clients are enhanced and new clients are attracted. Ethics is good for business.

Setting High Standards

The tradition represented by AIMR has been instrumental in advancing high professional standards in North America and, increasingly, the world. A few facts tell the story. In 1963, 268 individuals in the United States and Canada were the first to earn the right to use the CFA charter. Today, more than 24,000 investment professionals from more than 55 countries have earned the CFA designation, with more on the way to join their ranks. Over 58,500 candidates were enrolled to take one of the three levels of the CFA examinations in June of 1999. One-third of those candidates resided in 75 countries outside North America. The CFA designation truly sets the global standard for investment integrity.

An important goal of AIMR is to ensure that the organization and its members are globally recognized as representing and promoting the highest ethical standards, and the organization has taken the initiative in developing global standards for its members and for the firms that employ its members. The Code of Ethics and Standards of Professional Conduct are the bedrock of this project. Upon this foundation, AIMR has developed four additional distinct sets of professional standards: the AIMR Performance Presentation Standards℠; the Global Investment Performance Standards℠; the AIMR Soft Dollar Standards; and the AIMR Personal Investing Task Force Report.

AIMR was an active participant in the formulation of the International Code of Ethics and Standards of Professional Conduct adopted in 1998 by the International Council of Investment Associations. In addition, AIMR assisted the International Accounting Standards Committee in developing international accounting and financial disclosure standards. These activities are a logical extension of AIMR's mission to serve investors by promoting high ethical standards in the investment industry.

Because AIMR is a volunteer organization, its advocacy work relies to an extraordinary degree on the goodwill of its members to devote their time on the organization's behalf. Such goodwill is also in abundance among AIMR members acting in an individual capacity to extend ethical integrity. Setting corporate policies on ethics and standards of practice is perhaps the most important area in which members bring their energies to bear. Members also have an active role in the policy-making activities of governments, regulatory agencies, and other professional organizations on matters of ethics.

U.S. Supreme Court Justice Potter Stewart once remarked that ethics is "knowing the difference between what you have a right to do, and what is the right thing to do." Within this subtle observation is the essence of the task at hand. The law sets the benchmark for permissible behavior. If an activity is against the law, it is unethical, and AIMR members should always comply with applicable law. Members should also be aware that the laws and regulations of multiple countries may apply to securities trading in global markets. The mere fact that a particular course of action is legal, however, does not automatically make it ethical. Members of AIMR are held to a higher standard. AIMR's Code of Ethics affirms a set of principles that govern appropriate behavior. The Standards of Professional Conduct provide the minimum rules of conduct to which each member must adhere.

AIMR's Professional Conduct Program

A significant aspect of AIMR's efforts to promote and implement ethical standards is the Professional Conduct Program (PCP). The PCP's primary efforts in the area of ethics and professional conduct are to

- promote high standards of ethics and professional conduct globally;
- use newsletters, seminars, publications, and society programs to educate members on day-to-day ethical issues;
- increase ethical awareness within the investment profession by advocating adoption of the Code of Ethics and Standards of Professional Conduct by all investment management and research organizations;
- illustrate how to apply the Code and Standards in daily investment practices;
- take a leadership role in the development of a globally accepted code of ethics and standards of professional conduct;
- bring disciplinary action against members who violate the Code and Standards.

Code and Standards. AIMR became the primary professional organization for securities analysts, investment managers, and others related to the investment decision-making process on January 1, 1990, when the Financial Analysts Federation (FAF) and the Institute of Chartered Financial Analysts (ICFA) combined. One of AIMR's first actions was to adopt the Code and Standards that the FAF and the ICFA had long shared. AIMR enforces the Code and Standards, and responsibility for practicing within the context of the Code and Standards is assumed by AIMR members, CFA charterholders, and candidates in the CFA Program. In 1999, the FAF and ICFA were fully integrated into AIMR.

Today, the responsibility for formulating and reviewing the Code and Standards rests with AIMR's Standards and Policy Committee. The SPC draws its membership from a broad spectrum of organizations in the securities field, including brokers, investment advisors, banks, and insurance companies. In most instances, the SPC members also have important supervisory responsibilities within their firms. The SPC scrutinizes the Code and Standards on a continuing basis for potential areas of improvement. This scrutiny, initiated by dedicated individual members of the SPC and AIMR staff members, inevitably results in proposals to amend the Standards and update the *Handbook*. Over time, AIMR's Code of Ethics and Standards of Professional Conduct have evolved to meet the needs and challenges of the ever-changing investment industry.

In 1999, the AIMR Board of Governors revised the wording of two of the Standards of Professional Conduct, Standard II(A) and Standard II(B), which address proper use of the CFA designation and misconduct involving the CFA Program. These revisions do not add any new duties and only clarify members' existing responsibilities.

Enforcement of the AIMR Code and Standards. AIMR's Professional Conduct Program is based on the principle of self-disclosure. Each AIMR member, CFA charterholder, and candidate in the CFA Program must sign an annual Professional Conduct Statement. By posing several specific questions regarding members' professional activities, the Professional Conduct Statement requires every member to state whether their professional conduct has been challenged in the past year. In addition to the Professional Conduct Statement, information received by AIMR relating to an individual's professional conduct, such as legal or regulatory proceedings or any complaints against a member, may initiate a professional conduct inquiry. Members are encouraged to report possible violations of the Code and Standards to the Professional Conduct Program.

AIMR's Bylaws and Rules of Procedure for Proceedings Related to Professional Conduct (Rules of Procedure) form the basic structure for enforcing the Code and Standards (see Appendix A). The Rules of Procedure are guided by the following principles: (1) fair process to the member and (2) confidentiality of proceedings. Under the Bylaws and

Rules, the AIMR Board of Governors maintains oversight and responsibility for the PCP through the Disciplinary Review Committee (DRC) and Standards and Policy Committee (SPC). The DRC is responsible for the enforcement of the Code and Standards, and the SPC is responsible for ethics education.

AIMR's Professional Conduct Program staff, under the supervision of AIMR's Designated Officer, conducts professional conduct inquiries. Anyone can write the PCP with a complaint regarding the professional conduct of any member, and the PCP will initiate an inquiry into the member's conduct to determine whether a violation of the Code or Standards has occurred. When an inquiry is initiated, the PCP conducts an investigation that may include a written explanation from the member; interviewing the member, complaining parties, and third parties; and collecting documents and records in support of its investigation. The Designated Officer, upon reviewing the material obtained during the investigation, may either dismiss the complaint, issue a cautionary letter, or institute proceedings to discipline the member.

If the Designated Officer determines that disciplinary action is appropriate, he or she is authorized to take the following sanctions, in increasing order of severity: private censure, public censure, suspension of membership, revocation of membership, and in the case of CFA charterholders, suspension or revocation of the CFA designation. Suspension or revocation of membership and/or the CFA designation may have significant consequences, including condemnation by the sanctioned members' peers and possible ramifications for employment. Candidates enrolled in the CFA Program who are found to have violated the Code and Standards may be suspended from further participation in the CFA program.

An AIMR member will be summarily suspended from membership and/or use of the CFA designation if the member: (1) is convicted, pleads guilty, or consents to a crime that is defined as a felony, or its equivalent, under the laws of the convicting jurisdiction; (2) is barred from the investment business; (3) fails to cooperate with AIMR in its investigation of the member's conduct; or (4) fails to complete, sign, and return to AIMR the required annual Professional Conduct Statement.

Appropriate notices of disciplinary action are published in the *AIMR Exchange* newsletter, which is sent to all members. When an AIMR member has been publicly sanctioned, AIMR may provide the sanctioned member's primary regulator(s) with copies of the notice of disciplinary action, the Stipulation Agreement, and/or the hearing panel report.

AIMR's Professional Conduct Program also enforces stringent professional conduct admissions criteria for individuals who wish to apply for AIMR membership or to enroll in the CFA program.

Ethics Education. In addition to enforcing the Code and Standards, the Professional Conduct Program strives to communicate AIMR's core values of ethics, professionalism, and education to AIMR members, employers, the investment profession, and the constituencies they serve. The PCP uses a variety of tools to meet this goal, including

- responding to inquiries from members and the investing public regarding ethics and professional conduct;
- regularly publishing professional conduct articles and notices in the *AIMR Exchange* newsletter;
- publishing the *AIMR Advocate*;
- drafting and promulgating a self-administered ethics exam for members and nonmembers to test their ethical awareness;
- commenting on a variety of proposals from regulators dealing with professional conduct;
- conducting presentations for societies and other groups of professionals on ethics and professional conduct;
- contributing to and editing the *Standards of Practice Casebook* (first edition, Charlottesville, VA, 1996);
- supporting the ethics/professional conduct portion of the CFA Program curriculum.

Standards of Practice Handbook. The *Standards of Practice Handbook* (SOPH) is the fundamental element of AIMR's ethics education effort and the primary resource for guidance in interpreting and implementing the Code and Standards. This *Handbook* is the cornerstone used in building the ethics Body of Knowledge.

The *Standards of Practice Handbook* seeks to educate members on how to apply the Code and Standards to their professional lives and thereby benefit their clients, employers, and the investing public in general. The *Handbook* explains the purpose of the Standards and how they apply in a variety of situations. The text discusses and amplifies each Standard and suggests procedures to prevent violations. The names contained in the examples provided in the "Application of the Standard" sections of each chapter are fictional and are not meant to refer to any actual person or entity. Unless otherwise stated, individuals in each example are AIMR members and/or holders of the Chartered Financial Analyst designation. Because factual circumstances vary so widely and often involve gray areas, the explanatory material and examples are not intended to be all inclusive.

Many situations described in the *Handbook* involve Standards that have legal counterparts; members are, therefore, strongly urged to discuss with their supervisors and legal and compliance departments the content of the Code and Standards and the members' general obligations under the Code and Standards.

Although the origin of the Code and Standards can be traced to the 1960s, the first edition of the *Handbook* was not published until 1982. Since then, AIMR has published seven revised editions. As with previous editions, this *Handbook* contains chapters that discuss each of the Standards and all their subsections. To reflect AIMR's growing global membership, this edition of the *Handbook* includes discussion and examples of a more global scope than in past editions. In addition, to reflect the growing professional diversity of AIMR membership, the SPC has added new applications and interpretations relevant to diverse disciplines of the investment industry, such as investment banking.

The seventh edition of the *Handbook* introduced a new section titled "Topical Studies." The intent of the topical studies is to cover extensively issues of significant interest to our members and to provide as much detailed guidance about an issue as is practical. Each topical study cross-references one or more appropriate standards. The studies are also intended, in recognition of the diversity of AIMR membership, to discuss many facets of the investment profession.

The eighth edition adds two new topical studies on the subjects of corporate governance and soft dollars. Each of the topical studies is the work of a special subcommittee or task force dedicated to establishing standards for investment professionals in a particular area. The topical studies do not establish additional requirements for members; instead, they set recommended procedures or standards for members to follow to achieve best practices in these areas.

Acknowledgments

A debt of gratitude is due to the many individuals who have collaborated on this and previous editions of the *Standards of Practice Handbook*. Over the years, the group that shepherded each edition to publication has gone under successive names: the Investment Analysis Standards Board; followed by the Professional Ethics and Responsibility Committee; and currently, the Standards and Policy Subcommittee of the Professional Standards and Policy Committee. Below is a list of the current and past members of those committees who generously donated their time and energy to these committees:

Theodore Aronson, CFA
Brierly W. Anderson, CFA*
Carl L.A. Beckers, CFA*
David W. Bodenberg, CFA
DeWitt Bowman, CFA
O.Whitfield Broome, Jr.
William A. Cornish, CFA
Edward H. Cronin, CFA
Patricia Doumas, CFA
Herbert H. Frost, CFA
Michael Even, CFA
Gay P. Gervin, CFA
William S. Gray III, CFA
Richard P. Halverson, CFA
John E. Hore, CFA
Douglas R. Hughes, CFA*
Julianne C. Iwesen-Niemann, CFA
William Jahnke
Samuel B. Jones, Jr., CFA*
William Koenig, CFA
James LaFleur, CFA
Richard W. Lambourne, CFA
Douglas Lempereur, CFA
Theodore R. Lilley, CFA
Charles Lovejoy, CFA
William R. Ludwick, CFA
John E. Mills, CFA
Bernadette B. Murphy
John Nagorniak, CFA
Ian Rossa O'Reilly, CFA
Carol Plucinnik-Allen, CFA
Claude N. Rosenberg
Evan Schulman
Paul Van Schyndel, CFA
Marion Smith
Nancy C. Smith, CFA
Burton M. Siegel, CFA
Michael L. Sjostrom, CFA
Anthony Spare, CFA
Nancy E. Stroker, CFA
Linda H. Taufen, CFA
Kenneth Trider, CFA
Heidi L. Whitfield, CFA

*denotes former chairperson

Copious thanks are also due to the past and present staff of the Association for Investment Management and Research, and in particular, Thomas A. Bowman, CFA, Michael S. Caccese, Jonathan J. Stokes, Mildred M. Hermann, and its past adviser, John G. Gillis.

A Final Word

The Code and Standards are available directly from AIMR and are also available on AIMR's World Wide Web home page on the Internet (http://www.aimr.org). The *Handbook* is available to all AIMR members on AIMR's web site, and copies of the *Handbook* can be ordered from PBD at 1-800-789-2467.

As noted, the development and interpretation of the Code and Standards is an evolving process and will be subject to continuing refinement. In time, this edition is likely to be superseded by another.

The committee hopes this eighth edition will be enlightening and useful in the AIMR professional standards program and in the professional practice of members.

The SPC recognizes that the presence of any set of ethical standards can create a false sense of security unless the documents are fully understood, enforced, and made a meaningful part of everyday professional activities. The *Standards of Practice Handbook* is intended to provide a useful frame of reference that lends substance to the understanding of professional behavior in the investment decision-making process.

This book cannot cover every contingency or circumstance, and it does not attempt to do so. In the final analysis, there is no substitute for integrity.

Standards and Policy Committee
Guy G. Rutherfurd, Jr., CFA, Chair

The Code of Ethics

Members of the Association for Investment Management and Research shall:

- Act with integrity, competence, dignity, and in an ethical manner when dealing with the public, clients, prospects, employers, employees, and fellow members.
- Practice and encourage others to practice in a professional and ethical manner that will reflect credit on members and their profession.
- Strive to maintain and improve their competence and the competence of others in the profession.
- Use reasonable care and exercise independent professional judgment.

Statement of
The Standards Of Professional Conduct

Standard I: Fundamental Responsibilities

Members shall:

A. Maintain knowledge of and comply with all applicable laws, rules, and regulations (including AIMR's Code of Ethics and Standards of Professional Conduct) of any government, governmental agency, regulatory organization, licensing agency, or professional association governing the members' professional activities.

B. Not knowingly participate or assist in any violation of such laws, rules, or regulations.

Standard II: Relationships with and Responsibilities to the Profession

A. Use of Professional Designation.

1. AIMR members may reference their membership only in a dignified and judicious manner. The use of the reference may be accompanied by an accurate explanation of the requirements that have been met to obtain membership in these organizations.

2. Those who have earned the right to use the Chartered Financial Analyst designation may use the marks "Chartered Financial Analyst" or "CFA" and are encouraged to do so, but only in a proper, dignified, and judicious manner. The use of the designation may be accompanied by an accurate explanation of the requirements that have been met to obtain the right to use the designation.

3. Candidates in the CFA Program, as defined in the AIMR Bylaws, may reference their participation in the CFA Program, but the reference must clearly state that an individual is a candidate in the CFA Program and cannot imply that the candidate has achieved any type of partial designation.

B. Professional Misconduct.

1. Members shall not engage in any professional conduct involving dishonesty, fraud, deceit, or misrepresentation or commit any act that reflects adversely on their honesty, trustworthiness, or professional competence.

2. Members and candidates shall not engage in any conduct or commit any act that compromises the integrity of the CFA designation or the integrity or validity of the examinations leading to the award of the right to use the CFA designation.

C. **Prohibition against Plagiarism.** Members shall not copy or use, in substantially the same form as the original, material prepared by another without acknowledging and identifying the name of the author, publisher, or source of such material. Members may use, without acknowledgment, factual information published by recognized financial and statistical reporting services or similar sources.

Standard III: Relationships with and Responsibilities to the Employer

A. **Obligation to Inform Employer of Code and Standards.** Members shall:

1. Inform their employer in writing, through their direct supervisor, that they are obligated to comply with the Code and Standards and are subject to disciplinary sanctions for violations thereof.

2. Deliver a copy of the Code and Standards to their employer if the employer does not have a copy.

B. **Duty to Employer.** Members shall not undertake any independent practice that could result in compensation or other benefit in competition with their employer unless they obtain written consent from both their employer and the persons or entities for whom they undertake independent practice.

C. **Disclosure of Conflicts to Employer.** Members shall:

1. Disclose to their employer all matters, including beneficial ownership of securities or other investments, that reasonably could be expected to interfere with their duty to their employer or ability to make unbiased and objective recommendations.

2. Comply with any prohibitions on activities imposed by their employer if a conflict of interest exists.

D. **Disclosure of Additional Compensation Arrangements.** Members shall disclose to their employer in writing all monetary compensation or other benefits that they receive for their services that are in addition to compensation or benefits conferred by a member's employer.

E. **Responsibilities of Supervisors.** Members with supervisory responsibility, authority, or the ability to influence the conduct of others shall exercise reasonable supervision over those subject to their supervision or authority to prevent any violation of applicable statutes, regulations, or provisions of the Code and Standards. In so doing, members are entitled to rely on reasonable procedures designed to detect and prevent such violations.

Standard IV. Relationships with and Responsibilities to Clients and Prospects

A. **Investment Process.**

A.1 **Reasonable Basis and Representations.** Members shall:

a. Exercise diligence and thoroughness in making investment recommendations or in taking investment actions.

b. Have a reasonable and adequate basis, supported by appropriate research and investigation, for such recommendations or actions.

c. Make reasonable and diligent efforts to avoid any material misrepresentation in any research report or investment recommendation.

d. Maintain appropriate records to support the reasonableness of such recommendations or actions.

A.2 **Research Reports.** Members shall:

a. Use reasonable judgment regarding the inclusion or exclusion of relevant factors in research reports.

b. Distinguish between facts and opinions in research reports.

c. Indicate the basic characteristics of the investment involved when preparing for public distribution a research report that is not directly related to a specific portfolio or client.

A.3 **Independence and Objectivity.** Members shall use reasonable care and judgment to achieve and maintain independence and objectivity in making investment recommendations or taking investment action.

B. **Interactions with Clients and Prospects.**

B.1 **Fiduciary Duties.** In relationships with clients, members shall use particular care in determining applicable fiduciary duty and shall comply with such duty as to those persons and interests to whom the duty is owed. Members must act for the benefit of their clients and place their clients' interests before their own.

B.2 Portfolio Investment Recommendations and Actions. Members shall:

a. Make a reasonable inquiry into a client's financial situation, investment experience, and investment objectives prior to making any investment recommendations and shall update this information as necessary, but no less frequently than annually, to allow the members to adjust their investment recommendations to reflect changed circumstances.

b. Consider the appropriateness and suitability of investment recommendations or actions for each portfolio or client. In determining appropriateness and suitability, members shall consider applicable relevant factors, including the needs and circumstances of the portfolio or client, the basic characteristics of the investment involved, and the basic characteristics of the total portfolio. Members shall not make a recommendation unless they reasonably determine that the recommendation is suitable to the client's financial situation, investment experience, and investment objectives.

c. Distinguish between facts and opinions in the presentation of investment recommendations.

d. Disclose to clients and prospects the basic format and general principles of the investment processes by which securities are selected and portfolios are constructed and shall promptly disclose to clients and prospects any changes that might significantly affect those processes.

B.3 Fair Dealing. Members shall deal fairly and objectively with all clients and prospects when disseminating investment recommendations, disseminating material changes in prior investment recommendations, and taking investment action.

B.4 Priority of Transactions. Transactions for clients and employers shall have priority over transactions in securities or other investments of which a member is the beneficial owner so that such personal transactions do not operate adversely to their clients' or employer's interests. If members make a recommendation regarding the purchase or sale of a security or other investment, they shall give their clients and employer adequate opportunity to act on the recommendation before acting on their own behalf. For purposes of the Code and Standards, a member is a "beneficial owner" if the member has

a. a direct or indirect pecuniary interest in the securities;

b. the power to vote or direct the voting of the shares of the securities or investments;

c. the power to dispose or direct the disposition of the security or investment.

B.5 Preservation of Confidentiality. Members shall preserve the confidentiality of information communicated by clients, prospects, or employers concerning matters within the scope of the client–member, prospect–member, or employer–member relationship unless the member receives information concerning illegal activities on the part of the client, prospect, or employer.

B.6 Prohibition against Misrepresentation. Members shall not make any statements, orally or in writing, that misrepresent

a. the services that they or their firms are capable of performing;

b. their qualifications or the qualifications of their firm;

c. the member's academic or professional credentials.

Members shall not make or imply, orally or in writing, any assurances or guarantees regarding any investment except to communicate accurate information regarding the terms of the investment instrument and the issuer's obligations under the instrument.

B.7 Disclosure of Conflicts to Clients and Prospects. Members shall disclose to their clients and prospects all matters, including beneficial ownership of securities or other investments, that reasonably could be expected to impair the member's ability to make unbiased and objective recommendations.

B.8 Disclosure of Referral Fees. Members shall disclose to clients and prospects any consideration or benefit received by the member or delivered to others for the recommendation of any services to the client or prospect.

Standard V. Relationships with and Responsibilities to the Investing Public

A. Prohibition against Use of Material Nonpublic Information. Members who possess material nonpublic information related to the value of a security shall not trade or cause others to trade in that security if such trading would breach a duty or if the information was misappropriated or relates to a tender offer. If members receive material nonpublic information in confidence, they shall not breach that confidence by trading or causing others to trade in securities to which such information relates. Members shall make reasonable efforts to achieve public dissemination of material nonpublic information disclosed in breach of a duty.

B. Performance Presentation.

1. Members shall not make any statements, orally or in writing, that misrepresent the investment performance that they or their firms have accomplished or can reasonably be expected to achieve.
2. If members communicate individual or firm performance information directly or indirectly to clients or prospective clients, or in a manner intended to be received by clients or prospective clients, members shall make every reasonable effort to assure that such performance information is a fair, accurate, and complete presentation of such performance.

Standard I: Fundamental Responsibilities

Members shall:

A. Maintain knowledge of and comply with all applicable laws, rules, and regulations (including AIMR's Code of Ethics and Standards of Professional Conduct) of any government, governmental agency, regulatory organization, licensing agency, or professional association governing the members' professional activities.

B. Not knowingly participate or assist in any violation of such laws, rules, or regulations.

Purpose and Scope of the Standard

The Standards of Professional Conduct cover many critical areas of the investment profession. However, because members engage in a wide variety of professional, financial, and/or business activities, the Code of Ethics and Standards of Professional Conduct cannot provide guidance for proper conduct in every circumstance. Standard I contains principles that apply to the general activities of members; Standards II–V address specific conduct. Standard I sets minimum standards of conduct in areas not specifically covered by Standards II–V by requiring members to comply with laws, rules, and regulations governing their conduct.

Standard I assists members in avoiding legal or ethical traps and violations of the Code and Standards. It also seeks to inculcate an ethical culture among members. Within their responsibilities to and relationships with the profession, the investment process, clients and prospects, and the public, members should always aspire to the highest ethical conduct. Therefore, although the text of Standards II–V is directed at setting the minimum standards of professional conduct, members are expected to aim higher.

Standard I(A) states the responsibility of AIMR members, holders of the Chartered Financial Analyst designation, and candidates in the CFA Program to comply with the laws and rules of governments, governmental agencies, and self-regulatory organizations. AIMR believes that a *minimum* level of professional responsibility and conduct dictates that members be aware of and comply with laws, rules, and regulations governing their conduct. In addition to complying with the law, members are to be aware of and comply with the requirements of the Code and the Standards as well as the laws and regulations of foreign jurisdictions. (The international application of the Code and Standards is outlined in **Exhibit 1**.) In general, members in all countries should comply at all times with the Code and

Exhibit 1. International Application of the Code and Standards

Members who practice in multiple jurisdictions may be subject to varied securities laws and regulations. **RULE OF THUMB:** If applicable law is more strict than the requirements of the Code and Standards, members, CFA charterholders, and candidates in the CFA Program must adhere to applicable law; otherwise, they must adhere to the Code and Standards. The following chart provides illustrations involving a member who may be subject to the securities laws and regulations of three different countries:

NL = no securities laws or regulations
LS = securities laws and regulations that are *less* strict than the Code and Standards
MS = securities laws and regulations that are *more* strict than the Code and Standards

Applicable Law	Duties	Explanation
Member resides in NL, does business in LS; LS law applies.	Member must adhere to the Code and Standards.	Because applicable law is less strict than the Code and Standards, the member must adhere to the Code and Standards.
Member resides in NL, does business in MS; MS law applies.	Member must adhere to the law of MS.	Because applicable law is more strict than the Code and Standards, member must adhere to the more strict applicable law.
Member resides in LS, does business in NL; LS law applies.	Member must adhere to the Code and Standards.	Because applicable law is less strict than the Code and Standards, the member must adhere to the Code and Standards.
Member resides in LS, does business in MS; MS law applies.	Member must adhere to the law of MS.	Because applicable law is more strict than the Code and Standards, the member must adhere to the more strict applicable law.
Member resides in LS, does business in NL; LS law applies, but it states that law of locality where business is conducted governs.	Member must adhere to the Code and Standards.	Because applicable law states that the law of the locality where the business is conducted governs and there is no local law, the member must adhere to the Code and Standards.
Member resides in LS, does business in MS; LS law applies, but it states that law of locality where business is conducted governs.	Member must adhere to the law of MS.	Because applicable law of the locality where the business is conducted governs and local law is more strict than the Code and Standards, the member must adhere to the more strict applicable law.

Exhibit 1. (Continued)

Applicable Law	Duties	Explanation
Member resides in MS, does business in LS; MS law applies.	Member must adhere to the law of MS.	Because applicable law is more strict than the Code and Standards, member must adhere to the more strict applicable law.
Member resides in MS, does business in LS; MS law applies, but it states that law of locality where business is conducted governs.	Member must adhere to the Code and Standards.	Because applicable law states that the law of the locality where the business is conducted governs and local law is less strict than the Code and Standards, the member must adhere to the Code and Standards.
Member resides in MS, does business in LS with a client who is a citizen of LS; MS law applies, but it states that the law of the client's home country governs.	Member must adhere to the Code and Standards.	Because applicable law states that the law of the client's home country is less strict than the Code and Standards, the member must adhere to the Code and Standards.
Member resides in MS, does business in LS with a client who is a citizen of MS; MS law applies, but it states that the law of the client's home country governs.	Member must adhere to the law of MS.	Because applicable law states that the law of the client's home country governs and the law of the client's home country is more strict than the Code and Standards, the member must adhere to the more strict applicable law.

Standards. A member must adhere to applicable law, however, if the legal requirements are more strict than those of the Code and Standards.

Some members may live, work, and provide investment services to clients living in a country that has no securities laws or has securities laws that are less strict than the Code and Standards. Members cannot engage in conduct that constitutes a violation of the Code and Standards but that may otherwise be legally acceptable in their country. In the absence of any applicable securities laws or when the Code and Standards impose a higher degree of responsibility than applicable securities laws and regulations, members must adhere to the Code and Standards.

The more interesting question arises when members live in a country with securities laws that are less strict than the Code and Standards but the members provide investment services to persons residing in countries with more strict laws and regulations. Should the member adhere to the Code and Standards or the laws and regulations of the country that are more strict than the Code and Standards? The answer depends on which law governs the member's conduct. In this case, assuming that the law of the client's country preempts the law of the member's country, the member must comply with the laws and regulations of the client's country because those laws are more strict than the Code and Standards.

A member might live in a country with securities laws that are more strict than the Code and Standards but provide investment services to clients residing in a country with lenient securities laws. If the client's country laws control the member's activities but are less strict than the Code and Standards, the member must adhere to the Code and Standards.

What law applies will depend on the particular facts and circumstances of each case. For instance, in the United States, the Securities and Exchange Commission (SEC) analyzes each case using a "conduct" and "effects" test when applying the Investment Advisers Act of 1940 (Advisers Act). When a sizable amount of advisory services takes place in the United States or when the advisory services have effects in the United States, the Advisers Act applies. Thus, when a registered advisor, foreign or domestic, deals with clients in the United States and a sizable amount of advisory services is likely to take place in the United States, the Advisers Act applies because significant conduct and effects will occur in the United States. When a registered advisor deals with a client outside the United States but a sizable amount of advisory services are likely to take place in the United States, the Advisers Act applies. In general, the SEC will not apply the Advisers Act to a foreign advisor's dealings with non-U.S. clients, but when a foreign advisor's dealings with non-U.S. clients operate to defraud its U.S. clients, such as when the advisor is "front-running" trades of U.S. clients, the Advisers Act applies because the acts affect a U.S. client.

When either a foreign or domestic advisor is multinational—that is, has offices outside its foreign or domestic base—application of the Advisers Act depends on whether a sizable amount of advisory service takes place or has a significant effect in the United States. If the effect in the United States is sufficiently significant or the conduct significantly important, the SEC will assert regulatory jurisdiction under the Advisers Act. Because of the fact-specific nature of these issues, the SEC addresses questionable matters on a case-by-case basis.

Members should ensure that they have appropriate knowledge of the laws and regulations of all countries in which they trade securities, provide investment advice, analyze corporate securities, or provide other investment services. When in doubt in a particular case, a member should seek the advice of counsel concerning the legal requirements.

Standard I(B) states the responsibility of AIMR members, CFA charterholders, and candidates in the CFA Program to avoid participating in legal and ethical violations committed by others. Standard I(B) applies when members know, or should know, that their conduct may contribute to a violation of applicable laws, rules, regulations, or the Code and Standards.

Members are responsible for violations they *knowingly* participate in or assist. Although members are presumed to know all applicable laws, rules, and regulations, AIMR acknowledges that members may not recognize violations if they are not aware of all the facts giving rise to the violations.

The Code and Standards do not require that members report legal violations to the appropriate governmental or regulatory organizations, but such disclosure may be prudent in certain circumstances.

Application of the Standard

Example 1. Allen works for a brokerage firm and is responsible for an underwriting of securities. A company official gives her information indicating that the financial statements filed with the registration statement may overstate the issuer's earnings. She seeks the advice of the brokerage firm's general counsel.

> *Comment*: Because she sought advice of counsel, she can defend herself against allegations that she violated Standard I as long as she (1) has reason to believe that her attorney is both competent to render the advice sought and unbiased and (2) she follows the attorney's advice without any material variation.

Example 2. Brown's employer, an investment banking firm, is the principal underwriter for an issue of convertible debentures by the Courtney Company. Brown discovers that Courtney Company, in its prospectus, has concealed severe third-quarter losses in its foreign operations. The preliminary prospectus has already been distributed.

> *Comment*: Knowing that the preliminary prospectus is misleading, Brown should report his findings to the appropriate supervisory persons in his firm. If the matter is not remedied and Brown's employer does not dissociate his firm from the underwriting, Brown should sever all his connections with the underwriting. Brown should also seek legal advice to determine whether additional reporting or other action should be taken.

Example 3. Murray is a financial analyst and an outside director of Allied Corporation. The Allied board of directors learns that the company management has made foreign political contributions without disclosing them in its financial statements to regulators or the stockholders. Murray consults her employer's counsel and determines that these unreported foreign political contributions will result in illegally misleading financial statements. Despite her urging at meetings with Allied directors and management, the board of directors votes not to disclose the secret contributions.

> *Comment*: Murray should promptly dissociate herself from Allied Corporation's actions by resigning as a director and, with advice of counsel, should consider making the appropriate regulators aware of the situation.

Example 4. Collins is an investment analyst for a major New York-headquartered stock brokerage firm. He works in a developing country with a rapidly modernizing economy and a budding capital market. Local securities laws are embryonic—in form and content—and include no punitive prohibitions against insider trading.

> *Comment*: Collins should be mindful of the risks that a small market and the absence of a fairly regulated flow of information to the market represent to his ability to obtain information and make timely judgments. He should include this factor in formulating his advice to clients. In handling material nonpublic information that accidentally comes into his possession, he should follow the AIMR Code and Standards [see Standard V(A)].

Example 5. Jameson, a U.S. citizen and CFA charterholder, works for a multinational investment advisor based in the United States. Jameson lives and works as a registered investment advisor in the tiny, but wealthy, island nation of Karramba. Karramba's securities laws state that no investment advisor registered and working in that country can participate in initial public offerings (IPOs) for the advisor's personal account. Jameson, believing that as a U.S. citizen working for a U.S.-based company she need only comply with U.S. law, has ignored this Karramba law. In addition, Jameson believes that, as a charterholder, so long as she adheres to the Code and Standards' requirement that she disclose her participation in any IPO to her employer and clients when such ownership creates a conflict of interest, she is operating on ethical high ground.

> *Comment*: Jameson is in violation of Standard I. As a registered investment advisor in Karramba, Jameson is prevented by Karrambian

securities law from participating in IPOs regardless of the law of her home country. In addition, because the law of the country in which she is working is more strict than the Code and Standards, she must follow the strict requirements of the local law rather than the requirements of the Code and Standards.

Procedures for Compliance

Members can acquire and maintain knowledge about applicable laws, rules, and regulations in the following ways:

- Maintain current files. Members should maintain, or encourage their employer to maintain, current reference copies of applicable statutes, rules, regulations, and important cases in a readily accessible manner. The employer should be encouraged to distribute such information to members for this purpose.
- Keep informed. Members should establish, or encourage their employer to establish, a procedure by which employees are regularly informed about changes in applicable laws, rules, regulations, and case law. In many instances, the employer's counsel can provide such information in the form of memoranda distributed to each member in the organization.
- Review procedures. Members should review, or encourage their employer to review, written compliance procedures on a regular basis to ensure that they reflect current law and provide adequate guidance to employees concerning what is permissible conduct under the law. Compliance procedures for specific problem areas are discussed in the chapters of this *Handbook* that discuss and interpret the relevant Standards.

When members suspect a client or a colleague of planning or engaging in ongoing illegal activities, members should take the following actions:

- Determine legality. Consult counsel to determine whether the conduct is, in fact, illegal.
- Dissociate from any illegal or unethical activity. If the member has reasonable grounds to believe that imminent or ongoing client or employee activities are illegal or unethical, the member should dissociate from these activities and urge the firm to attempt to persuade the perpetrator(s) to cease such conduct. Note that the activities of not only a firm's paid employees are relevant but also the activities of, for example, interns who are working without pay simply for experience or people on retainer to whom specific projects may have been outsourced under contract. Members can dissociate themselves from

the illegal or unethical activities by reporting the activities to the appropriate authorities. Inaction combined with continuing association with those involved in illegal conduct may be construed as participation, or assistance, in the illegal conduct.

Standard II: Relationships with and Responsibilities to the Profession

Standard II(A)—Use of Professional Designation

1. AIMR members may reference their membership only in a dignified and judicious manner. The use of the reference may be accompanied by an accurate explanation of the requirements that have been met to obtain membership in these organizations.
2. Those who have earned the right to use the Chartered Financial Analyst designation may use the marks "Chartered Financial Analyst" or "CFA" and are encouraged to do so, but only in a proper, dignified, and judicious manner. The use of the designation may be accompanied by an accurate explanation of the requirements that have been met to obtain the right to use the designation.
3. Candidates in the CFA Program, as defined in the AIMR Bylaws, may reference their participation in the CFA Program, but the reference must clearly state that an individual is a candidate in the CFA Program and cannot imply that the candidate has achieved any type of partial designation.

Purpose and Scope of the Standard

Standard II(A) states the responsibility of AIMR members, CFA charterholders, and candidates in the CFA Program to use the CFA designation or refer to their candidacies in the CFA Program properly and in a manner that does not mislead the investing public or others.

The Chartered Financial Analyst designation is a professional designation granted by AIMR to persons that AIMR considers qualified for the professional practice of financial analysis. To be granted the right to use the CFA or Chartered Financial Analyst designation, persons must satisfy the following requirements imposed by AIMR:

- Successfully complete the CFA Program.
- Make an ongoing commitment to abide by the requirements of AIMR's Professional Conduct Program.
- Maintain active membership in AIMR.

If a CFA charterholder fails to meet any one of these requirements, including failure to file an annual professional conduct statement or failure to pay dues for any year, the right to use the CFA designation is automatically suspended. Once suspended, individuals MAY NOT hold themselves out as CFA charterholders. Holding oneself as a CFA charterholder includes

- placing the designation "CFA" or "CFA Charterholder" after one's name on a resume, business card, brochure, or other published material;
- orally referencing oneself as a current/active/practicing CFA charterholder; or
- displaying the CFA charter in an office or work environment.

Obtaining the CFA charter is a significant achievement. It signifies that the investment professional successfully completed a comprehensive program, including three examinations covering a defined body of knowledge fundamental to the practice of investment management. For employers, clients, customers, and the public to recognize this achievement and the professionalism expected of a charterholder is important. Thus, charterholders must use the designation properly and in a dignified and judicious manner. The same is true for references to membership in AIMR. Membership includes those who are regular and affiliate members. Standard II(A) attempts to prevent uses of the designation that mislead employers, clients, prospects, and the public regarding the meaning and significance of the membership references.

Standard II(A) applies to (1) the use of the designation Chartered Financial Analyst, or the CFA mark, and references to membership in AIMR and (2) all related explanations or descriptions, including letterheads and business cards, resumés, directory listings, printed advertising, descriptive firm brochures, and oral statements to clients and prospects.

When used in conjunction with the CFA Program's services, the CFA mark does not serve simply as an acronym or generic term for certified analysts; rather, the CFA mark is an exclusive, unique mark of AIMR that is registered with the U.S. Patent and Trademark Office. The CFA mark must be referenced properly if AIMR is to maintain exclusive control of its use. The CFA mark must be used as an adjective, not a noun, and should never be used in the plural or the possessive. For example, to refer to oneself as a "CFA" or a "Chartered Financial Analyst" is improper. A proper use of the designation would be to state that one is a "CFA charterholder" or that one "earned the right to use the CFA designation." Charterholders are not given the CFA but awarded the right to use the CFA designation. **Exhibit 2** provides examples of correct and incorrect use of the designation.

The Chartered Financial Analyst and CFA marks are registered in several other countries, including Canada, China, Japan, South Korea, and Indonesia. Registration of the marks is pending in many other countries, and AIMR continues to register the marks globally.

Candidates for the CFA Designation. Each candidate in the CFA Program must adhere to the proper ethical, as well as legal, use of the Chartered Financial Analyst and CFA marks as professional designations. Standard II(A) limits use of the CFA designation to those who have passed all three levels of the CFA Program, have received their charters, and are charterholders in good standing. There is no designation for someone who has passed Level I, Level II, or Level III of the CFA examinations. Candidates may state, however, that they have completed Level I, II, or III, as the case may be, of the CFA Program. For purposes of this standard, a person is a candidate in the CFA Program if

- the person's application for registration in the CFA Program has been accepted by AIMR, as evidenced by issuance of a notice of acceptance, and the person is enrolled to sit for a specified examination; and
- the person has not (1) received exam results, (2) voluntarily removed him or herself from the CFA Program, (3) failed to sit for the exam, or (4) otherwise been removed from the CFA Program.

Application of the Standard

Example 1. Jones and Whittle, portfolio managers in a bank trust department, are awarded the right to use the CFA designation. The bank wishes to place a newspaper advertisement recognizing their accomplishment.

> *Comment*: An advertisement consistent with Standard II(A) would be limited to a statement of facts regarding the designation and/or regarding AIMR as the conferring organization. For example, the advertisement could indicate that Jones and Whittle were required to pass three examinations totaling 18 hours over a minimum of three years and could include a brief summary of the various areas of knowledge tested. The bank should follow the same approach regarding description of AIMR and the member society if the bank desires to reference Jones and Whittle's memberships in these organizations.

Example 2. An advertisement for ACA Investment Advisors states that all principals are CFA charterholders and all passed the three examinations on their first tries. The ad claims that they are an elite within an elite, having accomplished what few in the investment profession have done, and that, therefore, ACA's clients may expect superior performance from the firm.

> *Comment*: ACA's advertisement does not represent use of the designation in a dignified and judicious manner and exceeds the CFA

charterholder's permissible explanation specified in Standard II(A). To imply that CFA charterholders will achieve better investment results is misleading, and to imply that those who pass the exams on the first try will be more successful than those who do not is inappropriate.

Example 3. Overby, an investment counselor, states in her firm's written promotional material that she is a CFA candidate. She has indeed enrolled in the program, but she has not taken an examination since failing Level I five years previously and she is not registered to take the next exam.

Comment: Even though Overby enrolled in the CFA Program, she is not a candidate for the CFA charter because she is not registered to take the next scheduled exam. Earning the CFA charter or referencing the candidacy process implies achievement of, or a striving toward, a recognized level of competence and ethical behavior. Candidates who have successfully completed one or more levels may state this accomplishment in promotional materials, but the statement should be couched in terms that avoid potential misrepresentation. Overby may not imply that her candidacy is current. Instead, Overby must make clear that she was a candidate at one time but is not currently enrolled in the CFA Program.

Example 4. Everly has passed Level II of the CFA examination. While studying for Level III, he circulates a resumé stating that he has "completed Chartered Financial Analyst II" and indicates that he holds the designation "CFA II."

Comment: Everly has violated Standard II(A). AIMR does not award a designation for passage of a particular level of the CFA Program. He may state that he passed Level II of the CFA exam or that he is a Level III candidate in the CFA Program.

Example 5. Bailey submitted a resumé and cover letter for a position at Jacobson & Maass. In his cover letter Bailey stated, "I am a CFA with more than sixteen years of experience in fixed income."

Comment: Bailey violated Standard II(A) by using the CFA mark as a noun instead of an adjective. Bailey should have stated, "I am a CFA charterholder" or "I am a holder of the right to use the Chartered Financial Analyst designation."

Example 6. Jacobs, a CFA charterholder, resigns his position as an investment analyst and spends the next two years traveling abroad. Because he is not actively engaged in the investment profession, he does not pay his annual AIMR dues. At the conclusion of his travels, Jacobs becomes a self-employed analyst, accepting assignments as an independent contractor. Without reinstating his AIMR membership by paying annual dues, he prints business cards and stationery that display the CFA designation after his name.

> *Comment*: Jacobs' use of the CFA designation was suspended when he stopped paying dues. Therefore, he no longer was able to state or imply that he was an active CFA charterholder. Jacobs' use of the CFA designation in this instance is a violation of Standard II(A). When Jacobs resumes paying AIMR dues, his right to use the CFA designation will be reinstated.

Example 7. Harrison received his CFA charter in 1965. He was actively involved in the investment profession until 1997, when a serious health condition forced him into retirement. As he was no longer employed in the profession, Harrison let his AIMR membership dues lapse. In 1999, his former employer awarded him a lifetime achievement and excellence award for his contributions to his employer and to the profession. In the presentation of the award, his employer stated that Harrison was awarded the CFA charter in 1965.

> *Comment*: Although Harrison's right to use the CFA designation was suspended when he stopped paying dues in 1997, stating that he was awarded the CFA charter in 1965 is a matter of fact and does not imply that he is a current or practicing CFA charterholder.

Procedures for Compliance

On letterheads and business cards and in directory listings, only the mark CFA or the words Chartered Financial Analyst should appear after the charterholder's name. The same rule applies for membership in AIMR. Moreover, for the designation to appear in type larger than that used for the charterholder's name is inconsistent with Standard II(A).

Any description or explanation of the designation—in printed media, electronic media, or in formal oral presentations to clients or others—should be limited to a concise description of the requirements to obtain the right to use the designation and/or a concise description of the conferring organization: AIMR.

Once a CFA charterholder stops paying dues, the right to use the CFA designation is suspended. Individuals can no longer use the CFA designation after their names or refer to themselves as a holder of the

Chartered Financial Analyst designation. Individuals may state the year the designation was received and the years they were active, dues-paying charterholders.

Candidates may state, "I am a Level I (II or III) candidate in the CFA Program." A self-declared candidate for a given level should be enrolled to take the exam within the year. Candidates should not cite the expected date of exam completion. Final award of the charter is subject to CFA Program requirements and AIMR Board approval. A candidate who has passed Level III but has not yet received notice of having earned the CFA charter may state, "I have passed all three levels of the CFA Program and will be eligible for the CFA charter upon completion of the required work experience" (or give another accurate statement explaining why the charter has not yet been awarded).

An individual who has passed one or more levels of the CFA Program but is not currently registered may say, "I passed Level I (II or III) of the CFA Program in the year _____."

An appropriate step to ensure compliance with Standard II(A) is for a firm's investment and research departments to inform the firm's legal, compliance, public relations, and marketing departments, in writing, of the requirements for the right to use the CFA designation and provide a description of AIMR and the requirements for membership in AIMR.

Exhibit 2. Correct and Incorrect Use of the Chartered Financial Analyst and CFA Marks

Principle	Correct	Incorrect
The CFA and Chartered Financial Analyst designations must always be used as adjectives, never as nouns or common names.	He is one of two CFA charterholders in the company. He earned the right to use the Chartered Financial Analyst designation.	He is one of two CFAs in the company. He is a Chartered Financial Analyst.
Always capitalize the letters "CFA."	Jane Smith, CFA	Jane Smith, C.F.A. John Doe, cfa
Do not alter the designation to create new words or phrases.	John Jones, CFA	John, a CFA-type portfolio manager. The focus is on Chartered Financial Analysis. CFA equivalent program. Swiss-CFA
The designation must not be used as part of the name of a firm.	John Jones, Chartered Financial Analyst	Jones Chartered Financial Analysts, Inc.
The CFA designation should not appear larger than the charterholder's name.	Jane Smith, CFA John Doe, Chartered Financial Analyst	Jane Smith, **CFA** John Doe, **Chartered Financial Analyst**
Candidates in the CFA Program must not cite the expected date of exam completion and award of charter.	Level I candidate in the CFA Program.	Chartered Financial Analyst (CFA), September 2005.
No designation exists for someone who has passed Level I, Level II, or Level III of the exam. The CFA designation should not be referred to as a degree.	Passed Level I of the CFA examination in 1998.	CFA Level I. CFA degree expected in 2004.
A candidate who has passed Level III but has not yet received his/her charter cannot use the CFA or Chartered Financial Analyst designation.	I have passed all three levels of the CFA Program and may be eligible for the CFA charter upon completion of the required work experience.	CFA (Passed Finalist)

Standard II: Relationships with and Responsibilities to the Profession

Standard II(B)—Professional Misconduct

1. Members shall not engage in any professional conduct involving dishonesty, fraud, deceit, or misrepresentation or commit any act that reflects adversely on their honesty, trustworthiness, or professional competence.
2. Members and candidates shall not engage in any conduct or commit any act that compromises the integrity of the CFA designation or the integrity or validity of the examinations leading to the award of the right to use the CFA designation.

Purpose and Scope of the Standard

Standard II(B) states the responsibility of AIMR members, CFA charterholders, and candidates in the CFA Program to refrain from conduct that exhibits a lack of honesty, trustworthiness, or fitness to practice as an investment professional or that impairs the integrity of the CFA designation or the exams that lead to the award of the right to use the CFA designation. Whereas Standard I addresses the overall obligation to comply with the laws, rules, and regulations that govern their professional activities, the scope of Standard II(B) extends beyond technical compliance with laws and regulations. Standard II(B) addresses personal integrity and prohibits individual behavior that reflects adversely on the entire profession.

Violations of Standard II(B) include conviction of a felony or crime punishable by more than one year in prison or a misdemeanor involving moral turpitude (lying, cheating, stealing, or other dishonest conduct), whether or not the offenses relate to a member's professional activities. Standard II(B) also addresses dishonest activities that do not result in criminal convictions. Repeated convictions for misdemeanors or acts reflecting negatively on professional competence, no matter how inconsequential, that indicate a disrespect for the law may also fall within the scope of Standard II(B). Likewise, Standard II(B) prohibits any conduct that undermines confidence that the CFA charter represents a level of achievement based on merit and ethical conduct.

Application of the Standard

Example 1. Sasserman is a trust investment officer at the Dime Bank in a small affluent suburb. He enjoys lunching every day with friends at the

Country Club, where his clients have observed him having numerous drinks. Back at work after lunch, he clearly is intoxicated while making investment decisions. His clients make a point of handling any business with Sasserman in the morning because they distrust his judgment after lunch.

> *Comment*: Sasserman's excessive drinking at lunch and subsequent intoxication at work constitute a violation of Standard II(B) because this conduct has raised questions among his clients about his professionalism and competence. His behavior thus reflects poorly on him, his bank, and the investment industry.

Example 2. Spicolli is employed as an analyst with the investment counseling firm of Ridgemont & High. She has been arrested for erratic driving after a 10th-year college reunion. A search of her car reveals three ounces of marijuana in the car. Spicolli is charged with possession of a controlled substance—a misdemeanor under state law. This is the third time in a year that she has faced minor drug-possession charges. Although the president of her firm is far from pleased with Spicolli's conduct, he does not believe it is affecting her day-to-day work. He tells Spicolli she may continue to work at the firm provided that there are no more such "incidents."

> *Comment*: Spicolli violated Standard II(B) because her conduct reflected adversely on her fitness as a CFA charterholder. Although her supervisor did not believe Spicolli's conduct warranted discipline, Spicolli's repeated and serious violations of laws involving possession of illegal substances that can interfere with judgment and job performance violated Standard II(B). Convictions of even minor offenses might rise to the level of violating Standard II(B) if committed with a frequency suggesting gross disregard for the law.

Example 3. Hoffman, a security analyst at ATZ Brothers, Inc., a large brokerage house, submits reimbursement forms over a two-year period to ATZ's self-funded health insurance program for more than two dozen bills, of which most have been altered to increase the amount due. An investigation by the firm's director of employee benefits uncovers the conduct. ATZ subsequently terminates Hoffman's employment and notifies AIMR.

> *Comment*: Despite the absence of a criminal conviction, Hoffman violated Standard II(B) because he engaged in intentional and calculated conduct that adversely reflected on his honesty.

Example 4. Black, who writes research reports on the automotive industry, volunteers much of her spare time to local charities. The board of one of the charitable institutions decides to buy five new vans to deliver hot lunches to low-income elderly persons. Black offers to donate her time to handle purchasing agreements. To pay a long-standing debt to a friend who operates an automobile dealership—and to compensate herself for her trouble—she agrees to a price 20 percent higher than normal and splits the surcharge with her friend. The director of the charity ultimately discovers the scheme and tells Black that her services, donated or otherwise, are no longer required.

> *Comment*: Black engaged in conduct involving dishonesty, fraud, and misrepresentation in violation of Standard II(B).

Example 5. Nero, a member analyst at Holistic Advisers LLC, serves as a proctor for the administration of the CFA examination in his city. In the course of his service, he reviews a copy of the Level II examination on the evening prior to the exam's administration and provides information concerning the examination questions to two candidates who are also employees of Holistic.

> *Comment*: Nero and the two candidates violated Standard II(B). By providing information concerning the examination questions to two candidates, Nero provided an unfair advantage to the two candidates and undermined the integrity and validity of the Level II examination as an accurate measure of the knowledge, skills, and abilities necessary to earn the right to use the CFA designation. By accepting the information, the candidates also compromised the integrity and validity of the Level II exam and undermined the ethical framework that forms a key part of the designation.

Procedures for Compliance

Generally, complying with Standard II(B) is a matter of the member's own personal integrity and moral character. Each member needs to be aware of the professional implications and consequences of all personal actions. In addition, members and candidates must adhere to all rules and procedures related to the CFA designation or the administration of the CFA exams.

The public and private regulatory framework provides additional incentives, however, to maintain a high standard of ethical conduct. Agencies such as the Securities and Exchange Commission, the Ontario Securities Commission, the Investment Management Regulatory Organization, stock exchanges, and other self-regulatory organizations require disclosure of a wide variety of information on behavior that would preclude an individual from engaging in the securities business. Members should encourage their employers to

- make clear that any personal behavior that reflects poorly on the individual involved, the institution as a whole, or the investment industry will not be tolerated;
- adopt a code of ethics to which every employee must subscribe; and
- conduct background checks on potential employees to ensure that they are of good character and not ineligible to work in the investment industry because of past infractions of the law.

Standard II: Relationships with and Responsibilities to the Profession

Standard II(C)—Prohibition against Plagiarism

Members shall not copy or use, in substantially the same form as the original, material prepared by another without acknowledging and identifying the name of the author, publisher, or source of such material. Members may use, without acknowledgment, factual information published by recognized financial and statistical reporting services or similar sources.

Purpose and Scope of the Standard

Standard II(C) states the responsibility of AIMR members, CFA charterholders, and candidates in the CFA Program to avoid plagiarism in the preparation of material for distribution to employers, associates, clients, prospects, or the general public. Plagiarism is defined as copying or using in substantially the same form materials prepared by others without acknowledging the source of the material or identifying the author and publisher of such material. The only permitted exception is the use of factual information published by recognized financial and statistical reporting services or similar sources.

The investment profession uses myriad financial, economic, and statistical data in the investment decision-making process. Through various publications and presentations, the investment professional is constantly exposed to the work of others and to the temptation to use it without proper acknowledgment.

Plagiarism in investment management can take various forms. The simplest and most flagrant example is to take a research report or study done by another firm or person, change the names, and release the material as one's own original analysis. This action is a clear violation of Standard II(C) and various regulations. Other practices include (1) using excerpts from articles or reports prepared by others, either verbatim or with only a slight change in wording without acknowledgment, (2) citing specific quotations supposedly attributable to "leading analysts" and "investment experts" without specific reference, (3) presenting statistical estimates of forecasts prepared by others with the source identified but without qualifying statements or caveats that may have been used, (4) using charts and graphs without stating their sources, and (5) copying proprietary computerized spreadsheets or algorithms without seeking the cooperation or authorization of their creators.

By blindly adopting the ideas and words of others without acknowledgment, members also risk violation of Standard IV(A.1) by making recommendations that may not have a reasonable basis and may not avoid material misrepresentations.

The following statement pertaining to the predecessor of Standard II(C) was adopted and published by the FAF Board of Directors in 1980 and reaffirmed by the AIMR Board of Governors in 1990:

> The Board of Governors calls to the attention of all members the seriousness with which it views plagiarism. Standard II(C) of the Standards of Professional Conduct provides that a financial analyst who prepares material for distribution must not copy or use in substantially the same form material prepared by others without due acknowledgment. Failure to abide by Standard [II(C)] is plagiarism. Plagiarism is an offense to the profession and the public; in many cases, it is also a violation of the copyright laws and will expose the offender to civil suit. A writer who quotes from another writer must in most cases obtain permission and give proper attribution for the quotation. A writer must not only avoid verbatim copying without acknowledgment, but must also avoid using passages with alterations that seek to disguise or conceal the origin but which do not materially change the form of expression.

The terminology of the standard easily gives the impression that it is directed at written materials. However, the standard also applies to plagiarism in oral communications, such as through group meetings; visits with associates, clients, and customers; use of audio/video media (which is rapidly increasing); and telecommunications, such as through electronic data transfer and the outright copying of electronic media.

One of the insidious practices in the investment field has been the preparation of research reports based on multiple sources of information without acknowledging the sources. Such information would include, for example, ideas, statistical compilations, and forecasts combined to give the appearance of original work. Of course, there is no monopoly on ideas, but the fair financial analyst should give credit when it is clearly due. Analysts should be warned against the use of undocumented forecasts, earnings projections, asset values, and the like. Sources should be revealed or at least the research studies should state, "Our analysis indicates (or shows) that...," to bring the responsibility directly back to the author of the report or the firm involved. Statements of fact should be documented.

The standard provides, however, that "factual information published by recognized financial and statistical reporting services or similar sources" can be used without an acknowledgment. This provision was introduced to eliminate laborious references to information already in the public realm.

The permission to use recognized sources of factual information without acknowledgment is susceptible to abuse and must be used with discretion. The term "recognized" is defined broadly as a source worthy of confidence or one that is reliable and generally accepted or viewed by the investment profession globally or regionally or by a particular industry segment as a recognized source. For instance, it is generally accepted that recognized sources include factual materials supplied by Standard & Poor's Corporation and Moody's Investors Service. Members should be careful not to use without acknowledgment materials supplied by sources that have not established a credible record over a considerable period or supplied by sources that do not have a clearly identifiable staff of professionals who prepare financial and statistical reports.

Whether information must be attributed to primary sources also depends on whom the member is representing when she or he is disseminating the information. For example, the managing partners of an investment firm may relate any findings of the investment firm's research staff to a client without specific attribution because the partners represent the firm in this exchange. If the same individuals are representing themselves, or their own views (as expert witnesses, for example), they must attribute any of their firm's research to its source(s).

Application of the Standard

Example 1. Grant, a research analyst for a Canadian brokerage firm, has specialized in the Canadian mining industry for the past 10 years. She recently read an extensive research report on Deep Shaft Mining, Ltd., by Barton, another analyst. Barton provided extensive statistics analyzing the mineral reserves, production capacity, selling rates, and marketing factors affecting Deep Shaft's operations. He also noted that initial drilling results on a new ore body, which had not been made public, might show the existence of mineral zones that could increase the life of Deep Shaft's main mines, but Barton cited no specific data as to the initial drilling results. Grant called an officer of Deep Shaft, who gave her the initial drilling results over the telephone. The data indicated that the expected life of the main mines would be tripled. Grant added these statistics to Barton's report and circulated it as her own report within her firm.

> *Comment*: Grant plagiarized Barton's report by reproducing large parts of it in her own report without acknowledgment. Moreover, if the Barton report was copyrighted, Grant very likely violated that copyright. She may also have violated Standard V(A), Prohibition

against Use of Material Nonpublic Information, by including material nonpublic information in the report.

Example 2. Swanson is a senior analyst in the investment research department of Ballard and Company. Apex Corporation has asked Ballard to assist in acquiring the stock of Campbell Company, a financial consulting firm, and to prepare a report recommending that stockholders of Campbell agree to the acquisition. Another investment firm, Davis and Company, had already prepared a report for Apex analyzing both Apex and Campbell and recommending an exchange ratio. Apex has given the Davis report to Ballard officers, who have passed it on to Swanson, who has reviewed the Davis report along with other available material on the Apex and Campbell companies. From his analysis, he concludes that the common stocks of Campbell and of Apex represent good value at their current prices; he believes, however, that the Davis report does not consider all the factors a Campbell stockholder would need to know to make a decision. Swanson reports his conclusions to the partner in charge, who tells him to "use the Davis report, change a few words, sign your name, and get it out."

Comment: If Swanson does as requested, he will violate Standard II(C). He could refer to those portions of the Davis report with which he agrees, if he identifies Davis as the source, and add his own analysis and conclusions to the report before signing and distributing it. If the partner is an AIMR member, he has violated Standard I by assisting in the violation of the Standards of Professional Conduct and has violated Standard III(E), Responsibilities of Supervisors, by rendering inappropriate supervision.

Example 3. Chippendale, a quantitative analyst for Double Alpha, Inc., returns in great excitement from a seminar. In that seminar, Jorrely, a well-publicized quantitative analyst at a national brokerage firm, discussed one of his new models in great detail, and Chippendale is intrigued by the new concepts. She proceeds to test this model, making some minor mechanical changes but retaining the concept, until she produces some very positive results. She quickly announces to her supervisors in Double Alpha that she has discovered a new model and that clients and prospective clients alike should be informed of this positive finding as ongoing proof of Double Alpha's continuing innovation and ability to add value.

Comment: Although Chippendale tested Jorrely's model on her own and even slightly modified it, she must still acknowledge the original source of the idea. Chippendale can certainly take credit for the final, practical results; she can also support her conclusions with her own test. The credit for the innovative thinking, however, must be awarded to Jorrely.

Example 4. The research staff of Hudson Portfolio Management (HPM) has developed a unique and simple way to measure the downside risk of equity portfolios. Tillman, the president and majority owner of HPM, has been discussing this project with many of HPM's clients and prospective clients. As word of the new methodology spreads, Tillman is asked to appear as an expert witness on portfolio risk in more and more public situations. Although Tillman is a strong supporter of the research done internally at HPM and he is now well versed in its implications and intricacies, he did not directly contribute to the development. He does not regularly share this fact with clients or those hearing his expert testimony.

Comment: When speaking with clients and prospects, Tillman need not explicitly attribute the new methodology to his staff; he is representing HPM and, therefore, is within his rights to discuss HPM's research without attribution. As an expert witness, however, Tillman is no longer representing HPM but, rather, himself. Thus, he must attribute any of HPM's research to HPM and to the team that carried out the research. Such attribution will not only give credit to the developers of the risk-measurement concepts but will also define the limits of Tillman's expertise.

Example 5. After six years of employment as a portfolio manager with Stiles Financial, Neville decided to start his own business. Prior to his departure from Stiles Financial, Neville took certain steps to begin his new business, including the drafting of marketing materials for his new venture. In creating marketing materials for his new firm, Neville copied, with only minor changes, several portions of Stiles' marketing materials.

Comment: Neville violated Standard II(C) by copying another company's marketing materials without permission and without proper credit. Neville may have also violated Standard III(B) by misappropriating his former employer's property.

Procedures for Compliance

In preparing research reports or conclusions of analysis, members should take the following steps:

- Maintain copies. Keep copies of all research reports, articles containing research ideas, material with new statistical methodology, and other materials that were relied on in preparing the research report.
- Attribute quotations. Attribute to their sources any direct quotations,

including projections, tables, statistics, model/product ideas, and new methodologies prepared by persons other than recognized financial and statistical reporting services or similar sources.

- Attribute summaries. Attribute to their sources paraphrases or summaries of material prepared by others. For example, the author of a research report on Brown Company, in order to support his analysis of Brown's competitive position, may summarize another analyst's report of Brown's chief competitor, but the author of the Brown report should acknowledge in his own report his reliance on the other analyst's report.

Standard III: Relationships with and Responsibilities to the Employer

The Employer–Employee Relationship Defined

An employee is someone in the service of another who has the power or right to control and direct the employee in the material details of how the work is to be performed. A written or implied contract may or may not exist between employee and employer, and actual receipt of monetary compensation is not required for an employer–employee relationship.

Existence of an employer–employee relationship rests in large measure on the degree of control exercised by the hiring party. In determining whether a person is an employee, members should consider the following factors: (1) extent of the employer's control and supervision over the worker; (2) kind of occupation, nature of skills required, and whether the skills are acquired in the workplace; (3) responsibility for costs of operation; (4) method and form of payment and benefits; and (5) length of job commitment and/or expectations.

Standard III: Relationships with and Responsibilities to the Employer

Standard III(A)—Obligation to Inform Employer of Code and Standards

Members shall:

1. Inform their employer in writing, through their direct supervisor, that they are obligated to comply with the Code and Standards and are subject to disciplinary sanctions for violations thereof.
2. Deliver a copy of the Code and Standards to their employer if the employer does not have a copy.

Purpose and Scope of the Standard

Standard III(A) states the responsibility of AIMR members, holders of the Chartered Financial Analyst designation, and candidates in the CFA Program to inform their employer that they are obligated to comply with the Code of Ethics and Standards of Professional Conduct in their professional activities and are obligated to deliver a copy of the Code and Standards to their employer.

AIMR believes that calling employers' attention to the Code and Standards may help prevent the implementation of firm policies and procedures that conflict with the Code and Standards. AIMR considers the responsibility required by Standard III(A) to be an integral part of professional practice. Disseminating the Code and Standards and holding them out as a minimum rule of conduct enhances ethical awareness and promotes professional honesty and respect. Individual members, their employers, their clients, and the participants and beneficiaries of accounts—all benefit from Standard III(A).

Standard III(A) requires that members take steps to notify their employer in writing of the Code and Standards that control members' professional practices. "In writing" includes any form of communication that can be documented (for example, communication via computer e-mail that can be retrieved and documented). "Employer" means "immediate supervisor."

Notifying an employer of the Code and Standards gives the employer the opportunity to adopt the Code and Standards or develop for the firm similar ethical standards or internal guidelines. If the employer has publicly acknowledged, in writing, adoption of AIMR's Code and Standards as part of its firm policies, then the member need not give the formal written notification as required by Standard III(A).

Supervisors in many organizations periodically circulate copies of the Code and Standards to members of their departments. Many supervisors stress the need to be familiar and comply with these documents and often require a written response from all recipients acknowledging that they have recently reviewed the materials. An increasing number of organizations also circulate supplemental information on areas covered by the Code and Standards. In addition, many employers conduct seminars and refresher programs for employees on standards of professional responsibility. In organizations where size or other factors make such procedures impractical, copies of the Code and Standards can be posted on a bulletin board or other suitable place.

Members are often supervised by other members or work among several members. In such situations, members often assume that "someone else will take care of it." Each member must assume personal responsibility for Standard III(A). In most cases, the ultimate responsibility for compliance with Standard III(A) falls on the most senior member (in organizational responsibility) who reports to a nonmember. Organizational decisions that might result in placing individual employees/members in a position of conflict with the Code and Standards are likely to occur at a senior level. It is important, therefore, that senior management and the legal and compliance departments of organizations that employ AIMR members and candidates keep aware of the Code and Standards. Because the legal department in any organization serves in an important advisory capacity to senior management, that department might be an appropriate source of appeal for a member with lower organizational status should senior management appear to make decisions that might require the member to violate the Code and Standards.

Application of the Standard

Example 1. Jones, president of XYZ Trust Company and not an AIMR member or CFA charterholder, is contacted by a partner of a brokerage firm and asked to sell XYZ's large holding of Ajax Corporation bonds at a substantial premium over market, with a severe time limit on the transaction. Jones calls in Smith, the director of the investment department. Jones and Smith agree the price is attractive, considering the economic conditions and value to the accounts. They conclude that they do not have enough time, however, to contact all accounts. Consequently, they decide that none should be contacted and that the bonds should be sold from the discretionary accounts only. Brown, a portfolio manager, complains to Smith about leaving out the other accounts, and Smith tells her to "forget it or speak to Jones." Brown informs Jones that the action might violate the

Code and Standards. Jones replies that she is unaware of what standards Brown is talking about but will check them out later. Before she does so, however, the bonds are sold from the discretionary accounts.

> *Comment*: Smith violated Standard III(A) because she did not take steps to ensure that Jones was aware of the existence and content of the Code and Standards. Jones should have been provided with a copy of the Code and Standards and informed of Brown's (and Smith's) compliance obligations under penalty of disciplinary sanctions. Brown would have violated Standard III(A) if she had not reminded Smith about this obligation, even though Smith is a CFA charterholder and herself subject to the Code and Standards. Subordinate employees cannot assume that their supervisors are aware of the obligation, even if the supervisor is a member.
>
> Complying with Standard III(A) might not have prevented what occurred in this example, but it certainly would have provided a valid reason to appeal Jones's decision. If XYZ's legal department had been made aware of the existence and content of the Code and Standards before the incident, Brown could have appealed to the department for support. This course of action might have been easier for Brown than confronting Jones and Smith and might have been of greater influence on them.
>
> Smith also violated Standard IV(B.3), Fair Dealing, by treating discretionary accounts differently from nondiscretionary accounts.

Example 2. Johnson, who is a senior partner of ABC Securities, a small brokerage firm, is not an AIMR member or CFA charterholder. Johnson has learned that her firm will be a participant in a large stock offering. She tells Black, her analyst and a member of AIMR, to update Black's last report on the stock, which was somewhat unfavorable, and to make the report more exciting and more favorable to the offering company. Black follows Johnson's instructions and rewrites the report with a more favorable opinion.

> *Comment*: Black violated Standard III(A) because he failed to make Johnson aware of the existence of the Code and Standards. Black should have provided Johnson a copy of the Code and Standards and informed her of his compliance obligation under penalty of disciplinary sanctions. In addition, by rewriting the report and not disclosing the firm's participation in the stock offering, Black also violated Standard IV(A.1), Reasonable Basis and Representations, and Standard IV(B.7), Disclosure of Conflicts to Clients and Prospects.

Procedures for Compliance

Members should provide a written notice to their supervisor advising them of their obligation to abide by the Code and Standards. The notice should also suggest that their employer adopt the Code and Standards and disseminate them throughout the firm, as illustrated in **Exhibit 3**. Members should maintain a written record of their notification.

Exhibit 3. Sample Memorandum

XYZ Trust Company

Memo to: John Jones, President
Date: August 29, 20__
Subject: Association for Investment Management and Research Code of Ethics and Standards of Professional Conduct

Enclosed is a copy of the AIMR Code of Ethics and Standards of Professional Conduct. According to Standard III(A), all AIMR members, CFA charterholders, and candidates in the CFA Program are required to take steps to ensure that their employers are informed of the member's obligation to comply with the Code and Standards.

As a CFA charterholder [candidate in the CFA Program; AIMR member], I am required to abide by AIMR's Code and Standards. AIMR may take disciplinary sanctions against me if I do not abide by the Code and Standards.

I believe it would be in the interest of XYZ and its staff that all employees adhere to the Code and Standards as well as all company regulations on these subjects. If you are interested in more information about the Code and Standards and corporate adoption of the Code and Standards to promote ethical conduct in the workplace, I will be happy to help you contact AIMR's Professional Conduct Program.

Catherine Smith, CFA
Director, Investments

cc: Trust Legal Office
All Division Heads
All Research Analysts
All Portfolio Managers

Standard III: Relationships with and Responsibilities to the Employer

Standard III(B)—Duty to Employer

Members shall not undertake any independent practice that could result in compensation or other benefit in competition with their employer unless they obtain written consent from both their employer and the persons or entities for whom they undertake independent practice.

Purpose and Scope of the Standard

Standard III(B) states the responsibility of AIMR members, CFA charterholders, and candidates in the CFA Program to abstain from independent competitive activity that could conflict with the business of the member's employer.

An employee must protect the interests of his or her firm by refraining from any conduct that would injure the firm, deprive it of profit, or deprive it of the advantage of the employee's skills and ability.

Standard III(B) does not preclude a member from entering into an independent business while still employed. However, the member must secure written permission from both the employer and the outside entity to undertake independent practice.

"Practice" means any service that the employer currently makes available for remuneration. "Undertaking independent practice" means engaging in competitive business, as opposed to making preparations to begin such practice. Therefore, a departing employee is generally free to make arrangements or preparations to go into a competitive business before terminating the relationship with the employee's employer provided that such preparations do not breach the employee's duty of loyalty.

When investment professionals plan to leave their current employers, they have a duty to act in the employers' best interests and not engage in any activities that would conflict with this duty until their resignations become effective. Basic guidelines for those members who plan to compete are difficult to define. The circumstances of each case must be reviewed to distinguish permissible preparations from violations of duty for which liability may be imposed. Activities that might constitute a violation, especially in combination, include the following:

- misappropriation of trade secrets;
- misuse of confidential information;
- conspiracy to bring about mass resignation of other employees;

- solicitation of employer's clients prior to cessation of employment;
- planning that involves a conspiracy or is characterized by secrecy and deceit;
- self-dealing (appropriating for one's own property a business opportunity or information belonging to one's employer);
- misappropriation of clients or client lists;
- a change from the original understanding among client, employer, and employee.

Standard III(B) applies to activity being conducted that could result in compensation. Actual receipt of monetary compensation is not required for Standard III(B) to apply.

A wide variety of business relationships exist within the investment industry. For instance, a member can be retained as an employee or independent contractor. Members must determine whether they are employees or independent contractors to determine the applicability of Standard III(B). This issue will be decided largely by the degree of control exercised by the employing entity over the member. Factors determining control include whether the member's hours, work location, and other parameters of the job are set; whether facilities are provided to the member; whether the member's expenses are reimbursed; whether the member holds himself or herself out to other employers for additional work; and the number of clients or employers the member works for.

A member's duties within an independent contractor relationship are governed by the oral or written agreement between the member and the client. Members should take care to define clearly the scope of their responsibilities and the expectations of each client within the context of each relationship. Once the member establishes a relationship with a client, the member has a duty to abide by the terms of the agreement.

Application of the Standard

Example 1. Boggs, a portfolio manager for ABC Trust Company, is asked by a neighbor, Gray, to "take a look at the pension fund portfolio of my small manufacturing company." Gray, as president of the company, acts as trustee of the pension plan and has invested the funds based on her own limited financial knowledge. She has not sought the services of Boggs's employer or any other professional investment manager because she believes the plan is too small to interest anyone. Boggs reviews the portfolio on Saturday and develops a number of recommendations, which she discusses with Gray on Sunday at Gray's house. Boggs is surprised at the size of the fund, which is as large as ABC Trust's other retirement accounts. Gray is impressed with Boggs's thorough analysis and asks if she will do a similar review again in three months. As a gesture of appreciation, Gray sends Boggs an expensive gift, which Boggs accepts. After the next review and meeting, Gray insists that Boggs accept a check for an amount in excess of the quarterly fee ABC Trust would have charged an account of this size. This arrangement is mutually satisfactory, and quarterly meetings continue for a number of years. Boggs does not inform her employer of the service she is performing for Gray.

> *Comment*: Boggs is violating Standard III(B) by not seeking written consent from ABC Trust Company to provide services for Gray. Because of the size of the account, Gray's willingness to pay for professional assistance, and Gray's request for continuous review, Boggs is in competition with her employer. The performance of these services on Boggs's own time is not relevant. The written consent of both ABC Trust and Gray are the requirements for Boggs to accept compensation without violating Standard III(B).

Example 2. Adams, a registered investment advisor, does business as a sole proprietorship with four clients. He is interested, however, in affiliating with a brokerage firm. When he is offered a position as an employee with Star Brokerage Services in the advisory department, he accepts. He continues to maintain his individual business as well.

> *Comment*: Adams should obtain the written consent of his new employer to maintain and be independently compensated by his old clients. Adams should also disclose in writing to each of his clients and prospective clients his employment by Star Brokerage Services.

Example 3. Black is employed by Drew Brokers, Inc. Unbeknownst to Drew Brokers, Black is also working with Acme, Inc., to make a sale in a private transaction of a block of securities owned by the principal stockholder of Acme, and Black has arranged for a buyer of those securities. Upon completion of the sale, Black is to receive a negotiated fee from the seller. The transaction has not been completed, however, nor any compensation paid to Black when Drew Brokers discovers Black's activities and alleges that Black is in violation of Standard III(B) because no consent has been obtained from Drew or Acme.

> *Comment*: Black's conduct is a violation of Standard III(B). Black has not received consent from Drew, Acme, or the principal stockholder, and if completed, the transaction could result in compensation. Black is in competition with her employer because Drew Brokers engages in the same business as Black is planning.

Example 4. Magee manages pension accounts for Trust Assets, Inc., but has become frustrated with the working environment and has been offered a position with Fiduciary Management. Before resigning from Trust Assets, Magee asks four big accounts to leave that firm and open accounts with Fiduciary. Magee also persuades several prospective clients to sign agreements with Fiduciary Management. Magee had previously made presentations to these prospects on behalf of Trust Assets, Inc.

> *Comment*: Magee has violated the employee–employer principle requiring that he act solely for his employer's benefit. Magee's duty is to Trust Assets as long as he is employed there. The solicitation of current clients and prospective clients is unethical and violates Standard III(B).

Example 5. Hightower has been employed by Jason Investment Management Corporation for 15 years. He began as an analyst but assumed increasing responsibilities and is now a senior portfolio manager and a member of the firm's investment policy committee. Hightower has decided to leave Jason Investment and start his own investment management business. He has been careful not to tell any of Jason's clients that he is leaving, because he does not want to be accused of breaching his duty to Jason by soliciting Jason clients before his departure. Hightower is planning to copy and take with him the following documents and information he developed or worked on while at Jason: (1) the client list, with addresses, telephone numbers, and other pertinent client information, (2) client statements, (3) sample marketing presentations to prospective clients containing Jason's performance record, (4) Jason's recommended list of securities, (5) computer models to determine asset allocations for accounts with different objectives, (6) computer models for stock selection, and (7) personal computer spreadsheets for Hightower's major corporate recommendations that he developed when he was an analyst.

> *Comment*: Hightower holds a position of trust and has a duty to his employer. Except with the consent of their employer, departing employees may not take employer property, which includes books, records, reports, and other materials, and may not interfere with their employer's business opportunities. Taking any employer records, even those the member prepared, violates Standard III(B).

Example 6. Winston manages all-equity portfolios at Target Asset Management (TAM), a large, established investment counselor. Ten years ago, Philpott & Company, which manages a family of global bond mutual funds, acquired TAM in a diversification move. After the merger, the combined operations prospered in the fixed-income business while the equity management business at TAM languished. Lately, a few of the equity pension accounts that had been with TAM before the merger have terminated their relationships with TAM. One day, Winston finds on her voice mail a message from a concerned client, "Hey! I just read in the latest issue of Wall Street Rag that Philpott is close to announcing the sale of your firm's equity management business to Rugged Life. What is going on?" Not being aware of any such deal, Winston and her associates are stunned. Their internal inquiries are met with denials from Philpott management, but the rumors persist. Feeling left in the dark, Winston contemplates leading an employee buyout of TAM's equity management business.

> *Comment*: An employee-led buyout of TAM's equity asset management business would be consistent with Standard III(B) because it would rest on the permission of the employer and, ultimately, the clients. In this kind of case, however, in which employees suspect the senior managers or principals are not truthful or forthcoming, members should consult legal counsel to determine their best alternatives.

Example 7. Cheap Chuckles, Inc., manages an equity fund for insurance companies. Because of the size of the firm (and its parsimonious nature), Cheap Chuckles does not employ any full-time research staff; instead, it allows outsiders to bring research to the firm in exchange for receiving the trading commission. McPickle supplies research exclusively to Cheap Chuckles, but he also puts together merger and acquisition deals for a variety of clients. Because Cheap Chuckles does not employ him for M&A work, he believes he is free to take his deals to whoever will pay him the highest commission or finders fee and keep the fees to himself.

> *Comment*: Because McPickle is an independent contractor, whether he has breached a duty to Cheap Chuckles depends on the terms of their agreement and the nature of the research requested by Cheap Chuckles. If Cheap Chuckles has hired McPickle to research stocks that are potential M&A candidates, he has a duty to identify those stocks to Cheap Chuckles prior to undertaking independent efforts to put together an M&A deal. If Cheap Chuckles has hired McPickle only to provide general research on a particular industry and, in the course of that research, McPickle discovers a potential M&A candidate, McPickle is free to arrange a deal without informing Cheap Chuckles.

Example 8. Clay, who is unemployed, wants part-time consulting work while seeking a full-time analyst position. During an interview at Phere Associates, a large institutional asset manager, Clay is told that the firm has no immediate research openings but would be willing to pay her a flat fee to complete a study of the wireless communications industry within a given period of time. Clay would be allowed unlimited access to Phere's research files and would be welcome to come in and use whatever support facilities are available during normal working hours. Phere's research director does not seek any exclusivity for Clay's output, and the two agree to the arrangement on a handshake. As Clay nears completion of the study, she is offered an analyst job in the research department of Dowt & Company, a brokerage firm, and she is pondering submitting the draft of her wireless study for publication by Dowt.

> *Comment*: Although she is under no written contractual obligation to Phere, Clay has an obligation to let Phere act on the output of her study before Dowt & Company or Clay uses the information to their own advantage. That is, unless Phere gives written permission to Clay waiving rights to her wireless report, Clay would be in violation of Standard III(B) if she were to immediately recommend to Dowt the same transactions recommended in the report to Phere. Furthermore, Clay must not take from Phere any research file material or other property that she may have used. Finally, Clay has an obligation not to exaggerate or misrepresent to prospective employers, in her resumé or in describing the nature of her present consulting business, the limited ties that she has with Phere.

Example 9. Madeline, a recent graduate of UCLA and a candidate in the CFA Program, spends her summer as an unpaid intern at Murdoch and Lowell. Murdoch and Lowell are attempting to bring the firm into compliance with the AIMR-PPS℠ standards, and Madeline is assigned to assist in their efforts. Two months into her internship, Madeline applies for a job at McMillan & Company, which has plans to become AIMR-PPS compliant. Madeline accepts the job with McMillan. Before leaving Murdoch, she copies the software she helped develop, as she believes this software will assist her in her new position.

> *Comment*: As a candidate in the CFA Program, Madeline is bound by AIMR's Code of Ethics and Standards of Professional Conduct. Even though Madeline doesn't receive monetary compensation for her services at Murdoch, she is considered an employee because she receives compensation and benefits in the form of work experience and knowledge. By copying the software, Madeline violated Standard III(B) because she misappropriated Murdoch's property without permission.

Procedures for Compliance

Members who plan to engage in independent practice for compensation should provide written statements to their employer describing the types of service the members will render prospective independent clients, the expected duration of the services, and the compensation for the services. Members should not render services until receiving written consent from their employer to all of the terms of the arrangement.

A member also should disclose to prospective clients the identity of the member's employer, clarify that the member is performing independently of that employer, and state the fees or charges the member's employer would make for rendering the same services. The member should not render services until the client gives consent in writing indicating that the client has read and understood the member's written disclosure statement.

Members contemplating seeking other employment should not contact existing clients or potential clients prior to leaving their employer. In addition, they should not take records or files to a new employer without the written permission of the previous employer.

Standard III: Relationships with and Responsibilities to the Employer

Standard III(C)—Disclosure of Conflicts to Employer

Members shall:

1. Disclose to their employer all matters, including beneficial ownership of securities or other investments, that reasonably could be expected to interfere with their duty to their employer or ability to make unbiased and objective recommendations.
2. Comply with any prohibitions on activities imposed by their employer if a conflict of interest exists.

Purpose and Scope of the Standard

Standard III(C) protects employers and, indirectly, clients by requiring AIMR members, CFA charterholders, and candidates in the CFA Program to report to employers any conflict of interest.

Unlike Standard IV(B.7), which deals exclusively with situations creating a conflict of interest in formulating investment advice and focuses on protecting the client, Standard III(C) deals with conflicts of interest in any actions or decisions of a member and focuses on responsibility to the employer. By reporting conflicts of interest, members should give their employer enough information to assess the impact of the conflict. By complying with employer guidelines, members allow their employers to avoid potentially embarrassing and costly violations.

Many investment firms restrict their employees' actions and investment freedom to avoid conflicts and ensure that client interests come first. Standard III(C) requires that members obey such internal directives and specifies that members use their own judgment to report any potential conflicts that are not covered by their employer's guidelines. Reportable situations include conflicts that would interfere with rendering unbiased investment advice and conflicts that would cause a member not to act in the employer's best interest.

The principles that apply to Standard IV(B.7) also apply to the investment recommendation portion of Standard III(C). Ownership of stocks analyzed or recommended, participation in outside boards, and financial and other pressures that may influence a decision are to be promptly reported to the employer so that their impact can be assessed and a decision made on how to resolve the conflict.

The mere appearance of conflict of interest may create problems for a member and the member's employer. Therefore, many of the conflicts mentioned in the preceding paragraph and others could be explicitly prohibited by the employer. For example, many employers restrict personal trading, outside board membership, and related activities to prevent situations that might not normally be considered problematic from a conflict-of-interest point of view but could give the appearance of a conflict of interest. Standard III(C) specifies that every member must honor these restrictions; members must avoid such conflicts and, if they occur inadvertently, must report them promptly so that the employer and the member can resolve them as quickly and effectively as possible.

Standard III(C) also deals with a member's conflicts of interest that might be detrimental to the employer's business. Any potential conflict situation that could prevent clear judgment in or full commitment to the execution of the member's duties to the employer should be reported to the member's employer and promptly resolved.

Application of the Standard

Example 1. Green is a telecommunications analyst at Alpha, Inc., an investment manager that caters to large pension funds and foundations. Green is considering a small purchase of DRAM, Inc., a computer chip manufacturer, for his personal portfolio. Green knows that Alpha's policy prohibits all personnel from trading in any equities traded on a U.S. exchange (DRAM trades on the New York Stock Exchange). He also knows that Alpha has no intention of trading in DRAM and that, even if it did, he would have no impact on the DRAM investment decision because he does not cover the computer chip industry. Green believes that his purchase would be sufficiently small to have no material impact on DRAM's trading patterns. Given these considerations, Green decides to purchase shares in DRAM and believes he has no need to report that transaction to Alpha's compliance officer.

Comment: In choosing to ignore his employer's trading prohibitions, Green is violating Standard III(C). It is not Green's prerogative to decide unilaterally that Alpha's prohibition against trading in exchange-listed securities can be ignored because his purchase will not create a conflict of interest. He should realize that Alpha's policies are designed not only to prevent material conflict of interest but also to prevent the appearance of impropriety. Green could discuss his wish to purchase DRAM stock with Alpha's compliance officer and request that Alpha make an exception in this case. Without such an exception, however, Green is prohibited from purchasing DRAM. If he makes the purchase, Green should report the transaction immediately to his compliance officer to determine how best to unwind the transaction and to determine if disgorgement of any profit is warranted.

Example 2. Corky, a senior portfolio manager for Universal Management, recently became involved as a trustee with the Chelsea Foundation, a very large not-for-profit foundation in her hometown. Universal is a small money manager (assets under management of approximately $100 million) catering to individual investors. Chelsea has assets in excess of $2 billion. Corky does not believe informing Universal of her involvement with Chelsea is necessary.

Comment: By failing to inform Universal of her involvement with Chelsea, Corky violated Standard III(C). Given the large size of the endowment at Chelsea, Corky's new role as a trustee can reasonably be expected to be time-consuming, to the possible detriment of Corky's portfolio responsibilities with Universal. As a trustee, Corky also may become involved with the investment decisions at Chelsea. Therefore, Corky should have discussed becoming a trustee at Chelsea with her compliance officer or supervisor at Universal before accepting the position and should have disclosed the degree to which she would be involved in investment decisions at Chelsea.

Example 3. Smith covers East European equities for Marlborough Investments, an investment management firm with a strong presence in emerging markets. While on a business trip to Russia, Smith learns that investing in Russian equity directly is difficult but that equity-linked notes that replicate the performance of the underlying Russian equity can be purchased from a New York-based investment bank. Believing that his firm would not be interested in such a security, Smith purchases a note linked to a Russian telecommunications company for his own account without informing Marlborough. A month later, Smith decides that the firm should consider investing in Russian equities using equity-linked notes, and he prepares a write-up on the market that concludes with a recommendation to purchase several of the notes. One note recommended is linked to the same Russian telecom company that Smith holds in his personal account.

Comment: Smith violated Standard III(C) by failing to disclose his ownership of the note linked to the Russian telecom company. Smith should have disclosed the investment opportunity to his employer and looked to his company's policies on personal trading to determine whether it was proper for him to purchase the note for his own account. By purchasing the note, Smith may or may not have impaired his ability to make an unbiased and objective assessment of the appropriateness of the derivative instrument for his firm. Smith's failure to disclose the purchase to his employer impaired his employer's ability to render an opinion regarding whether the ownership of the security constituted a conflict of interest that might have affected future recommendations. Once he recommended the notes to his firm, Smith compounded his problems by not disclosing that he owned the notes in his personal account—a clear conflict of interest.

Example 4. Roberts is a portfolio manager at Katama Investments, an advisory firm specializing in managing assets for high-net-worth individuals. Katama's trading desk uses a variety of brokerage houses to execute trades on behalf of its clients. Roberts asks the trading desk to direct a large portion of its commissions to Naushon, Inc., a small broker/dealer run by a business school classmate of Roberts. Katama's traders have found Naushon to be not very competitive on pricing, and although Naushon generates some research for its trading clients, Katama's other analysts have found most of Naushon's research not especially useful. Nevertheless, the traders do as Roberts asks, and in return for receiving a large portion of Katama's business, Naushon recommends the investment services of Roberts and Katama to its wealthiest clients. This arrangement is not disclosed to either Katama or the clients referred by Naushon.

Comment: Roberts violated Standard III(C) by failing to inform her employer of the referral arrangement and violated Standard IV(B.8), Disclosure of Referral Fees, by failing to disclose the arrangement to the clients referred by Naushon. If Katama is paying Naushon higher-than-average commissions for little in the way of added benefit, then Roberts also violated Standard IV(B.1), Fiduciary Duties.

Procedures for Compliance

Members should report any beneficial interest they may have in securities and any corporate directorships, trustee positions, or other special relationships that they may have that could reasonably be considered a conflict of interest with their responsibilities to their employer. Members should discuss with their compliance officer or supervisor, before taking action, any action by the member that could lead to such conflict.

Standard III: Relationships with and Responsibilities to the Employer

Standard III(D)—Disclosure of Additional Compensation Arrangements

Members shall disclose to their employer in writing all monetary compensation or other benefits that they receive for their services that are in addition to compensation or benefits conferred by a member's employer.

Purpose and Scope of the Standard

Standard III(D) states the responsibility of AIMR members, CFA charterholders, and candidates in the CFA Program to provide complete disclosure to their employer of the sources and nature of compensation or other benefits received by them for services rendered. Compensation and benefits include direct compensation by the client and any indirect compensation or other benefits received from third parties. The stipulation "in writing" includes any form of communication that can be documented (for example, communication via computer e-mail that can be retrieved and documented).

Members must disclose outside compensation/benefits to employers because such arrangements may affect loyalties and objectivity and create potential conflicts of interest. Disclosure allows an employer to consider the outside arrangements when evaluating the actions and motivations of members. Moreover, the employer is entitled to have full knowledge of compensation/benefit arrangements to assess the true cost of the outside services members are providing. Written disclosure requirements discourage the use of devices such as compensation in kind, through products or services, and reimbursement of expenses that conceal benefits.

Application of the Standard

Example 1. White, a portfolio analyst for Adams Trust Company, manages the account of Cochran, a client. White is paid a salary by his employer, and Cochran pays the trust company a standard fee based on the market value of assets in her portfolio. Cochran proposes to White that "any year that my portfolio achieves at least a 15 percent return before taxes, you and your wife can fly to Florida at my expense and use my condominium during the third week of January." White does not inform his employer of the arrangement and vacations in Florida the following January as Cochran's guest.

Comment: White violated Standard III(D) by failing to inform his employer in writing of this supplemental, contingent compensation arrangement. The nature of the arrangement could have resulted in partiality to Cochran's account, which could have detracted from White's performance with respect to other accounts he handles for Adams Trust.

Example 2. Jones sits on the board of directors of Exercise Unlimited, Inc. In return for his services on the board, Jones receives unlimited membership privileges for his family at all Exercise Unlimited facilities. Jones does not disclose this arrangement to his employer, as he does not receive monetary compensation.

Comment: Jones violated Standard III(D) by failing to disclose to his employer benefits received in exchange for his services on the board of directors. Jones may also be obligated to disclose his participation on Exercise Unlimited's board to clients and prospective clients under Standard IV(B.7).

Procedures for Compliance

Members should make an immediate written report to their employer specifying any compensation they receive or propose to receive for services in addition to compensation or benefits received from their primary employer. This written report should state the terms of any oral or written agreement under which a member will receive additional compensation; terms include the nature of the compensation, the amount of compensation, and the duration of the agreement.

Standard III: Relationships with and Responsibilities to the Employer

Standard III(E)—Responsibilities of Supervisors

Members with supervisory responsibility, authority, or the ability to influence the conduct of others shall exercise reasonable supervision over those subject to their supervision or authority to prevent any violation of applicable statutes, regulations, or provisions of the Code and Standards. In so doing, members are entitled to rely on reasonable procedures designed to detect and prevent such violations.

Purpose and Scope of the Standard

Standard III(E) states the responsibility of AIMR members, CFA charterholders, and candidates in the CFA Program to take steps to prevent persons acting under their supervision from violating the law or the Code and Standards.

Any investment professionals who have employees subject to their control or influence—whether or not the employees are AIMR members, CFA charterholders, or candidates in the CFA Program—exercise supervisory responsibility. Members are expected to have in-depth knowledge of the Code and Standards and to apply this knowledge in discharging their supervisory responsibilities.

The conduct that constitutes reasonable supervision in a particular case depends on the number of employees supervised and the work performed by those employees. Some members who supervise large numbers of employees cannot personally evaluate the conduct of their employees on a continuing basis. Although these members may delegate supervisory duties, such delegation does not relieve members of their supervisory responsibility. Their responsibilities under Standard III(E) include instructing those to whom supervision is delegated about methods to prevent and detect violations.

Members with supervisory responsibility must make reasonable efforts to detect violations of laws, rules, regulations, and the Code and Standards. They exercise reasonable supervision by establishing and implementing written compliance procedures and ensuring that those procedures are followed through periodic review. If a member has adopted reasonable procedures and taken steps to institute an effective compliance program, then the member may not be in violation of Standard III(E) if the member is unable to detect violations that occur despite these efforts. The fact that violations do occur may indicate, however, that the compliance procedures are inadequate. In addition, in some cases, merely enacting such procedures may not be sufficient to fulfill the duty imposed by Standard III(E). A member may be in violation of Standard III(E) if he or she knows or should know that the procedures designed to detect and prevent violations are not being followed.

Members with supervisory responsibility also are expected to understand what constitutes an adequate compliance system for their firms and to make reasonable efforts to see that appropriate compliance procedures are established, documented, communicated to covered personnel, and followed. "Adequate" procedures are those designed to meet industry standards, regulatory requirements, the requirements of the Code and Standards, and the circumstances of the firm. Once compliance procedures are established, the supervisor must also make reasonable efforts to ensure that the compliance procedures are monitored and enforced.

To be effective, compliance procedures must be in place prior to the occurrence of a violation of the law or the Code and Standards. Although compliance procedures cannot be designed to anticipate every potential violation, they should be designed to anticipate the activities most likely to result in misconduct. Each compliance program must be appropriate for the size and nature of the organization. Competitors' compliance procedures or other industry programs should be reviewed to ensure that procedures meet the minimum industry standards.

A member with supervisory responsibility should bring an inadequate compliance system to the attention of the firm's senior managers and recommend corrective action. If the member clearly cannot discharge supervisory responsibilities because of the absence of a compliance system or because of an inadequate compliance system, the member should decline in writing to accept supervisory responsibility until the firm adopts reasonable procedures to allow the member to adequately exercise such responsibility.

Once a supervisor learns that an employee has violated or may have violated the law or the Code and Standards, the supervisor must promptly initiate an investigation to ascertain the extent of the wrongdoing. Relying on an employee's statements about the extent of the violation or assurances that the wrongdoing will not recur is not enough. Reporting the misconduct up the chain of command and warning the employee to cease the activity are also not enough. Pending the outcome of the investigation, a supervisor should take steps to ensure the violations will not be repeated, such as placing limits on the employee's activities or increasing the monitoring of the employee's activities.

Application of the Standard

Example 1. Mattock, senior vice president and head of the research department of H&V, Inc., a regional brokerage firm, has decided to change her recommendation for Timber Products from buy to sell. In line with H&V's procedures, she orally advises certain other H&V executives of her proposed actions before the report is prepared for publication. As a result of his conversation with Mattock, Frampton, one of the executives of H&V accountable to Mattock, immediately sells Timber's stock from his own account and from certain discretionary client accounts. In addition, other personnel inform certain institutional customers of the changed recommendation before it is printed and disseminated to all H&V customers who have received previous Timber reports.

> *Comment*: Mattock failed to supervise reasonably and adequately the actions of those accountable to her. She did not prevent, or establish reasonable procedures designed to prevent, dissemination of or trading on the information by those who knew of her changed recommendation. She must ensure that her firm has procedures for reviewing or recording trading in the stock of any corporation that has been the subject of an undisseminated material change in recommendation. Adequate procedures would have informed the subordinates of their duties and detected sales by Frampton and selected customers.

Example 2. Miller is the research director for Jamestown Investment Programs. The portfolio managers have become critical of Miller and his staff because the Jamestown portfolios do not include any stock that has been the subject of a merger or tender offer. Ginn, a member of Miller's staff, tells Miller that she had been studying a local company, Excelsior, Inc., and recommends its purchase. Ginn adds that the company has been widely rumored to be the subject of a merger study by a well-known conglomerate and that discussions between them are under way. Miller directs Ginn to prepare a memo recommending the stock, which she does. Miller passes along Ginn's memo to the portfolio managers, noting that he has not reviewed the memo and is leaving town for a week. As a result of the memo, the portfolio managers buy Excelsior stock immediately. The day Miller returns to the office, Excelsior reports a sharp decline and the exchange suspends trading because of an influx of sell orders following a public announcement of declining earnings. Upon questioning Ginn, Miller learns that Ginn's only sources were her brother, who is an acquisitions analyst with Acme Industries, and the "well-known conglomerate" and that the merger discussions were planned but not held.

Comment: Miller violated Standard III(E) by not exercising reasonable supervision when he disseminated the memo without checking it to ensure that Ginn had a reasonable and adequate basis for her recommendations, as required by Standard IV(A.1), and that Ginn was not relying on material nonpublic information, as prohibited by Standard V(A).

Example 3. Edwards, a trainee salesman at Wheeler & Company, a major national brokerage firm, assists a customer in paying for the securities of High, Inc., by using anticipated profits from the immediate sale of the same securities. Despite the fact that High is not on Wheeler's recommended list, a large volume of its stock is traded through Wheeler in this manner. Mason is a Wheeler vice president responsible for supervising compliance with the securities laws in the sales department. Part of her compensation from Wheeler is based on commission revenues from the sales department. Although she notices the increased trading activity, she does nothing to investigate or halt it.

Comment: Mason's failure to adequately review and investigate purchase orders in High stock executed by Edwards and her failure to supervise the trainee's activities violated Standard III(E). Supervisors should be especially sensitive to actual or potential conflicts between their own self-interests and their supervisory responsibilities.

Example 4. Tabbing is first vice president and portfolio manager for Crozet, Inc., a registered investment advisory and registered broker/dealer firm. She reports to Henry, the president of Crozet. Crozet serves as the investment advisor and principal underwriter for ABC and XYZ public mutual funds. The two funds' prospectuses allow Crozet to trade financial futures for the funds for the limited purpose of hedging against market risks. Henry, extremely impressed with Tabbing's performance in the past two years, directs Tabbing to act as portfolio manager for the funds. For the benefit of its employees, Crozet has also organized the Crozet Employee Profit-Sharing Plan (CEPSP), a defined-contribution retirement plan under ERISA (the U.S. Employee Retirement Income Security Act of 1974). Henry assigns Tabbing to manage 20 percent of the assets of CEPSP. Tabbing's investment objective for her portion of CEPSP's assets is aggressive growth. Unbeknownst to Henry, Tabbing frequently places S&P 500 Index purchase and sale orders for the funds and the CEPSP without providing the futures commission merchants (FCMs) who take the orders with any prior or simultaneous designation of the account for which the trade has been placed. Frequently, neither Tabbing nor anyone else at

Crozet completes an internal trade ticket to record the time an order was placed or the specific account for which the order was intended. FCMs often designate a specific account only after the trade, when Tabbing provides such designation. Crozet has no written operating procedures or compliance manual concerning its futures trading, nor does its compliance department review such trading. Tabbing, after observing the market's movement, assigns to CEPSP the S&P 500 positions with more favorable execution prices, and she assigns positions with less favorable execution prices to the funds.

> *Comment*: Tabbing's actions violated Standard III(C), Disclosure of Conflicts to Employer, because Tabbing clearly had a conflict of interest between her responsibility to the mutual funds and her responsibility to the profit-sharing plan. Tabbing also violated Standard IV(B.3) concerning fair dealing with customers and clients and Standard IV(B.1) concerning fiduciary responsibilities. Henry, having placed Tabbing in this position, violated Standard III(E) by failing to adequately supervise Tabbing with respect to her S&P 500 trading. Henry further violated Standard III(E) by failing to establish record-keeping and reporting procedures to prevent or detect Tabbing's violations.

Example 5. Burrow is chair and CEO of Giant Brothers, Inc., a broker/dealer. Weems is Giant's president. Harris serves as vice chair of Giant and is responsible for the firm's fixed-income trading. Milland is the head of Giant's government bond trading desk, but she is not a member of AIMR. Burrow, Weems, and Harris discover that Milland recently submitted a false $1 billion bid in an auction of U.S. Treasury securities. Milland's purpose in submitting the false bid, in the name of a Giant customer without the customer's knowledge, was to enable Giant to evade the Treasury's restriction on a single bidder bidding for more than 35 percent of an auction amount. After the auction, Giant took into inventory not only securities that it bid for in its own name but also the securities acquired through the false bid made without the customer's knowledge. When Harris, Milland's immediate supervisor, confronts Milland with this information, Milland assures Harris that this bid was an isolated incident and will not happen again. Harris advises Milland that her actions will be reported to senior management but places no further restrictions on Milland's activities at the firm. Harris later discusses the matter with Burrow, Weems, and Giant's legal counsel. Counsel advises that Giant should report the false bid, which counsel considers to be an illegal act, to the regulatory authorities. Harris and Weems concur with counsel's recommendation but fail to report the conduct to any regulatory agency. An internal investigation reveals that numerous violations have occurred before and after the conduct discovered by Harris. The U.S. Securities and Exchange Commission subsequently investigates the matter. Burrow, Weems, and Harris attempt to place responsibility for investigating Milland's conduct on one another. Harris, Milland's immediate supervisor, states that he believed he had satisfied his supervisory responsibilities by making Burrow and Weems aware of Milland's actions. Weems states that he believed the responsibility to belong to Harris as Milland's immediate supervisor. Burrow indicates that she believed her subordinates would follow through with the necessary steps to handle the matter.

> *Comment*: Burrow, as CEO, bore ultimate responsibility for ensuring that a prompt and thorough inquiry into Milland's conduct was undertaken, including a review of all relevant documents and questioning of other Giant employees. Burrow was responsible for ensuring that the firm took steps to prevent further violations of the securities laws and to determine the scope of misconduct. Weems violated Standard III(E) by failing to ascertain whether action had, in fact, been taken once the conduct was reported and for failing to follow up when she learned that action had not been taken. Harris did not go far enough by simply advising Milland that her actions would be brought to the attention of Giant's senior executives. As Milland's immediate supervisor, Harris should have increased supervision of Milland and placed appropriate limitations on her activities pending the outcome of an internal investigation. Supervisors cannot rely on unverified representations made by employees regarding the extent of wrongdoing or the employee's assurances that the wrongdoing will not recur. When multiple supervisors are involved, it is imperative that the responsibilities of each in addressing the potential wrongdoing be clearly defined. Supervisors must make certain that steps are taken to ensure that wrongdoing is not repeated while an internal investigation is going on.

Procedures for Compliance

A supervisor complies with Standard III(E) by identifying situations in which legal violations or violations of the Code and Standards are likely to occur and establishing and enforcing compliance procedures to prevent such violations. Adequate compliance procedures should

- be contained in a clearly written and accessible manual that is tailored to the member's operations;
- be drafted so that the procedures are easy to understand;

- designate a compliance officer whose authority and responsibility are clearly defined and who has the necessary resources and authority to implement the firm's compliance procedures;
- describe the hierarchy of supervision and assign duties among supervisors;
- implement a system of checks and balances;
- outline the scope of the procedures;
- outline procedures to document the monitoring and testing of compliance procedures;
- outline permissible conduct;
- delineate procedures for reporting violations and sanctions.

Once a compliance program is in place, a supervisor should

- disseminate the contents of the program to appropriate personnel;
- periodically update procedures to ensure that the measures are adequate under the law;
- continually educate personnel regarding the compliance procedures;
- issue periodic reminders of the procedures to appropriate personnel;
- incorporate a professional conduct evaluation as part of the employee's performance review;
- review the actions of employees to ensure compliance and identify violators;
- take the necessary steps to enforce the procedures once a violation has occurred.

Once a violation is discovered, a supervisor should

- respond promptly;
- conduct a thorough investigation of the activities to determine the scope of the wrongdoing;
- increase supervision or place appropriate limitations on the wrongdoer pending the outcome of the investigation.

A supervisor that is an AIMR member, CFA charterholder, or candidate in the CFA Program should consider advising new employees—in writing—of the expectation that their conduct should meet high ethical standards. During briefing procedures, the Code and Standards should be given to all new employees. New employees might be informed of the existence of the AIMR self-administered Standards of Practice Exam included in the *Handbook* (see chapter with that title) so that they can test their understanding of professional conduct and ethical behavior and, by passing the examination, show proof of their knowledge.

Standard IV: Relationships with and Responsibilities to Clients and Prospects
A. Investment Process

Standard IV(A.1)—Reasonable Basis and Representations

Members shall:

a. Exercise diligence and thoroughness in making investment recommendations or in taking investment actions.

b. Have a reasonable and adequate basis, supported by appropriate research and investigation, for such recommendations or actions.

c. Make reasonable and diligent efforts to avoid any material misrepresentation in any research report or investment recommendation.

d. Maintain appropriate records to support the reasonableness of such recommendations or actions.

Purpose and Scope of the Standard

Standard IV(A.1) states the responsibility of AIMR members, holders of the Chartered Financial Analyst designation, and candidates in the CFA Program to perform diligent and thorough investigation appropriate to the circumstances for an investment recommendation or action. Members must establish a reasonable basis for every investment recommendation or action, exercise diligence in avoiding any material misrepresentation, and maintain such records and documentation as are appropriate to support that action or recommendation.

Standard IV(A.1) is meant to address the member–client relationship, the role of the member in the investment decision-making process, and the support the organization provides the investment professional in the performance of this role. These relationships, whether initiated by the investor (buy side) or by the broker/dealer (sell side), will dictate the nature of the diligence and thoroughness of the research and investigation required by Standard IV(A.1) and the records in support of the recommendation/action required by Standard IV(A.2). Members are in compliance if they recommend an investment transaction on the basis of their firm's research; the research of another party who exercised diligence and thoroughness in arriving at a decision; research prepared by a brokerage firm, bank, or investment service for general distribution; or quantitatively oriented research, such as computer-generated screening or ranking of universes of common stocks based on various sets of prescribed criteria. For part or all of the background information for general recommendations, a member may depend on reliable sources both within and outside the member's firm. With respect to an individual investment transaction, a member may rely on the same sources but also has the obligation to consider the transaction within the context of a client's entire portfolio, including client needs and preferences. Generally, the use of reliable sources should be disclosed.

Members engaged in corporate finance activities must perform diligent and thorough investigations appropriate to the circumstances with regard to initial public offerings (IPOs), private placements, and secondary offerings, including the proper pricing of any issues. Members must demonstrate a thorough understanding of the industry sector and the issuing company's role within that sector. Members are responsible for performing general industry analysis, company financial analysis, personnel reviews, and studies of use of proceeds, legal matters, potential conflicts of interest, capital structure, and environmental considerations.

Members must also make a reasonable and diligent effort to ensure that any research report finding or investment recommendation is accurate. If a member has reason to suspect that any information in a source is not accurate, the member should refrain from relying on that information.

The requirements for issuing conclusions on research will vary with the member's investment style, but the member has the responsibility to make reasonable efforts to cover all pertinent issues. In the case of fundamental analysis, such efforts normally would include an examination of historical earnings, ownership of assets, outstanding contracts, and other business factors. A quantitative analyst should concentrate on using valid statistical analysis techniques and on ensuring, to the greatest possible degree, that the conclusions are based on accurate and meaningful data and on as wide a sample as possible.

Members should take into consideration accounting and disclosure differences among countries. Variations in the scope and effectiveness of local securities regulations can sometimes lead to misunderstandings on the part of those participating in foreign markets about the nature and extent of the information available to make investment judgments and about the degree of protection afforded public investors. Members are obligated to identify differences between foreign and domestic markets, to consider them in their work, and to inform their clients of any relevant significant differences. Relevant factors include, but are not limited to, the following:

- differences in the basis for providing accounting figures;
- international variations in the timeliness, depth, quality, and comprehensiveness of corporate disclosures;

- the degree of public protection provided by securities laws and regulations;
- the general extent of regulatory compliance with laws and regulations;
- the degree of liquidity of foreign markets;
- tax withholding;
- difficulties in settling transactions and other custody issues;
- any other relevant factors, such as capital or currency controls.

Members should not, for example, compare financial ratios (such as return on equity, debt to equity, or net profit margin) prepared with figures presented under different accounting standards without examining the significance of the differences and, where appropriate, making adjustments to ensure comparability. Equally unprofessional would be for a member to ignore (and fail to inform clients of) the risks associated with trading in a foreign securities market if the market has no rules in place—enforced by local governments or stock exchanges—concerning the use by insiders of material nonpublic information.

To comply with Standard IV(A.1), the member must retain records that refer to the specific research analysis or quantitative system used as well as records that indicate reasons for any specific transaction. Members are required to maintain files, including work papers, indicating the scope of their research and reasons for their conclusions. Files should include details of where the data necessary for the analysis were obtained and an account of the method of analysis that is detailed enough to allow reconstruction of the method. Quantitative analysts should document the development and describe the purpose of algorithms used in any investment decision-making process. In the event of real-time or path-dependent quantitatively driven investment systems, the analyst must have the capability to reconstruct the variables and conditions leading up to and precipitating actual transactions and have a basis for demonstrating that these investment systems are functioning as intended.

Application of the Standard

Example 1. Martin, a quantitative analyst at Allen Brothers, an investment counseling firm, has completed an analysis of return patterns of out-of-favor, low-book-value stocks for the past five years. Based on the study, Martin's report recommends selling this class of stocks out of all portfolios for which client objectives allow such a move.

> *Comment*: Martin's recommendation is not based on thorough quantitative work; to be comprehensive, the work would need to extend over a longer time period. The study should be redone or the recommendation issued in such a manner as to make its limitations obvious.

Example 2. Jenner works on the fixed-income trading floor of a major investment bank. She supports the sales and trading effort by advising clients and traders about corporate credit trends and potential rating actions. Noticing that an automotive company is making a large acquisition, she calls the company to obtain more information. She also calls the rating agencies to gauge their responses. With this information in hand, she works up an advisory for interested clients about the credit implications of the company's action. Randall, a senior partner of the firm, has a good relationship with the auto company. He explodes when he discovers that Jenner has contacted the company without his knowing it. He tells Jenner she should never again contact one of "his" companies without his consent. Jenner believes that the restriction ties her hands in such a way that she cannot continue to do her job properly.

> *Comment*: Jenner has a responsibility to exercise diligence and thoroughness in forming investment judgments, but she needs to be sensitive to business considerations and balance them against her responsibility. Although Jenner can try to cooperate more effectively with Randall in obtaining needed information, Jenner must also let the firm's clients know when she is "conflicted" or otherwise unable to obtain the information necessary to draw a conclusion.

Example 3. Hawk manages the corporate finance department of Black & White Securities, Ltd. (B&W). The firm is anticipating that the government will soon close a tax loophole that currently allows oil and gas exploration companies to pass on drilling expenses to holders of a certain class of shares. Because market demand for the tax-advantaged class of stock is currently high, B&W decides to undertake several new equity financings at once before the loophole closes. Time is of the essence, but B&W lacks sufficient resources to conduct adequate research on all the prospective issuing companies; so, Hawk decides to estimate the IPO prices based on the relative size of each company and to justify the pricing later when her staff has time.

> *Comment*: B&W should have taken on only the work that it could adequately handle. By categorizing the issuers as to general size, Hawk has bypassed researching all the other relevant aspects that should be considered when pricing new issues. Such an omission can result in investors purchasing shares at prices that have no actual basis.

Example 4. Dhaliwal works for Cloudy Days Brokerage in the corporate finance group. He has just persuaded Starchy Resources, Ltd., to allow his firm to do a secondary equity financing at Starchy Resources stock's current price. Because the stock has been trading at higher multiples than similar companies with equivalent production, Dhaliwal presses the Starchy Resources managers to project what would be the maximum production they could achieve in an optimal scenario. Based on these numbers, he is able to justify the price they will be asking for the secondary issue. During a sales pitch to the brokers, Dhaliwal then uses these numbers as the base-case production levels Starchy Resources will achieve.

> *Comment*: When presenting information to the brokers, Dhaliwal should have given a range of production scenarios and the probability of Starchy Resources achieving each level. By giving the optimal production level as the likely level of production, he has misrepresented the chances of achieving that production level and seriously misled the brokers.

Example 5. Jennings is an international portfolio manager based in Boston, Massachusetts. A client of Jennings who had previously stipulated that all his money be invested in North American blue-chip securities requests that, in the future, Jennings manage his money on an international basis, with emphasis on securities in countries with high rates of economic growth.

> *Comment*: As an international fund manager, Jennings must be aware of relevant differences among countries in accounting, disclosure, and compliance standards; market liquidity; capital controls; taxation; and other factors. Jennings must be capable of incorporating such considerations into her assessments of potential risks and returns. Her client may well be unaware of these factors and their potential influence on the amount and volatility of his future investment returns. So, Jennings should explain these factors to her client and allow the client to consider them before altering his investment strategy.

Example 6. Witt is a CFA charterholder who has created an Internet site, with a chatroom area, to publish his recommendations. He views the site as a chance to attract new clients. In the chatroom, he almost always writes positively about technology stocks and recommends purchasing what the conventional wisdom of the markets have christened the "hot" Internet-related securities of the day.

> *Comment*: Witt's exuberance about technology and conventional wisdom of the markets, without more information, do not form a reasonable and adequate basis, supported by appropriate research and investigation, on which to base a recommendation. Therefore, Witt has violated Standard IV(A.1).

Procedures for Compliance

Members can comply with Standard IV(A.1) by addressing the following areas:

- Analyze basic characteristics. Before recommending a specific investment or investment discipline to a broad client group, a member should investigate the investment's basic characteristics. Furthermore, written records should indicate the characteristics (for example, quality ratings, terms such as "businessman's risk" or "speculative issue") and the basis for the recommendation (quantitative, fundamental, technical, etc.). A research report can serve as a record of the findings that support conclusions about a particular issue or group of securities. With respect to a quantitative investment discipline, the process should be illustrated in thorough detail, and any applicable backtesting data should be made available for inspection or review.
- Analyze portfolio needs. A member has the obligation to analyze clients' investment needs as well as the basic characteristics of investments. The analysis of a client's needs and circumstances is not a one-time matter but a continuing responsibility. As for the meshing of client characteristics and investment characteristics, members should keep in mind that a combination of several different investments is likely to provide a more acceptable level of risk exposure than is investing in one or two securities. Also, the basic characteristics of the entire portfolio will largely determine whether client factors are being served. Thus, the focus should be on the characteristics of the total portfolio rather than an issue-by-issue review.

At the outset of the relationship, the portfolio manager and client should develop a statement of investment objectives, and they should review this statement periodically (annually and when a major change in client circumstances occurs). These objectives should be set forth in writing. Each recommendation or transaction should be made in view of client objectives and the basic characteristics of the investment to be bought or sold.

- Maintain files. A member should maintain files to support investment recommendations. In addition to furnishing excellent reference materials for future work, research files play a key role in justifying investment decisions under later scrutiny. Files can serve as the ultimate proof that recommendations and actions, good or bad, were made based on the same methodology that drove the analyst's decisions.

If recommendations are based on a report from an outside source, the member should keep a copy of the report. If the member undertakes original research, the member should include details of where the necessary data were obtained and include enough information about the analytical method to allow the process to be reconstructed. In the case of fundamental research, the member should keep company-published data, industry data, and records of all management contacts. Records and files may be kept on paper or in electronic form. If kept in electronic form, members should maintain adequate backup.

Standard IV: Relationships with and Responsibilities to Clients and Prospects
A. Investment Process

Standard IV(A.2)—Research Reports

Members shall:

a. Use reasonable judgment regarding the inclusion or exclusion of relevant factors in research reports.

b. Distinguish between facts and opinions in research reports.

c. Indicate the basic characteristics of the investment involved when preparing for public distribution a research report that is not directly related to a specific portfolio or client.

Purpose and Scope of the Standard

Standard IV(A.2) states the responsibility of AIMR members, CFA charterholders, and candidates in the CFA Program to include in each research report those key factors that are instrumental to the investment recommendation presented in the report. A critical part of this requirement is to distinguish clearly between opinions and facts. In preparing a research report, the member should present the basic characteristics of the security being analyzed, which will allow the reader to evaluate the report and incorporate information the reader deems relevant into his or her investment decision-making process.

For the purposes of Standard IV(A.2), the term "report" is not confined to a written report of the type traditionally generated by an analyst researching a particular security, company, or industry. A report can be made via any means of communication, including in-person recommendation, telephone conversation, media broadcast, and transmission by computer (e.g., on the Internet). Furthermore, the nature of these communications is highly diverse—from one word ("buy" or "sell") to in-depth reports of more than a hundred pages. Brief communications must be supported by background reports or data that are available to interested parties. The information can range from chartist data to studies on specific projects, brief updates, and the like.

The report may contain a general recommendation about the market, asset allocation, or classes of investments (e.g., stocks, bonds, real estate) or relate to a specific security. If recommendations are contained in capsule form (such as a recommended stock list), members should notify clients that additional information and analyses are available from the producer of the report. Investment advice based on quantitative research and analysis should be supported by readily available reference material and should be applied in a manner consistent with previously applied methodology. Members should outline known limitations of the analysis and conclusions contained in the report. In evaluating the basic characteristics of the investment being recommended, members should consider in the report the principal risks inherent in the expected cash flows, which may include credit risk, financial risk (specifically, the use of leverage or financial derivatives), and overall market risk.

In company analyses, a member has a duty to gather comprehensive information about the company in question. As part of the analysis, the member may ask company management to review the report for factual inaccuracies. Members should take care to thoroughly review and analyze any information provided by the company. The objective in company analyses is to determine the nature of the issuer's (or the company's) earning power, cash flow, operating and financial strength and viability, and dividend potential. The member's analysis of earning power may include growth potential, the degree of cyclical sensitivity of the earning power, and the analyst's confidence in future projections. These considerations should be part of the analytical process the analyst follows to reach a conclusion about the basic characteristics of the specific investment security, but disclosure of these factors is not required.

Once the process has been completed, the member who prepares the report should select those elements important to the analysis and conclusions of the report so that the user can follow and challenge the report's reasoning. So long as the writer has done adequate investigation, the report writer may emphasize certain areas, touch briefly on others, and omit certain aspects deemed unimportant. For instance, a report may dwell on a quarterly earnings release or new-product introduction at the sacrifice of examining other fundamental matters in depth so long as the analyst stipulates clearly the limits to the scope of the report.

Standard IV(A.2) requires that opinion be separated from fact. Violations are most likely to occur when reports fail to separate the past from the future by not indicating that earnings estimates, changes in the outlook for dividends, and/or future market price information are opinions subject to future circumstances. In the case of complex quantitative analysis, analysts must clearly separate fact from statistical conjecture and identify the known limitations of the analysis.

Standard IV(A.2) also requires that every research report containing an investment recommendation include an indication of the investment's basic characteristics so that the reader can understand the nature of the security discussed in the report.

Application of the Standard

Example 1. Williamson, director of marketing for Country Technicians, Inc., is convinced that she has found the perfect formula for increasing Country Technician's income and diversifying its product base. Williamson plans to build on Country Technician's reputation as a leading money manager by marketing an exclusive and expensive investment advice letter to high-net-worth individuals. One hitch in the plan is the complexity of Country Technician's investment system—a combination of technical trading rules (based on historical price and volume fluctuations) and portfolio construction rules designed to minimize risk. To simplify the newsletter, she decides to include only each week's top five buy and sell recommendations and leave out details of the valuation models and the portfolio structuring scheme.

> *Comment*: Williamson's plans for the letter violate Standard IV(A.2) because she does not plan to include all the relevant factors behind the investment advice. Clients need to fully understand Country Technician's process and logic in order to implement the advice effectively. Without understanding the basis for a recommendation, clients cannot possibly understand its limitations or its inherent risks. In addition to violating Standard IV(A.2), Williamson violated Standard IV(B.2), Portfolio Investment Recommendations and Actions, by ignoring Country Technician's normal portfolio considerations and focusing purely on the recommendations.

Example 2. Dox is a mining analyst for East Bank Securities. He has just finished his report on Boisy Bay Minerals. Included in his report is his own assessment of the geological extent of mineral reserves likely to be found on the company's land. Dox completed this calculation based on the core samples from the company's latest drilling. According to Dox's calculations, the company has in excess of 500,000 ounces of gold on the property. Dox concludes his research report as follows: "Based on the fact that the company has 500,000 ounces of gold to be mined, I recommend a strong BUY."

> *Comment*: If Dox issues the report as written, he will violate Standard IV(A.2). His calculation of the total gold reserves for the property is an opinion, not a fact. Opinions should be distinguished from fact in research reports.

Example 3. Orange, an analyst at Government Brokers, Inc., which is a brokerage firm specializing in government bond trading, has produced a report that describes an investment strategy designed to benefit from an expected decline in U.S. interest rates. The firm's derivative products group has designed a structured product that will allow the firm's clients to benefit from this strategy. Orange's report describing the strategy indicates that high returns are possible if various scenarios for declining interest rates are assumed. Citing the proprietary nature of the structured product underlying the strategy, the report does not describe in detail how the firm is able to offer such returns in the scenarios, nor does the report address the likely returns of the strategy if, contrary to expectations, interest rates rise.

> *Comment*: Orange has violated Standard IV(A.2) because her report fails to describe properly the basic characteristics of the investment strategy, including how the structure was created and the degree to which leverage was embedded in the structure. The report should also have included a balanced discussion of how the strategy would perform in the case of rising as well as falling interest rates.

Example 4. Greene, an analyst with Aberdeen Securities, prepared a report on Window America, Inc. Greene then provided a copy of the report to the chairperson and CEO of Window America, requesting that she review it for any factual inaccuracies. The chairperson revised the analyst's report to reflect company revenue and earnings projections, but some of the changes made the report misleading. Greene circulated the reports with the revised projections.

> *Comment*: Greene violated Standard IV(A.2). Greene has a duty to gather comprehensive company information in order to make fully informed recommendations about Window America. Although this duty permits Greene to ask management of Window America to review the research report for inaccuracies, Greene should have taken care to examine and verify the information provided by the company. The report should have remained the product of Greene's own independent and objective analysis.

Example 5. Bell, a telecom equipment analyst for CTO Securities, issued a memo to be included in CTO's morning fax to the firm's clients:

> Descend Communications (56) preannounced its first quarter results, stating that earnings would be as much as 3¢ better than consensus analyst projections of 44¢ per diluted share because of strong domestic orders and good expense control. We have upgraded our rating to "buy" from "outperform" and have raised our 12-month price target to 70 from 65, using a P/E equal to its 40% growth rate applied to our new 1999 estimate of $1.75, up from $1.65 per share.

Later the same morning, Bell justified her rating upgrade to her sales force by saying that the "whisper number" for the first quarter had approached 47 cents some time ago but that she'd heard from a client that Descend might unexpectedly benefit by a couple extra cents from lower tax rates at its plant in Ireland. She states that she'd also read a message in an Internet chat room that the company was close to booking a huge order from a major European telephone service provider. She said that she raised her published first quarter projection to just match Descend's guidance but was willing to take a chance that the company had a good shot at beating even those revised numbers, judging from the strong rumors on the "Street."

> *Comment*: Bell violated Standard IV(A.2) by failing to distinguish between the facts offered in Descend's preannouncement and the pure conjecture and/or rumors gathered from sources whose authenticity might be highly questionable and whose accuracy she had apparently not yet bothered to verify. What is more, Bell did not include in her memo any reference to the additional information, no matter how spurious it may have been, so that her clients could evaluate for themselves how relevant those factors might be in rendering their own respective investment decisions.

Procedures for Compliance

Because the selection of relevant factors is an analytical skill, determination of whether a member has used reasonable judgment in excluding and including information in research reports depends heavily on case-by-case review rather than a specific checklist. To assist the after-the-fact review of a report, the member must maintain records indicating the nature of the research and should, if asked, be able to supply additional information to the client (or any user of the report) covering factors not included.

In drafting reports, members are likely to use a number of data bases from various sources. Members must take reasonable steps to assure themselves of the reliability, accuracy, and appropriateness of the data included in each report. If the data have been processed in any way (e.g., into financial ratios), a member should ascertain that such processing has been done in a manner consistent with the member's analytical purposes.

Acknowledgment of the source(s) should be made when appropriate as required under Standard II(C), Prohibition against Plagiarism. Regulatory agencies, self-regulating organizations, and exchanges have specific requirements relating to research reports that members should review and satisfy. Most firms have developed written compliance procedures incorporating these requirements and other matters deemed desirable. Members are strongly urged to encourage their firms to develop such procedures if they do not have them in place.

Standard IV: Relationships with and Responsibilities to Clients and Prospects
A. Investment Process

Standard IV (A.3)—Independence and Objectivity

Members shall use reasonable care and judgment to achieve and maintain independence and objectivity in making investment recommendations or taking investment action.

Purpose and Scope of the Standard

Standard IV(A.3) states the responsibility of AIMR members, CFA charterholders, and candidates in the CFA Program to maintain independence and objectivity so that their clients will have the benefit of their work and opinions unaffected by any potential conflict of interest or other circumstance adversely affecting their judgment. Every member should endeavor to avoid situations that might cause, or be perceived to cause, a loss of independence or objectivity in recommending investments or taking investment action.

External sources may try to influence the investment process by offering analysts and portfolio managers a variety of "perks." Corporations may be seeking expanded research coverage; issuers and underwriters may wish to promote new securities offerings; brokers typically want to increase commission business. The perks may include gifts, invitations to lavish functions, tickets, favors, job referrals, and so on. One type of perk that has gained particular notoriety is the allocation of shares in oversubscribed IPOs to investment managers for their personal accounts. This practice affords managers the opportunity to make quick profits that may not be available to their clients. Such a practice is prohibited under Standard IV(A.3). Modest gifts that do not exceed US$100 and entertainment are acceptable, but special care should be taken by member analysts and investment managers to resist subtle and not-so-subtle pressures to act in a manner possibly detrimental to their clients.

Gifts from clients can be distinguished from gifts given by entities seeking to influence a member to the possible detriment of clients. In a client relationship, the client has already entered some type of compensation arrangement with the member or the member's firm. A gift could be considered supplementary compensation. The potential for obtaining influence to the detriment of other clients, while present, is not as great as in situations where no compensation arrangement exists.

Therefore, members may accept "bonuses" or gifts from clients but must disclose to their employers gifts from clients exceeding US$100 in value. Disclosure allows a member's employer or clients to make an independent determination about the extent to which the gift may impinge on the member's independence and objectivity.

Members may also come under pressure from their own firms to, for example, issue favorable reviews of certain companies. In a full-service investment house, the corporate finance department may be an underwriter for a company's securities and be loath to antagonize that company by publishing negative research. The commercial side of a bank may derive substantial revenues from its lending/deposit relationships with a company, and bank managers may be tempted to influence the work of analysts in the investment department. The situation may be aggravated if the head of the company sits on the bank's or investment firm's board and attempts to interfere in investment decision making. Members acting in a sales/marketing capacity should be especially certain of their independence in selecting appropriate investments for their clients.

Members also must be aware that some of their professional or social activities within AIMR or its member societies may subtly threaten their independence or objectivity. When seeking corporate financial support for conventions, seminars, or even weekly society luncheons, the members responsible for the activities must evaluate both the actual effect of such solicitations on their independence and whether their objectivity might be perceived to be compromised in the eyes of their clients.

Application of the Standard

Example 1. Tyler, a mining analyst with Bullock Brokers, is invited by Precision Metals to join a group of his peers in a tour of mining facilities in several western states. The company arranges for chartered group flights from site to site and for accommodations in Spartan Motels, the only chain with accommodations near the mines, for three nights. Tyler allows Precious Metals to pick up his tab, as do the other analysts—with one exception. Adams, an employee of a large Boston trust company, insists on following his company's policy and pays for his motel room himself.

> *Comment*: The policy of Adams's company complies closely with Standard IV(A.3) by avoiding even the appearance of a conflict of interest, but Tyler and the other analysts were not necessarily violating Standard IV(A.3). In general, when allowing companies to pay for travel and/or accommodations under these circumstances, members must use their judgment—keeping in mind that such arrangements must not impinge on a member's independence and objectivity. In this

instance, the trip was strictly for business and Tyler was not accepting irrelevant or lavish hospitality. The itinerary required chartered flights, for which analysts were not expected to pay. The accommodations were modest. These arrangements are not at all unusual and did not violate Standard IV(A.3) so long as Tyler's independence and objectivity were not compromised. In the final analysis, members must consider both whether they can remain objective and whether their integrity might be perceived by their clients to have been compromised.

Example 2. Dillon, an analyst in the corporate finance department of her investment service firm, is making a presentation to a potential new business client that includes the promise that her firm will provide full research coverage of the potential client.

Comment: Dillon may agree to provide research coverage, but she must not commit herself to providing a favorable recommendation. Her recommendation (favorable, neutral, or unfavorable) must be based on an independent and objective investigation and analysis of the company and its securities.

Example 3. Fritz is an equity analyst with Hilton Brokerage who covers the mining industry. He has concluded that the stock of Metals & Mining is overpriced at its current level, but he is concerned that a negative research report will hurt the good relationship between Metals & Mining and the investment banking division of his company. In fact, a senior manager of Hilton Brokerage has just sent him a copy of a proposal his firm has made to Metals & Mining to underwrite a debt offering. Fritz needs to produce a report right away and doesn't know what to do.

Comment: Fritz's analysis of Metals & Mining must be objective and based solely on consideration of company fundamentals. Any pressure from other divisions of his company is inappropriate. This conflict could have been eliminated if, in anticipation of the offering, Hilton Brokerage had placed Metals & Mining on a restricted list for its sales force.

Example 4. As support for the sales effort of her corporate bond department, Wagner offers credit guidance to purchasers of fixed-income securities. Her compensation is closely linked to the performance of the corporate bond department. Near the quarter's end, Wagner's firm has a large inventory position in the bonds of Milton, Ltd.; it has been unable to sell the bonds because of Milton's recent announcement of an operating problem. Salespeople have asked her to contact large clients to push the bonds.

Comment: Unethical sales practices create significant potential violations of the Code and Standards. Wagner's opinion of the bonds of Milton should not be clouded by internal pressure or compensation. In this case, Wagner should refuse to push the Milton bonds because she must be able to justify any recommendations she makes.

Example 5. Jorund is a securities analyst following airline stocks and a rising star at her firm. Her boss has been carrying a buy recommendation on International Airlines and asks Jorund to take over coverage of that airline. He tells Jorund that under no circumstances should the prevailing buy recommendation be changed.

Comment: Jorund must be independent and objective in her analysis of International Airlines. If she believes that her boss's instructions have compromised her, she has two options: tell her boss that she cannot cover the company under these constraints or pick up coverage of the company, reach her own independent conclusions, and if they conflict with her boss's opinion, share the conclusions with her boss or other supervisors in the firm so that they can make appropriate recommendations. Jorund should issue only recommendations that she supports.

Example 6. Grant, a portfolio manager for Tisbury Investments, directs a large amount of his commission business to Broad Street & Company, a New York-based brokerage house. In appreciation for all the business, Broad Street gives Grant two tickets to the Super Bowl in Miami, two nights at a nearby Florida resort, several meals, and transportation via limousine to the game. Grant fails to disclose receiving this package to his supervisor at Tisbury.

Comment: Grant has violated Standard IV(A.3) because accepting these perks (worth considerably more than US$100) may impede his independence and objectivity. Every member should endeavor to avoid situations that might cause, or be perceived to cause, a loss of independence or objectivity in recommending investments or taking investment action. By accepting the trip from Broad Street, Grant has opened himself up to the accusation that he may give the broker favored treatment in return.

Example 7. Greenhaus manages the portfolio of Knowlden, a client of Tisbury. Greenhaus achieves an annual return for Knowlden that is consistently better than that of the benchmark return she and the client previously agreed to. As a reward, Knowlden offers Greenhaus two tickets to Wimbledon and the use of Knowlden's house in London for a week. Greenhaus discloses this gift to her supervisor at Tisbury.

> *Comment*: Greenhaus is in compliance with Standard IV(A.3) because she disclosed the gift, exceeding US$100 in value, from one of her clients. Members may accept bonuses or gifts from clients exceeding $100 in value, so long as they disclose them to their employers, because gifts in a client relationship are deemed less likely to affect a member's objectivity and independence than gifts in other situations. Disclosure is required, however, so that supervisors can monitor such situations to guard against employees favoring a gift-giving client to the detriment of other fee-paying clients (such as by allocating a greater proportion of IPO stock to the gift-giving client's portfolio).

Example 8. Wayne is the investment manager of the Gotham City Employees Pension Plan. He recently completed a successful search for a firm to manage the foreign equity allocation of the plan's diversified portfolio. He followed the plan's standard procedure of seeking presentations from a number of qualified firms and recommended that his board select Penguin Advisors because of their experience, well-defined investment strategy, and performance record, which was compiled and verified in accordance with AIMR's Performance Presentation Standards. Since the plan selection of Penguin, a reporter from the Gotham City Record has called to ask if there is any connection between this action and the fact that Penguin was one of the sponsors of an "investment fact-finding trip to Asia" that Wayne made earlier in the year. The trip was one of several conducted by the Pension Investment Academy, which had arranged the itinerary of meetings with economic, government, and corporate officials in major cities in several Asian countries. The Pension Investment Academy obtains support for the cost of these trips from a number of investment managers, including Penguin Advisors; the Academy then pays the travel expenses of the various pension plan managers on the trip and provides all meals and accommodations. The president of Penguin Advisors was one of the travelers on the trip.

> *Comment*: Although Wayne can probably put to good use the knowledge he gained from the trip in selecting portfolio managers and other areas of managing the pension plan, his recommendation of Penguin Advisors may be tainted by the possible conflict incurred when he participated in a trip partly paid for by Penguin Advisors and when he was in the daily company of the president of Penguin Advisors. To avoid violating Standard IV(A.3), Wayne's basic

expenses for travel and accommodations should have been paid by his employer or the pension plan, contact with the president of Penguin Advisors should have been limited to informational or educational events only, and the trip, the organizer, and the sponsor should be a matter of public record. Even if his actions are not in violation of Standard IV(A.3), Wayne needs to be sensitive to the public perception of the trip when reported in the paper and the extent to which the subjective elements of his decision may be affected by the familiarity that the daily contact of such a trip would encourage. This advantage would probably not be shared by competing firms.

Procedures for Compliance

Members should follow certain practices and should encourage their firms to establish certain procedures to avoid violations of Standard IV(A.3):

- Protect integrity of opinions. Members and their firms should establish policies stating that every research report on issues by a corporate client reflects the unbiased opinion of the analyst. Firms should also design compensation systems that protect the integrity of the investment decision process by maintaining the independence and objectivity of analysts.
- Disclose all corporate relationships. Members should disclose relationships in which any analyst, officer, partner, or employee of the securities firm is a director of a company and disclose whether the firm underwrites the securities of that company and/or makes a market in them.
- Disclose personal holdings/beneficial ownerships. Members should disclose interests in all the members' affiliated entities or accounts and those accounts over which the member has control (e.g., a spouse or other relative's account).
- Create a restricted list. If the senior managers at a member's firm are unwilling to permit dissemination of adverse opinions about a corporate client, the firm should remove the controversial company from the research universe and put it on a restricted list so that the firm disseminates only factual information about the company.
- Restrict special cost arrangements. When attending meetings at an issuer's headquarters, a member should pay for commercial transportation and hotel charges. No corporate issuer should reimburse a member for air transportation. Members should encourage issuers to limit the use of corporate aircraft to situations in which commercial transportation is not available or in which efficient movement could not otherwise be arranged. Members should take particular care that when

frequent meetings are held between an individual issuer and an individual member, the issuer is not always the host of the member.

- Limit gifts. Members should limit the acceptance of gratuities and/or gifts to token items. US$100 is the maximum acceptable value for a gift or gratuity. Standard IV(A.3) does not preclude customary, ordinary, business-related entertainment so long as its purpose is not to influence or reward members.
- Restrict investments. Members should restrict (or encourage their investment firms to restrict) employee purchases of equity or equity-related IPOs. Strict limits should be imposed on investment personnel acquiring securities in private placements.
- Review procedures. Members should implement (or encourage their firms to implement) effective supervisory and review procedures to ensure that analysts and portfolio managers comply with policy relating to their personal investment activities.

Standard IV: Relationships with and Responsibilities to Clients and Prospects B. Interactions with Clients and Prospects

Standard IV (B.1)—Fiduciary Duties

In relationships with clients, members shall use particular care in determining applicable fiduciary duty and shall comply with such duty as to those persons and interests to whom the duty is owed. Members must act for the benefit of their clients and place their clients' interests before their own.

Purpose and Scope of the Standard

Standard IV(B.1) states the responsibility of AIMR members, CFA charterholders, and candidates in the CFA Program to understand and adhere to the fiduciary responsibility they assume with each client. A fiduciary is an individual or institution charged with the duty of acting for the benefit of another party in matters coming within the scope of the relationship between them. The duty required in fiduciary relationships exceeds that which is acceptable in many other business relationships because the fiduciary is in a position of trust. Fiduciaries owe undivided loyalty to their clients and must place client interests before their own.

Standard IV(B.1) relates principally to those members who have discretionary authority or responsibility for the management of a client's assets or who have other relationships of special trust. The investment manager's fiduciary responsibility to a client includes a duty of loyalty and a duty to exercise reasonable care. Investment actions should be carried out for the sole benefit of the client and in a manner the manager believes to be in the best interest of the client, given the known facts and circumstances.

The first step in fulfilling a fiduciary duty is to determine what the responsibility is and to whom it is owed. Members should take particular care in determining the identity of the "client" to whom the duty of loyalty is owed. In the context of an investment manager managing the personal assets of an individual, the client is easily identified. When the manager is responsible for the portfolios of pension plans or trusts, however, the client is not the person or entity who hires the manager but, rather, the beneficiaries of the plan or trust. The duty of loyalty is owed to the beneficiaries.

A fiduciary must also be aware of whether it has "custody" or effective control of client assets. If so, a heightened level of fiduciary duty arises. A fiduciary will be considered to have custody if the fiduciary has any direct or indirect access to client funds. Fiduciaries must manage any pool of assets in their control in accordance with the terms of the governing documents (such as trust documents and investment management agreements), which are the primary determinant of a fiduciary's powers and duties. Whenever their actions are contrary to provisions of those instruments or applicable law, fiduciaries are exposed to liability through litigation brought by parties at interest.

Situations involving potential conflicts of interest with respect to fiduciary responsibility can be extremely complex because they can involve a number of competing interests. Fiduciary standards apply to a large number of persons in varying capacities, but the exact duties may differ in many respects, depending on the nature of the relationship with the client or the type of account under which the assets are managed.

Individual clients. The fiduciary duty to the individual client is especially important because the knowledge and information of the professional investment manager may be greater than the knowledge and information of the client. This disparity places the individual client in a vulnerable position of trust. The manager in these situations has the responsibility to ensure that the client's objectives and expectations for the performance of the account are realistic and suitable to the client's circumstances and that the risks involved are fully understood and appropriate. In most circumstances, recommended investment strategies should relate to the long-term objectives of the client. Particular care should be taken to ensure that the goals of the investment manager or the firm in placing the business, selling products, or executing security transactions do not conflict with the best interests of the client.

Trusts. In the United States, for more than a century, the investment actions of fiduciaries have been subject to the test of the "Prudent Man Rule" as interpreted by U.S. courts. As enacted into legislation by most states, the Prudent Man Rule holds that

> a fiduciary shall exercise the judgment and care, under the circumstances then prevailing, which men of prudence, character and intelligence exercise in the management of their own affairs, not in regard to speculation but in regard to the permanent disposition of their funds, considering the probable income as well as the probable safety of their capital. (Model Prudent Man Investment Act)

As enunciated, this concept is clearly oriented toward personal trust accounts. Trustees must be impartial between income beneficiaries and remaindermen, whose interests are distinct, and must achieve an equitable balance between current income and the preservation of principal in real terms.

Charitable organizations and public pension plans. The standard fiduciary duty for charitable organizations and public pension plans may be different from the duties imposed on trustees of private trusts or managers of corporate pension plans, even though many charitable and public plans have been placed under ERISA (Employee Retirement Income Security Act of 1974) type standards in recent years (see discussion of ERISA standards in "Corporate Pension Plans" subsection). Members, however, must always put their fiduciary obligation first in all dealings. In addition, as fiduciaries, members must always avoid all real or potential conflicts of interest, forgo using opportunities for their own benefit at the expense of those to whom the fiduciary duty is owed, and refrain from all types of self-dealing.

Many charitable organizations and public pension plans have spending and investment policies. The member who is a fiduciary for these organizations must follow any guidelines set out by the organization for the management of its assets. Some organizations have strict investment policies that limit investment options to certain types or classes of investments or prohibit investments in certain securities. Other organizations have aggressive policies that do not prohibit investments by type but, instead, set criteria on the basis of the portfolio's total risk and return. In addition, government regulation of charitable organizations and public pension plans has increased as these organizations have grown in size and importance to the economy. Members who hold a fiduciary position for these organizations must examine applicable law, client agreement, and client guidelines for guidance as to their duties.

Fiduciaries at charitable organizations based in the United States may be bound by the Uniform Management of Institutional Funds Act (UMIFA). Charities governed by UMIFA are able to invest in a wide variety of assets and are not restricted by "legal list" statutes (statutes that limit investments to those securities specifically enumerated in the statute), which may restrict the investments of fiduciaries at other organizations. Fiduciaries at UMIFA charities are held to a standard of ordinary business care and prudence under the facts and circumstances prevailing at the time of the actions or decisions. The "standard of ordinary business care" is generally comparable to that of a director of a business corporation rather than that of a private trustee. Corporate directors are governed by the "business judgment rule," whereas trustees are governed by the Prudent Man Rule, generally a much higher standard. Fiduciaries must consider long- and short-term institutional needs in carrying out the charitable purpose, the charity's present and anticipated financial requirements, expected total return on its investments, trends in security price levels, and general economic conditions.

Corporate pension plans. ERISA establishes the fiduciary principles for U.S. corporate pension plans. ERISA is very specific in its definition of fiduciaries and their responsibilities, and investment managers of U.S. corporate pension plans are generally subject to ERISA's fiduciary provisions. Under ERISA, fiduciaries must

- act solely in the interest of, and for the exclusive purpose of benefiting, the plan participants and beneficiaries;
- act with the care, skill, prudence, and diligence of a prudent person acting in like capacity;
- diversify the plan's investments to protect it from the risk of substantial loss;
- act in accordance with the provisions of the plan documents to the extent that the documents comply with ERISA;
- refrain from engaging in prohibited transactions.

ERISA's fiduciary standard differs from the common-law standard in that investment decisions are judged in the context of the total portfolio rather than to individual investments within the portfolio. The statutory duty is satisfied with respect to a particular investment if the fiduciary has thoroughly considered the investment's place in the whole portfolio, the risk of loss and opportunity for gains, and the diversification, liquidity, cash flow, and overall return requirements of the pension plan or the portion of the pension plan assets for which the manager is responsible.

In a pension plan, the duty of a fiduciary is to the plan participants and their beneficiaries rather than to the plan sponsor that has the power to hire and fire the investment manager. If urged to make investments that might be of direct benefit to a sponsoring company or to the community at large (social investments), the manager must ensure that such investments are legal and do not impair the integrity of the funds in question or the financial security of the participants/beneficiaries.

Pooled funds and separate accounts. Managers of pooled funds, including mutual funds and unit investment trusts, owe a fiduciary duty to the fund's investors. These duties are no different from the fiduciary duties of managers of separate accounts. Possible abuses include, but are not limited to, front running, participation on favorable terms in oversubscribed IPOs and direct placements, disproportionate allocation of trades, and conflicts of interest arising out of situations in which fund managers serve as corporate directors.

Board service raises some particularly interesting questions even in the absence of inappropriate actions. A manager's fiduciary duty to the company of which the manager is a director may conflict with the manager's duty to the fund investors and account beneficiaries. For example, the manager's ability to trade the securities of that company may be limited, possibly to the detriment of the fund and the manager's other clients. On the other hand, when investment managers are in a position requiring the exercise of ownership rights, circumstances may arise in which the manager should seek representation on a board to protect the interests of the fund's investors and the advisor's other clients.

Corporate governance. Certain fiduciaries are obligated to vote proxies in an informed and responsible manner. A fiduciary who fails to vote, casts a vote without considering the impact of the question, or votes blindly with management on nonroutine governance issues (e.g., a change in firm capitalization) may violate the fiduciary's duty of loyalty. ERISA mandates a heightened awareness of this duty; the U.S. Department of Labor considers the voting of proxies to be an integral part of the management of plan investments. The responsibility to vote proxies remains with the trustee(s) except when a plan document has delegated the power to manage, acquire, or dispose of plan assets to an investment manager. The investment manager can avoid liability only if the management agreement or the plan document itself specifically precludes the investment manager from voting proxies. Accurate proxy voting records must be maintained, and the plan sponsor should be able to review not only voting procedures with respect to plan stock but also the actions that are taken in individual proxy voting situations. Members managing non-ERISA assets should follow similar practice.

Soft dollars. An investment manager often has discretion over the selection of brokers executing transactions. Conflicts arise when an investment manager uses client brokerage to purchase research services that benefit the investment manager, which is commonly called "soft dollars," "soft pounds," or "soft commissions."

Whenever a manager uses client brokerage to purchase goods or services that benefit the manager, the manager, as a fiduciary, must disclose to clients the method or policies followed by the manager in addressing the potential conflict. A manager who pays a higher commission than she or he would normally pay to purchase the goods or services is violating the fiduciary duties owed to the client. This practice is commonly referred to as "paying up" for services. Various countries' securities laws permit a manager to pay up for goods and services without violating the manager's fiduciary duty so long as the requirements of the law are followed. The requirements typically state that

- the goods or services purchased must be for "research service" (i.e., must assist the manager in the investment decision-making process);
- the commission paid must be reasonable in relation to the research and execution services received;
- the manager's soft dollar practice must be disclosed;
- at all times, the manager must seek best price and execution.

Members are urged to review their country's laws concerning soft dollar practices.

From time to time, a manager's client will direct the manager to use the client's brokerage to purchase goods or services for the client, a practice that is commonly called "directed brokerage." Because brokerage is an asset of the client and the brokerage is used to benefit that client, not the manager, such practice does not violate any fiduciary duty. In such situations, the manager is obligated to seek best price and execution and be assured by the client that the goods or services purchased with brokerage will benefit the account beneficiaries.

Application of the Standard

Example 1. First Country Bank serves as trustee for the Miller Company's pension plan. Miller is the target of a hostile takeover attempt by Newton, Inc. In attempting to ward off Newton, Miller's managers persuade Wiley, an investment manager at First Country Bank, to purchase Miller common stock in the open market for the employee pension plan. Miller's officials indicate that such action would be favorably received and would probably result in other accounts being placed with the bank. Although Wiley believes the stock to be overvalued and would not ordinarily buy it, he purchases the stock to support Miller's managers, to maintain the company's good favor, and to realize additional new business. The heavy stock purchases cause Miller's market price to rise to such a level that Newton retracts its takeover bid.

At about the same time, Miller asks its shareholders to vote in favor of certain proxy proposals permitting changes in the corporate bylaws that would, if approved, virtually eliminate the possibility of a successful hostile takeover bid. Without giving the matter much attention, Wiley votes the proxy in favor of management.

> *Comment*: Standard IV(B.1) requires that a fiduciary, in evaluating a takeover bid, act prudently and solely in the interests of plan participants and beneficiaries. To meet this requirement, a member must carefully evaluate the long-term prospects of the company against

the short-term prospects presented by the takeover offer and by the ability to invest elsewhere. In this instance, Wiley, acting on behalf of his employer, the trustee, clearly violated Standard IV(B.1) by using the profit-sharing plan to perpetuate existing management, perhaps to the detriment of plan participants and the company's shareholders, and to benefit himself. Wiley's fiduciary responsibilities should take precedence over any ties to corporate managers and self-interest. A duty exists to examine such a takeover offer on its own merits and to make an independent decision. The guiding principle is the appropriateness of the investment decision to the pension plan, not whether the decision benefits Wiley or the company that hired him.

With respect to proxy solicitations, Wiley has a duty to examine management's proposals and to take whatever action he deems appropriate to protect the plan's investments, particularly in situations where management actions appear improper and could be construed to be substantially unfair to shareholders. By thoughtlessly voting with management in this situation, Wiley did not meet the requisite standard of care. When management proposals serve the best interests of the corporation and its shareholders or are consistent with the investment manager's reason for purchasing the investment, the proposals should be supported. In all proxy issues, the investment manager has a duty to make independent decisions and to view with objectivity that which is in the best interest of the beneficiary for whom the proxy is voted.

Example 2. JNI, a successful investment counseling firm, serves as investment manager for the pension plans of several large regionally based companies. Its trading activities generate a significant amount of commission-related business. JNI uses the brokerage and research services of many firms, but most of its trading activity is handled through a large brokerage company, Thompson, Inc., principally because of close personal relationships between the executives of the two firms. Thompson's commission structure is high in comparison with charges for similar brokerage services from other firms. JNI considers its research services and execution capabilities average. In exchange for JNI's directing its brokerage to Thompson, Thompson absorbs a number of JNI overhead expenses, including those for magazine subscriptions.

Comment: JNI executives breached their fiduciary duty by using client brokerage for nonresearch services that do not benefit JNI clients and by not obtaining best price and execution for their clients. Because JNI executives failed to uphold their fiduciary duty, they violated Standard IV(B.1).

Example 3. Everett, a struggling independent investment advisor, serves as investment manager for the pension plans of several widely dispersed companies. One of her brokers, Scott Company, is close to consummating management agreements with prospective new clients whereby Everett will manage the new client accounts and trade the accounts exclusively through Scott. One of Everett's existing clients, Crayton Corporation, has directed Everett to place securities transactions for Crayton's account exclusively through Scott. But to induce Scott to exert efforts to land more new accounts for Everett, she also directs transactions to Scott from other clients without their knowledge.

> *Comment*: Everett has an obligation at all times to seek best price and execution on all trades. Everett may direct new client trades exclusively through Scott Company as long as Everett receives best price and execution on the trades or receives a written statement from new clients that she is not to seek best price and execution and that they are aware of the consequence for their accounts. Everett may trade other accounts through Scott as a reward for directing clients to Everett only if the accounts receive best price and execution and the practice is disclosed in writing to the accounts. Because Everett did not disclose the directed trading, Everett has violated her fiduciary duty to her clients. [See also Standard IV(B.8), Disclosure of Referral Fees.]

Example 4. Jones is retained as an investment manager to Plan P to manage part of the plan assets. Jones directs the plan's brokerage transactions solely through broker Brown. In return, Brown provides research on tax-exempt securities to Jones. Although tax-exempt securities would not be a suitable investment for Plan P, Jones has determined that this research is useful to his managed accounts as a whole. Jones does not check to determine whether Brown is providing best price and execution and does not disclose his soft dollar practices to the plan sponsors.

> *Comment*: The use of Plan P brokerage to purchase research that benefits Jones while not seeking best price and execution and not disclosing this practice to Plan P is a breach of Jones's fiduciary duty to his clients. Under most securities laws, such practice is permitted even though the research service does not benefit Plan P. A manager can use client brokerage, including pension plan brokerage, to purchase research services that do not benefit the client whose brokerage is used to purchase the research so long as best price and execution are received, the commission paid is reasonable in relation to the services received, and the practice is disclosed. The Plan P sponsors, in

reviewing Jones's brokerage prices, could direct Jones to not use Plan P brokerage to purchase research services that do not benefit Plan P or Jones in supplying investment management services to Plan P.

Example 5. Frey, an investment officer at Moonlight Trust Company, is approached by the income beneficiary of a trust that permits no principal invasions. The beneficiary needs additional income for legitimate reasons, so Frey offers to buy Aaa-rated, high-coupon, pre-refunded municipal bonds for the trust just as she has for a number of her investment advisory accounts. Although the bonds are selling at a large premium, the current yield is very attractive compared with the yield on recent new issues of municipal bonds.

Comment: By paying a large premium for the bonds, Frey would be shifting principal to income and paying it out to the beneficiary to the detriment of the remainderman. This practice is unacceptable in a personal trust but is acceptable in an advisory account, in which the assets are owned outright by an individual and no differentiation is needed between income and principal.

Example 6. Rome, a trust officer for Paget Trust Company, was promoted to that position two years ago. Rome's supervisor is responsible for reviewing Rome's trust account transactions and her monthly reports of personal stock transactions. Rome has been using Black, a broker, almost exclusively for trust account brokerage transactions. Where Black makes a market in stocks, he has been giving Rome a lower price for personal purchases and a higher price for sales than he gives to Rome's trust accounts and other investors. Rome has been filing the monthly reports required by Paget's code of ethics only for those months in which she has no personal transactions, which is about every fourth month.

Comment: Rome is violating her fiduciary responsibility to the bank's trust accounts by using Black for brokerage transactions simply because Black gives Rome a discount on her personal purchases. Rome has also violated her firm's code of ethics by not properly completing her monthly trade reports. [The supervisor may have violated Standard III(E), Responsibilities of Supervisors, by failing to provide reasonable procedures for supervising Rome properly in her trading for trust accounts and failing to detect Rome's failure to report personal stock transactions.]

Example 7. Brown, an analyst with Providence Advisors, covers South American equities for the firm. She likes to travel to the markets for which she is responsible and decides to go on a briefing trip to Chile, Argentina, and Brazil sponsored by SouthAM, Inc. SouthAM is a research firm with a small broker/dealer affiliate that uses the clearing facilities of a larger New York brokerage house. SouthAM specializes in arranging South American trips for analysts during which they can meet with central bank officials, senior government ministers, local economists, and senior executives of corporations. SouthAM accepts commission dollars at a ratio of 2 to 1 against the hard-dollar cost of the research fee for the trip. SouthAM also arranges the ground package (hotels and meals), for which commission dollars can again be used for payment at a 2 to 1 ratio. Brown is not sure that SouthAM's execution is competitive but, without informing her supervisor, directs the trading desk at Providence to start giving commission business to SouthAM so she can take the trip. SouthAM has conveniently timed the briefing trip to coincide with the beginning of Carnival season, so Brown also decides to spend five days of vacation in Rio de Janeiro at the end of the trip. Brown includes the five days of hotel expenses in the ground package, for which commission dollars are used as payment.

Comment: Brown violated Standard IV(B.1) by not exercising her fiduciary duty to determine whether the commissions charged by SouthAM were reasonable in relation to the benefit of the research provided by the trip and by not determining that best execution and prices can be received from SouthAM. In addition, the ground package, even without the five extra days, is not part of the research effort because it does not assist in the investment decision-making process.

Brown also violated Standard IV(B.7), Disclosure of Conflicts to Clients and Prospects, by failing to disclose to clients and prospects that brokerage commissions would be used inappropriately to pay for ground arrangements and the five extra days' vacation in Rio de Janeiro. By not informing her employer, Brown also violated Standard III(C), Disclosure of Conflicts to Employer. In addition, this trip threatens Brown's ability to remain independent and objective, in violation of Standard IV(A.3).

Procedures for Compliance

As fiduciaries, members should ensure that they thoroughly analyze governing documents. Members should review investments periodically to ensure compliance with the terms of the governing documents. When questions arise over the interpretation of governing documents, members should seek legal advice. Members in a position to do so should incorporate in an ethics policy the concept of loyalty owed by a fiduciary.

Member's with control of client assets should

- submit to an independent audit at least once a year;
- submit to each client, at least quarterly, an itemized statement showing the funds and securities in the custody or possession of the member, plus all debits, credits, and transactions that occurred during the period;
- disclose to the client where the assets are to be maintained, as well as where or when they are moved;
- separate the client's assets from any other party's assets, including the member's own.

Members should establish policies and procedures with respect to proxy voting and the use of client brokerage, including soft dollars.

Members should receive approval from their employer before accepting corporate directorships. Members should review compensation arrangements and other special treatment by board directors to make certain that these arrangements do not create conflicts with their fiduciary duties. Any directorship should be disclosed to the appropriate parties.

If a member is uncertain about the appropriate course of action with respect to a client, the member should ask what he or she would expect or demand if the member were the client. If in doubt, a member should disclose the questionable matter in writing and obtain client approval.

Members who are investment managers and their firms should address the following topics when drafting their policies and procedures statements or manuals regarding fiduciary duties. Many of these topics are specifically addressed by other Standards and discussed elsewhere in this book. For further guidance, members should refer to "Topical Study: Fiduciary Duties."

- Follow all applicable rules and laws. Members must follow all legal requirements and applicable provisions of the *Standards of Practice Handbook.*
- Establish the investment objectives of the client. When taking investment actions, members must consider the appropriateness and suitability of the portfolio relative to (1) the client's needs and circumstances, or (2) the investment's basic characteristics, or (3) the basic characteristics of the total portfolio.
- Diversification. Members should diversify investments to reduce the risk of loss, unless diversification is not consistent with plan guidelines or is contrary to the account objectives.
- Deal fairly with all clients with respect to investment actions. Members must not favor some clients over others.

- Conflict of interest. Members must disclose all possible conflicts of interest so that clients can evaluate the conflict.
- Disclose compensation arrangements. Members must make their clients aware of all forms of manager compensation.
- Proxy solicitations. Members must determine who is authorized to vote shares and vote proxies in the best interest of the clients or beneficiaries.
- Confidentiality. Members must preserve the confidentiality of client information.
- Best execution. Members should provide their clients with the best execution reasonably available for securities trades. Best execution refers to executing client transactions so that the client's total cost is the most favorable under the particular circumstances at that time.
- Loyalty. Members must serve the best interest of the clients.

Standard IV: Relationships with and Responsibilities to Clients and Prospects B. Interactions with Clients and Prospects

Standard IV (B.2)—Portfolio Investment Recommendations and Actions

Members shall:

a. Make a reasonable inquiry into a client's financial situation, investment experience, and investment objectives prior to making any investment recommendations and shall update this information as necessary, but no less frequently than annually, to allow the members to adjust their investment recommendations to reflect changed circumstances.

b. Consider the appropriateness and suitability of investment recommendations or actions for each portfolio or client. In determining appropriateness and suitability, members shall consider applicable relevant factors, including the needs and circumstances of the portfolio or client, the basic characteristics of the investment involved, and the basic characteristics of the total portfolio. Members shall not make a recommendation unless they reasonably determine that the recommendation is suitable to the client's financial situation, investment experience, and investment objectives.

c. Distinguish between facts and opinions in the presentation of investment recommendations.

d. Disclose to clients and prospects the basic format and general principles of the investment processes by which securities are selected and portfolios are constructed and shall promptly disclose to clients and prospects any changes that might significantly affect those processes.

Purpose and Scope of the Standard

Standard IV(B.2) states the responsibility of AIMR members, CFA charterholders, and candidates in the CFA Program to consider carefully the needs, circumstances, and objectives of the client when determining the appropriateness and suitability of a given investment or course of investment action. Members must ensure that their clients are fully aware of the investment policies, strategies, and selection procedures that apply to the investment of the clients' assets.

Members should gather such client information as financial

circumstances, occupation, investment objectives, and risk tolerances at the inception of any client relationship. Without the identification of such client factors, members cannot judge whether a particular investment idea or investment course of action is suitable and appropriate for a particular client.

Such an inquiry should be repeated at least annually and prior to material changes to any specific investment recommendations or decisions on behalf of the client. The effort to determine the needs and circumstances of each client is not a one-time occurrence. Investment recommendations or decisions are usually part of an ongoing process that takes into account the diversity and changing nature of portfolio and client characteristics. The passage of time is bound to produce changes that are important with respect to investment objectives. For an individual client, such changes might include the number of dependents, personal tax status, the amount of wealth beyond that represented in the portfolio, and the extent to which compensation and other income provide for current income needs. With respect to an institutional client, such changes might relate to the magnitude of unfunded liabilities in a pension fund, the withdrawal privileges in an employee's savings plan, or the distribution requirements of a charitable foundation. Without efforts to update information concerning client factors, one or more factors could change without the investment manager's knowledge. Such information is to be acquired even in cases where prompt action is required.

Standard IV(B.2) is intended to cover all the broad categories of investment disciplines, including fundamental, quantitative, and technical approaches. For a client to have an adequate understanding of an investment product or service that is being offered, the member must disclose the key elements of and principles behind the investment process that the member uses to select securities or construct portfolios. Any significant changes to the process or changes of personnel that might affect the process must also be disclosed. Whether an investment manager bases individual security selection or portfolio construction on the abilities of one person, a committee, or quantitative models, Standard IV(B.2) is applicable to all investment disciplines. In large organizations, a suitability determination may be made by associates of the member who are involved with sales or business development. Ultimately, however, the member remains responsible for compliance with Standard IV(B.2).

An exception to the general rule that a member must obtain client information prior to taking investment action would be in the case of a client relationship having just been established, a portfolio of securities (or other investments) already existing for that client, and the proceeds of a maturing fixed-income issue becoming available. The prompt reinvestment of those proceeds in some cash-equivalent form is likely to be entirely reasonable and desirable under the circumstances. Variations of this same general case undoubtedly exist. In general, however, client information as described in this chapter is necessary for a member to determine whether there is reasonable basis for an investment.

One of the most important factors to be considered in matching appropriateness and suitability of an investment with a client's needs and circumstances is measuring that client's tolerance for risk. The investment professional must consider the possibilities of rapidly changing investment environments and their likely impact on a client's holdings, both individual securities and the collective portfolio. The risk of many investment strategies can and should be analyzed and quantified in advance.

The rapidly growing use of synthetic investment vehicles and derivative investment products has introduced particular issues of risk. Members should pay careful attention to the leverage often inherent in such vehicles or products when considering them for use in a client's investment program. Such leverage and limited liquidity, depending on the degree to which it is hedged, bears directly on the issue of suitability for the client.

The investment profession has long recognized that the combination of several different investments is likely to provide a more acceptable level of risk exposure than having all funds in a single investment. The unique characteristics (or risks) of an individual investment may become partially or entirely neutralized when combined with other individual investments within a portfolio. Some reasonable amount of diversification is thus the norm for many portfolios, especially those managed by individuals or institutions that have some degree of fiduciary responsibility.

A member should amply and adequately illustrate to clients and prospects the manner in which the member conducts the investment decision-making process. The member should keep existing clients and other interested parties informed with respect to changes to the chosen investment process on an ongoing basis. Only by thoroughly understanding the nature of the investment product or service can a client adequately decide whether changes to that product or service could materially affect the client's investment objectives.

Similarly, a member needs to understand the basic characteristics of the particular investment being considered. If the member is using quantitative methods that have been well established but contain no fundamental research, the member should disclose this fact to the client. Understanding the basic characteristics of the investment is of great importance in judging the suitability of each investment on a stand-alone basis, but it is especially important in determining the impact each investment will have on the characteristics of the portfolio. For instance, although the risk and return characteristics of shares of a stock seem to be the same for any investor if the stock is viewed in isolation, the implications of such an investment vary greatly depending on the other investments held. If the particular stock represents 90 percent of an individual's investments, with the balance in U.S. Treasury bills, the stock's importance in the portfolio is vastly different from the importance of the same amount of the stock held in a highly diversified common stock portfolio in which the stock represents only 2 percent of the holdings. The incorporation of options-related strategies into a portfolio may also alter the risk characteristics of the stock holding.

Application of the Standard

Example 1. Smith, an investment advisor, has as clients Robertson, 60 years old, and Lanai, 40 years old. Both clients earn roughly the same salary, but Robertson has a much higher risk tolerance because he has a large asset base. Robertson is willing to invest part of his assets very aggressively; Lanai wants only to achieve a steady rate of return with low volatility in order to pay for his children's education.

> *Comment*: In Robertson's case, whether Smith recommends risky investments such as emerging growth stocks, high-yield bonds, buying on margin, or using option strategies, Smith should acquaint Robertson with the downside risks along with the upside potential of any recommended transactions. Smith should make sure that Robertson recognizes the higher risks that might be assumed and that he agrees in writing to proceed as planned. These investments would not be suitable for Lanai, and Smith would be violating Standard IV(B.2) by applying Robertson's investment strategy to Lanai's account.

Example 2. Walters, an investment advisor, suggests to Crosby, a risk-averse client, the use of covered call options in her equity portfolio. The purpose would be to enhance Crosby's income and partially offset any untimely depreciation in paper value should the stock market or other circumstances act unfavorably on her holdings. Walters educates Crosby about all possible outcomes, including the risk of incurring an added tax liability if a stock rises in price and is called away and, conversely, the risk of her holdings losing protection on the downside if prices drop precipitously.

> *Comment*: When determining suitability of an investment, the primary focus should be on the characteristics of the client's entire portfolio,

not on an issue-by-issue analysis. The basic characteristics of the entire portfolio will largely determine whether the investment recommendations are taking client factors into account. Therefore, the most important aspects of a particular investment will be those that will affect the characteristics of the total portfolio. In this case, Walters properly considered the investment in the context of the entire portfolio and thoroughly explained the investment to the client.

Example 3. Newton has an annual income requirement of $200,000. With $125,000 coming from salary, his investment portfolio is expected to produce about $75,000 per annum. His investment advisor, Oliver, notes that because Newton's portfolio has a market value of $1,000,000, the average income yield required is 7 percent. Newton wants to know how every individual investment can possibly return 7 percent every year.

Comment: Oliver needs to explain that to reach the objective, the individual investments do not all need to produce a 7 percent current income yield. The important objective is that the investments combined produce Newton's $75,000 annual investment income. With the benefit of needed information about client factors, which Oliver has obtained, an investment professional is ready to proceed with the application of investment recommendations or to initiate investment actions with respect to a specific portfolio. The analyst or manager needs to understand the basic characteristics of the particular investment being considered in order to judge its suitability for the entire portfolio. Understanding the effects of the investment characteristics of various quantitative strategies on the whole portfolio is equally important.

Example 4. One of the unique characteristics of ACE Home Building Company is its adverse sensitivity to high interest rates. Merriam proposes including ACE stock in a portfolio that is heavily invested in public utility common stock (which is also sensitive to interest rates).

Comment: The portfolio produced by Merriam's proposed combination will have very different characteristics from those of a more diversified portfolio that combines the ACE stock with, for example, the stock of a company that generates most of its revenue from the management of money market funds. The principle is that investment managers should focus on the characteristics of the portfolio as a whole when taking investment actions. An individual investment may have unique characteristics (or risks) on a stand-alone basis that make it suitable or unsuitable within various portfolios because of the investment's positive or negative covariance with other holdings. Merriam might want to use one of the portfolio optimization programs that are available for judging the prospective impact of a particular investment in combination with the investments in Newton's existing portfolio. Such tools may be helpful in obtaining the proper balance of investments to meet various client factors—income requirements, total rate of return objectives, and risk tolerance.

Example 5. In a regular meeting with Jones, the portfolio managers at Blue Chip Investment Advisors are careful to allow some time to review his current needs and circumstances. In doing so, they learn that some significant changes have recently taken place. A wealthy uncle left Jones an inheritance that increased his net worth fourfold, to $1,000,000.

Comment: The inheritance significantly increased Jones's ability and willingness to assume risk and diminished the average yield required to meet his current income needs. Accordingly, the Blue Chip portfolio managers should consider a somewhat higher equity ratio for his portfolio than called for by the previous circumstances, and the managers' specific common stock recommendations might be heavily tilted toward low-yield, growth-oriented issues.

Example 6. May & Associates is an aggressive growth manager that has represented itself since its inception as a specialist at investing in small-capitalization domestic stocks. One of May's selection criteria is a maximum capitalization of $250 million for any given issue. After a string of successful years of superior relative performance, May has expanded its client base significantly, to the point at which assets under management exceed $3 billion. For liquidity purposes, May's chief investment officer (CIO) decides to lift the maximum permissible market-cap ceiling to $500 million and change the company's sales and marketing literature accordingly to inform prospective clients and third-party consultants.

Comment: Although the May CIO was correct to inform potentially interested parties about the change in investment process, she should also have notified May's existing clients. Among the latter group might be a number of clients who have retained May as a small-cap manager and also retained mid-cap and large-cap specialists in a multiple-manager approach. Such clients might regard May's change of criteria as a style change that could distort their overall asset allocations.

Example 7. Rather than lifting the ceiling for its universe from $250 million to $500 million, May & Associates extends its small-cap universe to include a number of foreign stocks.

> *Comment*: The same guidelines as in the comment to Example 6 apply: Standard IV(B.2) requires that May's CIO advise May clients of this change because the firm may have been retained by some clients specifically for its prowess at investing in domestic small-cap stocks. Other variations requiring client notification include introducing derivatives to emulate a certain market sector or relaxing various constraints, such as portfolio beta. In all such cases, member managers should disclose changes to all interested parties.

Example 8. RJZ Capital Management is a value-style active equity manager that selects stocks using a combination of four multifactor models. Because of favorable results gained from backtesting the most recent 10 years of available market data, the president of RJZ decides to replace a simple model of price to trailing 12-months earnings with a new dividend discount model, of the firm's own design, that will be a function of projected inflation rates, earnings growth rates, and interest rates.

> *Comment*: Because a new and different valuation model has been introduced to its selection process, RJZ's president should communicate the change to the firm's clients. RJZ is moving away from a model based on hard data toward a new model that is at least partly dependent on the firm's forecasting skills. Some clients could view such a model as a significant change rather than a mere refinement of RJZ's process.

Example 9. RJZ Capital Management loses the chief architect of its multifactor-model valuation system. Without informing its clients, RJZ decides to redirect its talents and resources toward developing a product for passive equity management, a product that will emulate the performance of a major market index.

> *Comment*: RJZ failed to disclose to clients a substantial change to its investment process, which is a violation of Standard IV(B.2). In addition, the president of RJZ must change its fees to reflect the change from active to passive equity management [see Standard IV(B.3), Fair Dealing with Customers and Clients, and Standard IV(B.6), Prohibition against Misrepresentation].

Example 10. At Fundamental Asset Management, Inc., the responsibility for selecting stocks for addition to the firm's "approved" list has just been shifted from individual security analysts to a committee consisting of the research director and three senior portfolio managers.

> *Comment*: Fundamental should disclose the process change to all interested parties. Some of Fundamental's clients might be concerned about the morale and motivation among the firm's best research analysts following the change. Moreover, clients might challenge the stock-picking track record of the portfolio managers and might even want to monitor the situation closely.

Procedures for Compliance

To fulfill the basic provisions of Standard IV(B.2), a member should put the needs and circumstances of each client and the client's investment objectives into an investment policy statement for each client. In formulating an investment policy for the client, the member should take the following into consideration:

- client identification—(1) type and nature of clients and (2) the existence of separate beneficiaries;
- investor objectives—(1) return objectives (income, growth in principal, maintenance of purchasing power) and (2) risk tolerance (suitability, stability of values);
- investor constraints—(1) liquidity needs, (2) expected cash flows (patterns of additions and/or withdrawals), (3) investable funds (assets and liabilities or other commitments), (4) time horizon, (5) tax considerations, (6) regulatory and legal circumstances, (7) investor preferences, circumstances, and unique needs, and (8) proxy voting responsibilities and guidance.

The investor's objectives and constraints should be maintained and reviewed periodically to reflect any changes in the client's circumstances. Annual review is reasonable unless business or other reasons dictate more or less frequent review.

Standard IV: Relationships with and Responsibilities to Clients and Prospects B. Interactions with Clients and Prospects

Standard IV(B.3)—Fair Dealing

Members shall deal fairly and objectively with all clients and prospects when disseminating investment recommendations, disseminating material changes in prior investment recommendations, and taking investment action.

Purpose and Scope of the Standard

Standard IV(B.3) states the responsibility of AIMR members, CFA charterholders, and candidates in the CFA Program to treat all clients and prospects fairly when disseminating investment recommendations or material changes in prior investment advice or when taking investment action with regard to general purchases, new issues, or secondary offerings. Only through the fair treatment of all parties can the investment management profession maintain the confidence of the investing public.

When an investment advisor has multiple clients, the potential exists for the advisor to favor one client over another. This favoritism may take various forms, from the quality and timing of services provided to allocation of investment opportunities.

The term "fairly" implies that the member must take care not to discriminate against any customers or clients when disseminating investment recommendations or taking investment action. Standard IV(B.3) does not state "equally" because members could not possibly reach all clients simultaneously—whether by mail, telephone, computer, facsimile, or wire. In addition, each client has unique needs, investment criteria, and investment objectives.

Standard IV(B.3) covers the conduct of two broadly defined groups of members—those who prepare recommendations and those who take investment action.

Investment recommendations. The first group includes those members whose primary function is the preparation of investment recommendations to be disseminated either to the public or within a firm for the use of others in making investment decisions. This group includes members employed by investment counseling, advisory, or consulting firms, banks, brokerage firms, and insurance companies if the members' primary responsibility is the preparation of recommendations to be acted upon by others, including those in the members' organizations.

An investment recommendation is any opinion expressed by a member in regard to purchasing, selling, or holding a given security or other investment. This opinion can be disseminated to customers or clients through an initial detailed research report, through a brief update report, by addition to or deletion from a recommended list, or simply by oral communication. A recommendation that is distributed to anyone outside the organization that initiated the recommendation is considered a communication for general distribution under Standard IV(B.3).

Standard IV(B.3) addresses the manner in which investment recommendations or material changes in prior recommendations are disseminated to clients. Each member is obligated to ensure that information is disseminated in such a manner that all clients have a fair opportunity to act upon every recommendation. In general, a material change in a firm's recommendation is one that could be expected to affect the investor's judgment or motivate an informed buyer or seller to take investment action. Although the definition of material change is subjective, a member should err on the side of materiality and, when in doubt, treat the change as material. This definition is similar to the definition of material information in the inside information rule [see Standard V(A), Prohibition against Use of Material Nonpublic Information]. A change of recommendation from buy to sell or sell to buy is generally material.

The duty to clients imposed by Standard IV(B.3) may be more critical when a firm changes its recommendation than when it makes an initial recommendation. For example, in its *Guide to Broker–Dealer Compliance*, the U.S. Securities and Exchange Commission states:

> Material changes in the broker/dealer's prior investment advice arising from subsequent research should be communicated to all current clients who the broker/dealer knows have purchased and may be holding securities on the basis of its earlier advice, at least under circumstances where to do so would not impose an unreasonable hardship on the broker. Persons placing orders contrary to a current firm recommendation should ordinarily be advised of the recommendation before the order is accepted.

Investment actions. The second group includes those members whose primary function is taking investment action (portfolio management) based on research recommendations prepared internally or received from external sources. Investment action, like investment recommendations, can affect market value. Consequently, Standard IV(B.3) states the obligation of each member when taking investment action to ensure that all clients and prospective clients are treated fairly in light of their investment objectives and circumstances, notwithstanding that the member may have discretionary power over certain accounts and not over others. When making investments in new offerings or in secondary financings, members should ensure the pro rata distribution of the issues to all customers for whom the investments are appropriate.

When new issues or secondary offerings are available or are being offered by the firm or if the firm is part of a selling syndicate, all clients for whom the security is appropriate are to be offered a chance to take part in the issue. If the issue is oversubscribed, then the issue is to be prorated to all subscribers. This action should be taken on a block basis to avoid odd-lot distributions. In addition, if the issue is oversubscribed, members should forgo any sales to themselves or their immediate families to free up additional shares for clients.

Members must make every effort to treat all clients, individuals, and institutions in a fair and impartial manner. A member may have multiple relationships with an institution; for example, a bank may hold many positions for a manager, such as corporate trustee, pension fund manager, manager of funds for individuals employed by the customer, loan originator, or creditor. A member must exercise care to treat all clients fairly, including those with whom multiple relationships do not exist.

Members must disclose to clients and prospects the allocation procedures they or their firms have in place and how the procedures would affect the client or prospect. The disclosure must be clear and complete so that the client can make an informed investment decision. Even when complete disclosure is made, however, members must put client interests first. A member's duty of fairness and loyalty to clients can never be overridden by client consent to patently unfair allocation procedures.

Treating clients fairly also means that members should not take advantage of their position in the industry to the detriment of clients. For instance, in the context of IPOs, members must make bona fide public distributions of "hot issue" securities (defined as securities of a public offering that trade at a premium in the secondary market whenever such trading commences because of the great demand for the securities). Members are prohibited from withholding such securities for their own benefit and may not use such securities as a reward or incentive to gain benefit.

Members also may not engage in trading ahead of the dissemination of research reports or investment recommendations to clients—a practice that creates a conflict with members' duties to clients.

Application of the Standard

Example 1. Ames, a well-known and respected analyst, follows the computer industry. In the course of his research, he finds that a small, relatively unknown company whose shares are traded over the counter has just signed significant contracts with some of the companies he follows. After a considerable amount of investigation, Ames decides to write a research report on the company and recommend purchase. While the report is being reviewed by the company for factual accuracy, Ames schedules a luncheon with several of his best clients to discuss the company. At the luncheon, he mentions the purchase recommendation scheduled to be sent early the following week to all the firm's clients.

> *Comment*: Ames violated Standard IV(B.3) by disseminating the purchase recommendation to the clients with whom he had lunch a week before the recommendation was sent to all clients.

Example 2. Eliot is an analyst with a brokerage firm that has a large investment advisory department. The department manages four mutual funds and numerous other discretionary and nondiscretionary accounts. For a number of years, Eliot has been recommending purchase of Harris Company as an excellent long-term investment. Many of her firm's brokerage and advisory clients and three of the mutual funds have purchased shares in the company on the basis of her recommendations. Two days before the firm's monthly research list, which includes buy, hold, and sell recommendations, is to be sent to the printer for distribution to all clients, Eliot learns from Harris Company's largest customer that the customer is not renewing a significant service contract with Harris that is scheduled to expire in six months. Eliot deduces that the loss of this contract will eventually have a material impact on Harris Company by damaging its long-term revenue and earnings growth. She does not have time to write a follow-up report on Harris, however, so she decides to change her recommendation from buy to hold rather than from buy to sell. Because she has on earlier occasions switched her rating from buy to hold based on relative price considerations, she does not feel compelled to broadcast this latest change. On the day the research list is delivered to the brokerage firm for mailing to customers, one of the mutual fund managers calls Eliot to inquire if her change is the result of price considerations or a change in fundamentals. She replies, "A change in fundamentals." She gives the same answer in a joint meeting of the research and investment management departments later that week. Immediately upon hearing the reason, but before the monthly research list is mailed, the fund manager and the other account managers sell all the Harris Company shares in their performance-oriented clients' portfolios over which they have complete discretion.

Comment: First, Eliot should have disclosed the reason for her change in investment recommendation through a summary report to be released with the research list. She should not have disclosed that information selectively to the mutual fund manager or the research and investment management departments. Second, even if Eliot added a follow-up to the report, the mutual fund manager and account managers should not have acted until after the report was disseminated.

Communicating with all clients and customers on a uniform basis presents practical problems for brokers and advisors because of differences in timing and methods of communication with the various types of customers and clients. Members should design an equitable system to prevent selective, discriminatory disclosure and should inform clients of what kind of communications they will receive.

Example 3. Rivers, president of XYZ Corporation, moves his company's growth-oriented pension fund to a particular bank primarily because of the excellent investment performance achieved by the bank's commingled fund for the prior five-year period. A few years later, Rivers compares the results of his pension fund with those of the bank's commingled fund. He is startled to learn that, even though the two accounts have the same investment objectives and similar portfolios, his company's pension fund has significantly underperformed the bank's commingled fund. Questioning this result at his next meeting with the pension fund's manager, Rivers is told that, as a matter of policy, when a new security is placed on the recommended list, Jackson, the pension fund manager, first purchases the security for the commingled account and then purchases it, on a pro rata basis, for all other pension fund accounts. Similarly, when a sale is recommended, the security is sold first from the commingled account and then sold on a pro rata basis from all other accounts. Rivers also learns that if the bank cannot get enough shares (especially the hot issues) to be meaningful to all the accounts, its policy is to place the new issues only in the commingled account.

Seeing that Rivers is neither satisfied nor pleased by the explanation, Jackson quickly adds that nondiscretionary pension accounts and personal trust accounts have a lower priority on purchase and sale recommendations than discretionary pension fund accounts. Furthermore, Jackson states, the company's pension fund had the opportunity to invest up to 5 percent in the commingled fund.

Comment: The bank's policy did not treat all customers fairly, and Jackson violated her fiduciary duty to her clients by giving priority to the growth-oriented commingled fund over all other funds and priority to discretionary accounts over nondiscretionary accounts. Jackson must execute orders on a systematic basis that is fair to all clients. In addition, trade allocation procedures must be disclosed to all clients from the beginning. Of course, in this case, disclosure of the bank's policy would not change the fact that the policy is unfair.

Example 4. Newtron works for a small regional securities firm. His work consists of corporate finance activities and investing for institutional clients. Arena, Ltd., is planning to go public. The partners have secured rights to buy a roller derby franchise and are planning to use the funds from the issue to complete the purchase. Because roller derby is the current rage, Newtron believes he has a hot issue on his hands. He has already personally secured a large loan in anticipation of taking 5 percent of the issue when it goes public and reselling the stock in the aftermarket. In addition, he has quietly negotiated some options for himself for helping convince Arena to do the financing. When he seeks expressions of interest, the institutional buyers oversubscribe the issue. Newtron, assuming that the institutions have the financial clout to drive the stock up, then fills all orders (including his own) and cuts back the institutional blocks.

Comment: Newtron has violated Standard IV(B.3) by not treating all customers fairly. He should not have taken any shares himself and should have prorated the shares offered among all clients. In addition, he should have disclosed that he had received options as part of the deal to his firm [see Standard III(C), Disclosure of Conflicts to Employer] and to his clients [see Standard IV(B.2), Portfolio Investment Recommendations and Actions].

Example 5. Preston, the chief investment officer of Guci Gulch Investments (GGI), a medium-sized money management firm, has been trying to retain a difficult client, Grouch Company. Management at the disgruntled client, which accounts for almost half of GGI's revenues, recently told Preston that if the performance of its account did not improve, it would find a new money manager. Shortly after this threat, Preston purchases mortgage-backed securities (MBS) for several accounts, including Grouch's. Preston is busy with a number of transactions that day, so she fails to allocate the trades immediately or write up the trade tickets. A few days later, when Preston is allocating trades, she notes that some of the MBS have significantly increased in price and some have dropped. Preston decides to allocate the profitable trades to Grouch and spread the losing trades among several other GGI accounts.

Even though Preston's actions improve the performance of the Grouch account, Grouch management is still not satisfied and continues to complain to Preston about performance. Loss of the account would be a significant blow to GGI, and with the quarter end fast approaching, Preston has only a little time left to improve performance. So, trying to resolve the issue once and for all, she enters into a cross-trade between Grouch and several of her other accounts. The cross-trade involves interest-only strips (IOs) purchased a month previously for five other accounts at a price of $4,000 per strip. Preston sells the strips out of those accounts and transfers them into Grouch's account at a price of $1,560 per strip. In contravention of her firm's stated policy, Preston has not obtained any independent bids from any brokers, and rather than obtaining a price quote from the broker, she has set the prices at which she instructs the broker to execute the cross-trades.

Comment: Preston failed to deal fairly with her clients in taking these investment actions. Preston should have allocated the trades prior to executing the orders, or she should have had a systematic approach to allocating the trades, such as pro rata, as soon after they were executed as practicable. In crossing trades, Preston should have obtained best price and execution for all clients and should not have favored one client over another. In general, members should not effect cross-transactions unless they follow certain procedures. Among other things, the member must disclose in writing to the client that the advisor may act as broker for, receive commissions from, and have a potential conflict of interest regarding both parties in agency cross-transactions, and after the written disclosure, the member should obtain from the client a written consent authorizing such transactions in advance.

Example 6. Webb manages a portfolio of securities for Afton Express, a registered investment company. Webb receives a call from his old college roommate, Hobson, who works as a broker/dealer for the Henley Brokerage Firm. Afton Express's portfolio managers frequently purchase securities from Henley brokers for their fund's portfolios, and Hobson tells Webb about a hot IPO for which Henley is part of the underwriting syndicate. Hobson offers Webb an opportunity to participate in the IPO but says that he needs Webb's answer right away because the IPO is available only to a limited number of investors. Webb decides to accept Hobson's offer and places an order for the hot issue. A week later, Hobson calls Webb and tells him that his decision to participate in the limited offering paid off; the new issue traded in the secondary market well above its original offering price.

Comment: Hobson violated Standard IV(B.3) by selling hot-issue securities to Webb, a person who may be in a position to direct future business to Hobson's firm. Members are not to benefit from the positions their clients occupy in the market. Webb also violated Standard IV(B.1). Members' fiduciary obligations must come first in all dealings. Because Webb was actively involved in the portfolio management of Afton's securities, a clear potential conflict existed between the interests of the fund and his own personal financial interests. By not pursuing the availability of the investment opportunity for the fund's shareholders, Webb put his self-interests ahead of his client and thereby violated Standard V(B.3).

Example 7. Mantera works in the trading department of a large broker/dealer. She learns that the research department of her firm has prepared a research report to be sent to clients that contains a recommendation to buy shares of ABC Company. Mantera buys a large block of ABC stock on behalf of the firm and congratulates herself on preparing for the customer demand that will appear once the report is released; she believes the stock will then be hard to acquire and that the increased demand will cause the price to rise. After Mantera has completed these trades, the firm presents the report to its clients. Then at a substantial profit to the firm, Mantera's firm fills customer orders from the inventory she acquired for the firm in the prerelease period.

Comment: Mantera's activities constitute a clear violation of Standard IV(B.3)'s prohibition against trading ahead of research reports.

Example 8. Saunders Industrial Waste Management publicly guides analysts that it is comfortable with an earnings per share projection of $1.15 for the quarter. The consensus earnings estimate for the quarter is $1.16 per diluted share. Roberts, an analyst at Coffey Investments, is confident that SIWM management does not believe this forecast is the actual earnings potential and has low-balled its estimate so that the real announcement would cause an "upside surprise" and boost the price of SIWM stock. The "whisper number" estimate discussed among knowledgeable analysts is $1.30 per share. Saunders repeats the $1.16 figure in his research report to all Coffey clients but informally discusses the whisper numbers with his large clients.

Comment: By not sharing his opinion regarding the potential for a significant upside earnings surprise with all clients, Saunders is not treating all clients fairly and is violating Standard IV(B.3).

Procedures for Compliance

Although Standard IV(B.3) refers to members' responsibility to deal fairly and objectively with their clients, members also have an obligation to ensure, within the limits of their employment, that their firms establish compliance procedures requiring all employees who disseminate investment recommendations or take investment actions to treat customers and clients fairly. At the very least, a member should recommend appropriate procedures to management if none are in place and make management aware of possible violations of fair-dealing practices within the firm when they come to the attention of the member.

The formality and complexity of such compliance procedures depend on the nature and size of the organization and the type of securities involved. An investment advisor who is a sole proprietor and handles only discretionary accounts may not disseminate recommendations to the public, but that advisor should have a formal procedure to ensure that all clients receive fair investment action.

Good business practice dictates that initial recommendations be made available to all customers who indicate an interest. Although a member need not communicate a recommendation to all customers, the selection process by which customers receive information should be based on suitability and known interest, not on any preferred or favored status. A common practice to assure fair dealing is to communicate recommendations within the firm and to customers simultaneously.

Members should consider the following points when establishing fair-dealing compliance procedures.

Limit the number of people involved. Members should make reasonable efforts to limit the number of people who are privy to the fact that a recommendation is going to be disseminated.

Shorten the time frame between decision and dissemination. Members should make reasonable efforts to limit the amount of time that elapses between the decision to make an investment recommendation and the time the actual recommendation is disseminated. If a detailed institutional recommendation is in preparation that might take two or three weeks to publish, a short summary report including the conclusion might be published. In an organization where both a research committee and investment policy committee must approve a recommendation, the meetings should be held on the same day, if possible. The process of reviewing, printing, and mailing reports, or faxing or distributing them by electronic mail, necessarily involves the passage of time, sometimes long periods of time. In large firms with extensive review processes, the time factor is usually not within the control of the analyst who prepares the report. Thus, many firms and their analysts communicate to customers and firm personnel the new or changed recommendations by a "flash." The communication technique might be fax, electronic mail, wire, or short written report.

Publish personnel guidelines for predissemination. Members must establish guidelines that prohibit personnel who have prior knowledge of an investment recommendation from discussing or taking any action on the pending recommendation.

Simultaneous dissemination. Members should establish procedures for dissemination of investment recommendations so that all clients are treated fairly—that is, informed at approximately the same time. For example, if a firm is going to announce a new recommendation, supervisory personnel should time the announcement to avoid placing any client or group of clients at unfair advantage relative to other clients. A communication to all branch offices should be sent at the time of the general announcement. When appropriate, the firm should accompany the announcement of a new recommendation with a statement that trading restrictions for the firm's employees are now in effect. The trading restrictions should stay in effect until the recommendation is evenly distributed.

Establish control over trading activity. Members should establish procedures to control and monitor the trading activities of firm personnel to ensure that transactions on behalf of customers and clients take precedence over transactions that will benefit the firm, its officers, partners, or employees. [See also Standard IV(B.6), Prohibition against Misrepresentation.]

Establish procedures for determining material change. Members should establish a procedure to determine whether a change in an investment recommendation is considered material. Although one individual could have responsibility for such a determination, to obtain diversity of opinions, involving more than one person in the decision is preferable.

Maintain a list of clients and their holdings. Members should maintain a list of all clients and the securities or other investments each client holds to facilitate notification of customers or clients of a change in an investment recommendation. If a particular security or other investment is to be sold, this list can be used to ensure that all holders are treated fairly in the liquidation of that particular investment.

Develop trade allocation procedures. When formulating procedures for allocating trades, members should develop a set of guiding principles that ensure

- fairness to advisory clients, both in priority of execution of orders and in the allocation of the price obtained in execution on block orders or trades;

- timeliness and efficiency in the execution of orders;
- accuracy of the member's records as to trade orders and client account positions.

With these principles in mind, members should develop or encourage their firm to develop written allocation procedures, with particular attention to procedures for block trades and new issues. Members should consider the following procedures:

- requiring orders and modifications or cancellations of orders to be in writing and time stamped;
- processing and executing orders on a first-in, first-out basis;
- developing a policy to address such issues as calculating execution prices and "partial fills" when trades are bunched, or blocked, for efficiency purposes;
- giving all client accounts participating in a block trade the same execution price and charging the same commission;
- when the full amount of the block order is not executed, allocating partially executed orders among the participating client accounts pro rata on the basis of order size;
- when allocating trades for new issues, obtaining advance indications of interest, allocating securities by client (rather than portfolio manager), and providing for a mechanical method for calculating allocations.

Members must make a bona fide public distribution of hot-issue securities. Members cannot withhold hot issues for their own benefit or to reward other persons who direct business to the member.

Disclose trade allocation procedures. The advisor should disclose to clients and prospective clients how it selects accounts to participate in an order and how it determines the amount of securities each account will buy or sell. Trade allocation procedures should be fair and equitable, and disclosure of inequitable allocation methods does not remedy this obligation.

Establish systematic account review. Member supervisors should review each account on a regular basis to ensure that no client or customer is being given preferential treatment and that the investment actions taken for each account are suitable for the account's objectives. Because investments should be based on individual needs and circumstances, an investment manager may have good reasons for placing a given security or other investment in one account while selling it from another account. However, firms should establish review procedures to detect whether one account is being used to bail a favored account out of a bad investment or whether the accounts are being churned.

Disclose levels of service. Members should disclose to all clients whether or not the organization offers two or more levels of service to clients for the same fee or different fees. For example, if an advisory service is offered on both a discretionary basis and a nondiscretionary basis, members should indicate that action may be taken for the discretionary accounts prior to taking the same action for nondiscretionary accounts because of the differences inherent in the accounts.

Standard IV: Relationships with and Responsibilities to Clients and Prospects B. Interactions with Clients and Prospects

Standard IV (B.4)—Priority of Transactions

Transactions for clients and employers shall have priority over transactions in securities or other investments of which a member is the beneficial owner so that such personal transactions do not operate adversely to their clients' or employer's interests. If members make a recommendation regarding the purchase or sale of a security or other investment, they shall give their clients and employer adequate opportunity to act on the recommendation before acting on their own behalf. For purposes of the Code and Standards, a member is a "beneficial owner" if the member has

a. a direct or indirect pecuniary interest in the securities;

b. the power to vote or direct the voting of the shares of the securities or investments;

c. the power to dispose or direct the disposition of the security or investment.

Purpose and Scope of the Standard

Standard IV(B.4) states the responsibility of AIMR members, CFA charterholders, and candidates in the CFA Program to give the interests of their clients and employers priority over their personal financial interests. Standard IV(B.4) is designed to prevent any potential conflict of interest or the appearance of a conflict of interest with respect to personal transactions.

Standard IV(B.4) covers the activities of all members who have knowledge of pending transactions that may be made on behalf of their clients or employer. Standard IV(B.4) also applies to members who have access to information during the normal preparation of research recommendations or who take investment actions. Members are prohibited from conveying such information to any person whose relationship to the member makes the member a beneficial owner of the person's securities.

A member may undertake transactions in accounts for which the member is a beneficial owner only after the member's clients and employer have had an adequate opportunity to act on the recommendation. Personal transactions include those made for the member's own account, for family (including spouse, children, and other immediate family members) accounts, and for accounts in which the member has a direct or indirect pecuniary interest, such as a trust or retirement account. Family accounts that are client accounts should be treated like any other firm account and should neither be given special treatment nor be disadvantaged because of an existing family relationship with the member. If a member has beneficial ownership in the account, however, the member may still be subject to preclearance or reporting requirements of the member's firm or applicable law.

Application of the Standard

Example 1. Jacobs, a research analyst, decides not to change a recommendation from buy/hold to sell because she wants to sell a personal holding in the stock and does not want to wait until all clients have the opportunity to sell first.

> *Comment*: Jacobs violated Standard IV(B.4) because her decision not to change her recommendation until she accomplished her own financial plans will result in losses to her clients if the value of the particular holding subsequently declines.

Example 2. A research analyst, Long, does not recommend purchase of a common stock for his employer's account because he wants to purchase the stock personally and does not want to wait until the recommendation is approved and the stock purchased by his employer.

> *Comment*: Long violated Standard IV(B.4) by taking advantage of his knowledge of the stock's value before allowing his employer to benefit from that information.

Example 3. A cash tender offer is announced by a company whose stock is held by Smith's employer and by Smith's father. Under the terms of the offer, the first 1 million shares tendered will be accepted in full at $28 a share and the next 1 million shares will be sold on a pro rata basis, also at $28 a share (which is 20 percent above the existing market price). Smith immediately calls her father with the news but waits a few days to tender her employer's holding.

> *Comment*: Smith violated Standard IV(B.4) by placing her father's financial interests above her employer's. As one of the first million sellers, Smith's father will receive $28 a share for all his shares, whereas, because of the delay in receiving the information, Smith's employer may receive $28 a share for only a portion of its holding.

Example 4. Baker, the portfolio manager of an aggressive-growth mutual fund, maintains accounts in his wife's maiden name at several brokerage firms with which the fund and a number of Baker's other individual clients do a substantial amount of business. Whenever a new hot issue becomes available, he instructs the brokers to buy it for his wife's account. Because such issues normally are scarce, Baker often acquires shares while his clients are not able to participate.

> *Comment*: Baker should acquire shares for his mutual fund first and only after doing so acquire them for his wife's account, even though he might in this way miss out on participating in new issues via his wife's account. He also should disclose the trading for his wife's account to his employer because this activity creates a conflict between his personal interests and his employer's interests [see Standard III(C), Disclosure of Conflicts to Employer].

Example 5. Toffler, a portfolio manager at Esposito Investments, manages the retirement account established with the firm by her parents. Whenever IPOs become available, she first allocates shares to all her other clients for whom the investment is appropriate; only then does she place any remaining portion in her parents' account, if the issue is appropriate for them. She has adopted this procedure so that no one can accuse her of playing favorites for her parents.

> *Comment*: Toffler has breached her fiduciary duty to her parents by treating them differently from her other accounts simply because of the family relationship. As fee-paying clients of Esposito Investments, Toffler's parents are entitled to the same treatment as any other client of the firm. If Toffler has beneficial ownership in the account, however, and Esposito Investments has preclearance and reporting requirements for personal transactions, she may have to preclear the trades and report the transactions to Esposito (see the topical study titled "Personal Investing").

Example 6. Michaels is an entry-level employee who holds a relatively low-paying job serving both the research and investment management departments of an active investment management company. He purchases a sports car and begins to wear expensive clothes after only a year of employment with the firm. The director of the investment management department, who has responsibility for monitoring the personal stock transactions of all employees, decides to investigate the situation. The director discovers that Michaels has parlayed a bank loan of $1,000 into a tidy sum of money by buying stocks just before they were put on the firm's recommended purchase list. Michaels was regularly given the firm's quarterly personal transaction form but declined to complete it.

Comment: Michaels violated Standard IV(B.4) by placing personal transactions ahead of client transactions. In addition, his supervisor violated the Standards by permitting Michaels to continue to perform his assigned tasks without first having signed the quarterly personal transaction form [see Standard III(E), Responsibilities of Supervisors]. Note also that if Michaels had communicated information about the firm's recommendations to a person who traded the security, that action would be a misappropriation of the information and a violation of Standard V(A), Prohibition against Use of Material Nonpublic Information.

Example 7. A brokerage's insurance analyst, Wilson, makes a closed-circuit report to her firm's branches around the country. During the broadcast, she includes negative comments about a major company within the industry. The following day, Wilson's report is printed and distributed to the sales force and public customers. The report recommends that both short-term traders and intermediate investors take profits by selling that company's stocks. Seven minutes after the broadcast, Noyen, head of the firm's trading department, closes out a long call position in the stock. Eight minutes later, Noyen establishes a sizable put position in the stock. Noyen claims she took this action to facilitate anticipated sales by institutional clients.

Comment: Noyen expected that both the stock and option markets would respond to the sell recommendation, but she did not give customers an opportunity to buy or sell in the options market before the firm itself did. By taking action before the report was disseminated, Noyen's firm could have depressed the price of the calls and increased the price of the puts. The firm could have avoided a conflict of interest if it had waited to trade for its own account until its clients had an opportunity to receive and assimilate Wilson's recommendations. As it is, Noyen's actions violated Standard IV(B.4).

Procedures for Compliance

Members should encourage their firms to prepare and distribute to firm personnel a code of ethics and compliance procedures, applicable to principals and employees, emphasizing their obligation to place the interests of clients above personal and employer interests. The form and content of such compliance procedures depend on the size and nature of each organization and the laws to which it is subject. In general, however, the code and procedures should do the following:

Define personal transactions. All employees need to be aware of what constitutes a personal transaction. Although a minimum definition is included in this discussion of Standard IV(B.4), in certain circumstances, including a stricter standard might be appropriate.

Define investment. The definition of "investment" for the purposes of the Standards is any medium by which placement of funds generally occurs with the expectation of preserving value and earning a positive return. Investments include not only bonds, common stocks, and related securities (such as convertible bonds, preferred stocks, warrants, options, puts and calls, and financial futures), but also such diverse vehicles as real estate; oil, gas, and other natural resources; commodities; currencies; and tangible property (such as works of art or other collectors' items).

Limit the number of access persons. Members and their firms should limit the number of "access," or "covered," persons—that is, persons who have knowledge of pending or actual investment recommendations or action. The firm's definition of access (covered) person should be broad enough to cover all people with that knowledge. Implementing "Fire Walls" (physical and procedural barriers to prevent the flow of information from one group to another) may be appropriate in certain organizations to limit the number of persons with such access. Because operational procedures may be changed or personnel reassigned, a systematic review (at least annually) of which personnel are access (covered) individuals is appropriate.

Define prohibited transactions. Members and their firms should clearly define prohibited transactions so that employees completely understand their obligations to clients and their employer. Participation by investment personnel in equity or equity-based IPOs should be restricted. For example, members' firms should impose strict limits on investment personnel acquiring securities in private placements. Managers should not be prevented, however, from purchasing government issues, such as municipal bonds and/or other government securities.

Each firm must determine specific requirements relating to "blackout" and restricted periods. Firm policies and procedures should prevent managers or employees who are involved in the investment decision-making process from initiating trades in a security for which their firms have a pending buy or sell order within a 24-hour period before the order is executed or canceled. All individuals who are involved in the investment decision-making process should be subject to the same restricted period.

Although AIMR advocates long-term investing for its members, members' firms should adopt provisions to address possible conflicts related to short-term trading. As a general rule, members and their firms should prohibit investment personnel from profiting in the purchase and sale or sale and repurchase of the same or equivalent securities within 60 calendar days. Members should establish clearance provisions whereby an independent review committee or designated senior officer within the firm has authority to approve a personal transaction within the 60-day period for exceptional or unusual circumstances. In addition to this clearance provision, members' firms should encourage the placement of firm and manager accounts at risk along with the investments of clients. Members' firms should establish their own policies regarding short-term trading so long as they disclose the policy prominently to clients and prospective clients.

Establish reporting and prior-clearance requirements. Members should establish a reporting system for all employees' personal transactions. The records should include the date and nature of the transaction, the price, and the name of the broker, dealer, or bank through which it was effected. Depending on circumstances, monthly reporting or more frequent requirements might be desirable. Members and their firms should require access (covered) persons to direct their brokers to supply duplicate copies of confirmations of all personal securities transactions and copies of periodic statements.

Procedures requiring prior approval for all personal investment transactions by employees will prevent any employee from unknowingly allowing a personal transaction to take precedence over those for clients or the employer.

Consider special situations. Members and their firms are advised to establish procedures for special situations. A review committee made up of senior firm officials and/or independent parties should review these situations to determine objectively whether the manager should act on the security in question.

Ensure that procedures will be enforced. Generally, authority to enforce firm procedures is the responsibility of a compliance officer; in a small organization, however, the responsibility might rest with the director of research, the head of the investment management department, the head of a trading department, or a combination of all three. Persons assigned to approve transactions should have a third party approve their personal investment transactions.

Contain disciplinary procedures. In fairness to all employees and as a deterrent to infractions of Standard IV(B.4), the members and their firms should establish a method of taking disciplinary action to enforce the code and compliance procedures. An internal investigation should be promptly conducted into any questionable trade. Disgorgement is recommended when a manager has purchased a security in violation of trading policy. It remedies the violation after the fact. Managers should disgorge all profits and assume any losses from the trade. AIMR encourages individual firms to determine the most appropriate method for allocating disgorged profits so long as monies accrued in the event of a personal trading violation do not benefit the individual manager or the firm.

Standard IV: Relationships with and Responsibilities to Clients and Prospects
B. Interactions with Clients and Prospects

Standard IV (B.5)—Preservation of Confidentiality

Members shall preserve the confidentiality of information communicated by clients, prospects, or employers concerning matters within the scope of the client–member, prospect–member, or employer–member relationship unless the member receives information concerning illegal activities on the part of the client, prospect, or employer.

Purpose and Scope of the Standard

Standard IV(B.5) states the responsibility of AIMR members, CFA charterholders, and candidates in the CFA Program to preserve the confidentiality of information communicated to them by their clients, prospects, and employers. Standard IV(B.5) is applicable when (1) the member receives information on the basis of his or her special ability to conduct a portion of the client's business or personal affairs and (2) the member receives information that arises from or is relevant to that portion of the client's business that is the subject of the special or confidential relationship. If the information concerns illegal activities by the client, however, the member may have an obligation to report the activities to the appropriate authorities.

The requirements of Standard IV(B.5) are not intended to prevent members from cooperating with an investigation by AIMR's Professional Conduct Program (PCP). Members shall consider the PCP an extension of themselves when requested to provide information about a client in support of a PCP investigation into their own conduct. Members are encouraged to cooperate with investigations into the conduct of others. Any information turned over to the PCP is kept in the strictest confidence. Thus, members will not be violating their duty under Standard IV(B.5) by forwarding confidential information to the PCP.

Furthermore, members are prohibited from executing settlement agreements that may prevent a customer or other party from providing information, documents, or testimony or otherwise cooperating with the PCP in its investigation of the member's alleged violations of the Code and Standards. Settlement agreements with confidentiality clauses should be written to expressly authorize both parties to respond without restriction or condition to any inquiry about the settlement or its underlying facts and circumstances by any securities regulator or the PCP. Members who refuse to provide requested information on the basis of confidentiality clauses in settlement agreements will be considered to be failing to cooperate with an investigation and subject to summary suspension of membership under AIMR's Bylaws.

Application of the Standard

Example 1. Connor, a financial analyst employed by Johnson Investment Counselors, Inc., provides investment advice to the trustees of City Medical Center. The trustees have given her a number of internal reports concerning City Medical's needs for physical plant renovation and expansion. They have asked Connor to recommend investments that would generate capital appreciation in endowment funds to meet projected capital expenditures. Connor is approached by a local businessman, Kasey, who is considering a substantial contribution either to City Medical Center or to another local hospital. Kasey wants to find out the building plans of both institutions before making a decision, but he does not want to speak to the trustees.

> *Comment*: The trustees gave Connor the internal reports so she could advise them on how to manage their endowment funds. Because the information in the reports is clearly both confidential and within the scope of the confidential relationship, Connor should refuse to divulge information to Kasey.

Example 2. Moody is an investment officer at the Lester Trust Company. He has an advisory customer who has talked to him about giving approximately $50,000 to charity to reduce his income taxes. Moody is also treasurer of the Home for Indigent Widows, which is planning its annual giving campaign. It hopes to expand its list of prospects, particularly those capable of substantial gifts. Moody recommends that the Home's vice president for corporate gifts call on his customer and ask for a donation in the $50,000 range.

> *Comment*: Even though the attempt to help the Home for Indigent Widows was well intended, Moody violated Standard IV(B.5) by revealing confidential information about his customer.

Example 3. Government officials approach Jones, the portfolio manager for Whiticker Company's pension plan, to examine pension fund records. They tell her that Whiticker's corporate tax returns are being audited and the pension fund reviewed. Two days earlier, Jones learned in a regular investment review meeting with Whiticker officers that potentially excessive and improper charges are being made to the pension plan by

Whiticker. Jones consults her employer's general counsel and is advised that Whiticker has probably violated tax and fiduciary regulations and laws by these charges to the pension fund.

> *Comment*: Jones should inform her supervisor of these activities, and her employer should take steps, with Whiticker, to remedy the violations. If that approach is not successful, Jones and her employer should seek advice of counsel to determine the appropriate steps to be taken. Jones may well have a duty to disclose the evidence she has of the continuing legal violations and to resign as asset manager for Whiticker.

Example 4. As part of an AIMR investigation into the conduct of Baker, the PCP requests certain records from Baker and his firm. Baker, stating that his duty under Standard IV(B.5) prevents him from disclosing confidential matters about his clients to AIMR, refuses to provide the requested information. He states further that he has entered into a settlement agreement with the client who originally brought the complaint that he disclosed on his professional conduct statement, and the agreement prevents him and his client from providing information about the matter to anyone, including AIMR.

> *Comment*: Baker would not be in violation of Standard IV(B.5) by providing confidential client information to the PCP as part of an investigation into Baker's conduct. Baker also cannot rely on the terms of the settlement agreement to thwart AIMR's efforts to investigate his conduct. If after this explanation he continues to refuse to cooperate with the investigation, Baker will be suspended from membership in AIMR and any member society. If he is a CFA charterholder, his right to use the CFA designation will be revoked.

Procedures for Compliance

The simplest, most conservative, and most effective way to comply with Standard IV(B.5) is to avoid disclosing any information received from a client except to authorized fellow employees who are also working for the client. In some instances, however, a member may want to disclose information received from clients that is outside the scope of the confidential relationship and does not involve illegal activities. Before making such a disclosure, a member should ask the following:

- In what context was the information disclosed? If disclosed in a discussion of work being performed for the client, is the information relevant to the work?
- Is the information background material that, if disclosed, will enable the member to improve service to the client?

Standard IV: Relationships with and Responsibilities to Clients and Prospects B. Interactions with Clients and Prospects

Standard IV (B.6)—Prohibition against Misrepresentation

Members shall not make any statements, orally or in writing, that misrepresent

a. the services that they or their firm are capable of performing;

b. their qualifications or the qualifications of their firm;

c. the member's academic or professional credentials.

Members shall not make or imply, orally or in writing, any assurances or guarantees regarding any investment except to communicate accurate information regarding the terms of the investment instrument and the issuer's obligations under the instrument.

Purpose and Scope of the Standard

Standard IV(B.6) states the responsibility of AIMR members, CFA charterholders, and candidates in the CFA Program to avoid misrepresentation of their services or qualifications and prohibits inappropriate assurances about any investment or its return. Misrepresentation can be defined as the act of representing improperly or imperfectly or giving a false impression. A misrepresentation is any untrue statement of a fact or any statement that is otherwise false or misleading.

Members should ensure that misrepresentation does not occur in oral representations, advertising (whether in the press or through brochures), electronic communications, or written materials (whether publicly disseminated or not). Written materials for a general audience include, but are not limited to, research reports, market letters, newspaper columns, and books. Electronic communications include, but are not limited to, Internet communications, Web pages, chat rooms, and e-mail.

Members who use Web pages should regularly monitor materials posted to the site to ensure the site maintains current information. Members should also ensure that all reasonable precautions have been taken to protect the site's integrity, confidentiality, and security and that the site does not misrepresent any information and provides full disclosure.

Standard IV(B.6) prohibits statements or implications that an investment is "guaranteed" or that superior returns can be expected in the future based on the member repeating past success. Standard IV(B.6) does not preclude truthful statements that some investments are, in fact, guaranteed in one way or another or that they have guaranteed returns, such as certain types of insurance contracts, short-term Treasury securities, and insured bank deposits.

Application of the Standard

Example 1. Rogers is a partner in the firm of Rogers and Black, a small firm offering investment advisory services. She assures Goff, a prospective client who has just inherited $1 million, that "we can perform all the financial and investment services you need." Rogers and Black is well equipped to provide investment advice but, in fact, cannot provide a full array of financial and investment services.

> *Comment*: Rogers has violated Standard IV(B.6) by orally misrepresenting the services her firm can perform for the prospective client. She should have limited herself to describing the range of investment advisory services Rogers and Black can provide and offering to help Goff obtain elsewhere the financial and investment services that her firm cannot provide.

Example 2. Brooks, a trainee at a brokerage firm, represents himself to several of his employer's clients as a "portfolio management specialist." Relying on his representations and advice, clients purchase securities and hold them while the securities decline in value.

> *Comment*: Brooks misrepresented his qualifications and violated Standard IV(B.6).

Example 3. White, a securities salesman for Johnson & Company, sells securities of Bland Development Company stating that "this strongly recommended investment will give you a 100 percent capital gain within six months and much more in the longer term." All that White knows about the company is that it has just licensed a patent to a major manufacturer of food containers for a new form of packaging.

> *Comment*: White's assurances are unsupported and violate Standard IV(B.6). He should have more information about the company before making any recommendation; he should disclose to clients that the gain cannot be assured; and he should warn investors of the risks of the investment.

Example 4. Cullen Brokerage Services, Inc., uses radio advertisements that claim investors can increase their returns by investing in money market funds rather than municipal bonds. The advertisements do not mention that the current after-tax yield on most money market funds is less than that on municipal bonds for investors in the highest personal tax brackets.

Comment: The advertisements are misleading to a large class of potential investors because they predict performance for all investors and do not distinguish the impact on investors in high tax brackets. Members at Cullen Brokerage Services who are responsible for the ads are thus violating Standard IV(B.6).

Example 5. When Marks sells mortgage-backed derivatives called interest only strips (IOs) to her public pension plan clients, she describes them as "guaranteed by the U.S. government." Purchasers of the IOs are entitled only to the interest stream generated by the mortgages, however, not the principal itself. The municipality's investment policies and local law require that securities purchased by the public pension plans be guaranteed by the U.S. government. Although the underlying mortgages are guaranteed, neither the investor's investment nor the interest stream on the IOs is guaranteed. When interest rates decline, causing an increase in prepayment of mortgages, the interest payments to the clients decline, and the clients lose approximately 50 percent of their investment.

Comment: Marks violated Standard IV(B.6) by misrepresenting the terms and character of the investment.

Example 6. McGuire is president and CEO of Market Strategy, Inc., an investment relations company. McGuire contracts with six publicly traded companies to electronically promote their stock. McGwire posts a profile and a strong buy recommendation for each company on Market Strategy's Internet site. McGuire also sends unsolicited Internet e-mail to 250,000 potential investors indicating that the stock is guaranteed to increase in value. The six companies compensate McGuire for the promotion with cash and stock. Neither the Internet site nor the e-mails disclose the compensation arrangement between McGuire and the six companies.

Comment: McGuire has violated Standard IV(B.6) because the Internet site and e-mails are misleading to potential investors. McGuire should not have guaranteed that the securities would increase in value. McGuire has also violated Standard IV(B.8) by not disclosing the existence of an arrangement with the six companies through which he receives compensation in exchange for his services.

McGuire may have also violated Standard IV(A.1) if he failed to perform a diligent and thorough investigation appropriate to the circumstances of his investment recommendations.

Procedures for Compliance

Members can prevent unintentional misrepresentations of the qualifications or services the member or the member's firm is capable of performing if each member understands the limit of the firm's or the individual's capabilities and the need to be accurate and complete in presentations. Firms can provide guidance for employees who make written or oral presentations to clients or potential clients by providing a written list of the firm's available services and a description of the firm's qualifications. This list should suggest ways of describing the firm's services, qualifications, and compensation that are both accurate and suitable for client or customer presentations. Firms can also help prevent misrepresentation by specifically designating which employees are authorized to speak on behalf of the firm. Whether or not the firm provides guidance, members should make certain that they understand the services the firm can perform and its qualifications.

In addition, each member should prepare a resumé of the member's own qualifications and a list of the services the member is capable of performing to use in accurate presentations to clients. Members should use a written resumé and job description of firm services when making a presentation to a client or prospective client to help the member focus on the firm's and the member's own strengths and limitations. Firms can aid member compliance by also periodically reviewing employee correspondence and documents that contain representations of individual or firm qualifications.

Standard IV: Relationships with and Responsibilities to Clients and Prospects B. Interactions with Clients and Prospects

Standard IV (B.7)—Disclosure of Conflicts to Clients and Prospects

Members shall disclose to their clients and prospects all matters, including beneficial ownership of securities or other investments, that reasonably could be expected to impair the member's ability to make unbiased and objective recommendations.

Purpose and Scope of the Standard

Standard IV(B.7) attempts to protect customers and prospects by requiring AIMR members, CFA charterholders, and candidates in the CFA Program to disclose fully all actual and potential conflicts of interest. All disclosures to clients should be made in plain language and in a manner designed to effectively communicate the information to clients and prospective clients. Once the member has made full disclosure, the member's clients and prospects will have all the data needed to evaluate the objectivity of the member's investment advice.

Members are required to maintain their objectivity when rendering investment advice or taking investment action. Investment advice may be perceived to be tainted in numerous situations. A potential conflict of interest exists whenever an analyst makes buy/sell recommendations. Can a member remain objective if, on behalf of the firm, the member obtains or assists in obtaining fees for services other than research? Can a member give objective advice if the member owns stock in the company that is the subject of an investment recommendation or if the member has a close personal relationship with the company managers? Requiring members to disclose all matters that reasonably could be expected to impair the member's objectivity allows clients and prospects to judge motives and biases for themselves.

In today's environment, a conflict, or the perception of a conflict, cannot be avoided in some circumstances. The most obvious conflicts of interest, which should always be disclosed, are special relationships between the member or the member's firm and an issuer (such as a directorship or consultancy), underwriting and financial relationships, broker/dealer market-making activities, and material beneficial ownerships of stock. A member must be aware of and disclose to clients and prospective clients material ownership in the member's firm's investment account, market-making activities, corporate finance relationships, and directorships. Disclosure of broker/dealer market-making activities alerts clients that a purchase or sale might be made from or to the broker/dealer's principal account and that the firm has a special interest in the price of the stock.

Service as a director poses three basic conflicts of interest. First, a conflict may exist between the fiduciary duties owed to clients and the duties owed to shareholders of the company. Second, investment personnel who serve as directors may receive the securities or the option to purchase securities of the company as compensation for serving on the board, which could raise questions about trading decisions that could increase the value of those securities. Third, board service creates the opportunity to receive material nonpublic information involving the company. Even though the material is confidential, the perception could be that information not available to the public might be communicated to a director's firm—whether broker, investment advisor, or other type of organization. When members providing investment services serve also as directors, they should be isolated from those making investment decisions by the use of Fire Walls or similar restrictions.

Many other circumstances give rise to actual or potential conflicts of interest. For instance, a sell-side analyst working for a broker/dealer may be encouraged, not only by members of her or his own firm but by corporate issuers themselves, to write research reports about particular companies. The buy-side analyst is likely to be faced with similar conflicts as banks exercise their underwriting and securities-dealing powers. The marketing division may ask an analyst to recommend the stock of a certain company in order to obtain business from that company.

The potential for conflict of interest also exists with broker-sponsored limited partnerships formed to invest venture capital. Increasingly, members are expected not only to follow issues from these partnerships once they are offered to the public but also to promote the issues in the secondary market after public offerings. Members and employers should attempt to resolve situations presenting potential conflicts of interest or disclose them in accordance with the principles set forth in Standard IV(B.7).

The most prevalent conflict relating to Standard IV(B.7) pertains to members' ownership of stock in companies that they recommend to clients and/or that are held by clients. Clearly, the easiest method for preventing a conflict is to prohibit members from owning any such securities, but this approach discriminates against members. Therefore, sell-side members should disclose any materially beneficial ownership interest in a security or other investment that the member is recommending. Buy-side members should disclose their procedures for reporting requirements for personal transactions. For the purposes of Standard IV(B.7), members beneficially own securities or other investments that they or a member of their immediate family own or that are held in trust for them or their immediate family.

Members also should disclose, with the approval of their employer, special compensation arrangements with the employer that might conflict with client interests, such as bonuses based on short-term performance criteria, commissions, incentive fees, performance fees, and referral fees. Members' firms are encouraged to include information on compensation packages in firms' promotional literature. If a member or the member's firm manages a portfolio for which the fee is based on a share of capital gains or capital appreciation (a performance fee), this information should be disclosed to clients. If the member or member's firm has outstanding agent options to buy stock as part of the compensation package for corporate financing activities, the amount and expiration date of these options should be disclosed as a footnote to any research report published by the member or member's firm.

Application of the Standard

Example 1. Ball, an analyst and a partner in his firm, is on the board of a public company. He does not disclose this fact when recommending the securities of that company.

> *Comment*: Ball is in violation of Standard IV(B.7). To comply, he must disclose his service on a company's board of directors to clients when he gives investment advice regarding the company to clients.

Example 2. Weiss is a research analyst with Farmington Company, a broker and investment banker. Farmington's merger and acquisition department has represented Whatco, a conglomerate, in all of its acquisitions for 20 years. From time to time, Farmington officers sit on the boards of directors of various Whatco subsidiaries. Weiss is writing a research report on Whatco.

> *Comment*: Weiss should disclose Farmington's special relationship with Whatco. Broker/dealer management of and participation in public offerings must be disclosed in research reports. Because the position of underwriter to a company presents a special past and potential future relationship with a company that is the subject of investment advice, it must be disclosed.

Example 3. The investment management firm of Dover & Roe sells a 25 percent interest in its partnership to a multinational bank holding company, First of New York. Immediately thereafter, President Prior of Dover & Roe changes her recommendation of First of New York's common stock from sell to buy and adds First of New York's commercial paper to Dover & Roe's approved list for purchase.

> *Comment*: Prior should disclose the new relationship with First of New York to all Dover & Roe clients. This relationship should also be disclosed to clients by the firm's portfolio managers when they make specific investment recommendations or take investment actions with respect to First of New York's securities.

Example 4. The head of the marketing division of Jones Investment Company, Sorenson, would like one of the Jones Investment analysts to recommend that clients buy stock in Xavier, Inc. Sorenson hopes to have Jones Investment selected as an investment manager of Xavier's employee benefit plans.

> *Comment*: Even if the purchase recommendation has no influence on Xavier's selection of an investment manager, it may adversely affect client investment decisions. Thus, Sorenson should have left the recommendation solely in the hands of Jones Investment's research department.

Example 5. Barton, a research analyst who follows firms producing small copiers, has been recommending purchase of Kincaid because of its innovative new line of copiers. After his initial report on the company, Barton inherits from a distant aunt $3 million of Kincaid stock, which now composes 85 percent of his new net worth. He has been asked to write a follow-up report on Kincaid.

> *Comment*: Barton should disclose his ownership of the Kincaid stock at the time of the follow-up report. The stock is a very high percentage of his net worth, and the total amount of its value is significant by a typical investor's standards.

Example 6. For her own account, Bolero is speculating in penny stocks and purchases 100,000 shares of Drew Mining, Inc., for 30 cents a share. She intends to sell these shares at the sign of any substantial upward price movement of the stock. A week later, her employer asks her to write a report on penny stocks in the mining industry to be published two weeks from then. Whether or not she owned Drew stock, Bolero would recommend it in her report as a buy, but the likely result is a surge of the price of the stock to the $2 range.

> *Comment*: Although this holding may not be material, Bolero should disclose it in the report and to her employer before writing the report because the gain for her will be substantial if the market responds strongly to her recommendation. The fact that she has only recently purchased the stock adds to the appearance that she is not entirely objective.

Example 7. Jacobs is a portfolio manager for several nondiscretionary pension funds at Trenton Trust Company. His wife is comptroller, treasurer, and a 20 percent shareholder of Miller Machine Parts, Inc., formerly a closely held corporation. Miller Machine Parts has been aggressively pursuing and winning foreign business and, a year ago, made a public offering to finance plant expansion. The market value of Mrs. Jacobs's holdings rose from $500,000 before the offering to $5 million one year after the offering. Trenton's research department recommends the stock to its trust officers and pension fund portfolio managers.

> *Comment*: For purposes of the Standards, Jacobs beneficially owns his wife's stock. He should disclose her ownership to his supervisor and to the trustees of all the pension funds he manages before buying Miller Machine Parts stock. Jacobs should also disclose any trading in the Miller stock by Mrs. Jacobs.

Example 8. Snead, a portfolio manager for Thomas Investment Counsel, Inc., specializes in managing defined-benefit pension plan accounts, all of which are in the accumulative phase and have long-term investment objectives. A year ago, Snead's employer, in an attempt to motivate and retain key investment professionals, introduced a bonus compensation system that rewards portfolio managers on the basis of quarterly performance relative to their peers and certain benchmark indexes. Now, an officer of Griffin Corporation, one of Snead's pension fund clients, asks why Griffin Corporation's portfolio seems to be dominated by high-beta stocks of companies that often appear among the most actively traded issues. No change in objective or strategy has been recommended by Snead during the year. Snead avoids answering the officer's question.

> *Comment*: Snead violated Standard IV(B.7) by failing to inform her clients of the changes in her compensation arrangement with her employer. Firms may pay employees on the basis of performance, but pressure by Thomas Investment Counsel to achieve short-term

performance goals was in basic conflict with the objectives of Snead's accounts.

Example 9. General Industries is conducting a search for a global bond manager for its pension fund and calls on Parsons, the head of fixed income at Ocala Advisors, to make a presentation to its investment committee. After making his presentation, Parsons receives a phone call from the head of the committee and learns that Ocala is the leading contender among those General Industries is considering for managing its global bond account. At about the same time, General Industries begins a hostile takeover attempt against Acme Metals, which is in the process of undertaking a friendly merger with Best Metals. Ocala owns a large position in Acme. Miller, Ocala's equity analyst covering the metals, believes that merging with Best Metals would be the better course of action for Acme because of the synergies that would result. Parsons calls Miller into his office, however, and pressures him to recommend that Ocala's proxy be voted with General Industries. Parsons does not want to lose the General Industries global bond business to another manager as a result of Ocala not voting its proxy in support of General Industries.

Comment: Parsons violated Standard IV(B.7) by failing to disclose to clients and prospects the conflict of interest that arose when General Industries began its hostile takeover attempt and by pressuring Miller to recommend voting the proxy in a manner that would benefit Ocala at the expense of the client. Although voting the proxy against General Industries' takeover will jeopardize the appointment of Ocala to manage General Industries' global bond allocation, Miller should be allowed to vote according to his beliefs. The interests of the client must prevail.

Example 10. Wayland Securities works with small companies doing IPOs and/or secondary offerings. Typically, these deals are in the $1 million to $5 million range, and as a result, the corporate finance fees are quite small. In order to compensate for the small fees, Wayland Securities usually takes "agents options"—that is, rights, exercisable within a two-year time frame, to acquire up to an additional 10 percent of the current offering. Following an IPO performed by Wayland for Shady Resources, Ltd., Hunter, the head of corporate finance at Wayland, is concerned about receiving value for her Shady Resources options. The options are one month from expiring and the stock is not doing well. She contacts Fitzpatrick in the research department of Wayland Securities, reminds him that he is eligible for 30 percent of these options, and indicates that now would be a good time to give some additional coverage to Shady Resources. Fitzpatrick agrees and immediately issues a favorable report.

> *Comment*: In order for Fitzpatrick not to be in violation of Standard IV(B.7), she would need to indicate as a footnote in the report the volume and expiration date of agent options outstanding. Furthermore, because she is personally eligible for some of the options, Fitzpatrick must disclose the extent of this compensation. She also should be careful that she does not violate her duty of independence and objectivity under Standard IV(A.3).

Example 11. Carter is a representative with Bengal International, a registered broker/dealer. Carter is approached by a stock promoter for Quick Quiche Company, who offers to pay Carter additional compensation for sales to his clients of Quick Quiche Company's stock. Carter accepts the sales promoter's offer but does not disclose the arrangements to his clients or to his employer. Carter sells shares of the stock to his clients.

> *Comment*: Carter has violated Standard IV(B.7) by failing to disclose to clients and prospective clients that he was receiving additional compensation for recommending and selling Quick Quiche stock. Because he did not disclose the arrangement with Quick Quiche to his clients, the clients were unable to evaluate whether Carter's recommendations to buy Quick Quiche were affected by this arrangement.
>
> Carter's conduct also violated Standard III(D) by failing to disclose to his employer monetary compensation received in addition to the compensation and benefits conferred by his employer. Carter should have disclosed the arrangement with Quick Quiche to his employer so that his employer could evaluate whether the arrangement created a conflict of interest or affected his objectivity and loyalty.

Procedures for Compliance

Many firms require employees to report all transactions by employees and their families for purposes of detecting conflicts of interest and trading on material nonpublic information. Whether such firm requirements exist or not, members should report to employers, clients, and prospects any material beneficial interest they may have in securities and any corporate directorships or other special relationships they may have with the companies they are recommending. Members should make these disclosures before they make any recommendations or take any action regarding such investments.

Standard IV: Relationships with and Responsibilities to Clients and Prospects B. Interactions with Clients and Prospects

Standard IV (B.8)—Disclosure of Referral Fees

Members shall disclose to clients and prospects any consideration or benefit received by the member or delivered to others for the recommendation of any services to the client or prospect.

Purpose and Scope of the Standard

Standard IV(B.8) states the responsibility of AIMR members, CFA charterholders, and candidates in the CFA Program to inform clients of any benefit received for referrals of customers and clients. Such disclosure will help the client (1) evaluate any partiality shown in any recommendation of services and (2) evaluate the full cost of the services.

Appropriate disclosure means advising the client or prospective client, before entry into any formal agreement for services, of any benefit given or received for the recommending of any services provided by the member. In addition, the member should disclose the nature of the consideration or benefit—for example, flat fee or percentage basis; one-time or continuing benefit; based on performance; benefit in the form of provision of research or other noncash benefit—together with the estimated dollar value. Consideration includes all fees, whether paid in cash, in soft dollars, or in kind.

Application of the Standard

Example 1. Brady Securities, Inc., a broker/dealer, has established a referral arrangement with Lewis Brothers, Ltd., an investment counseling firm. Under this arrangement, Brady Securities refers all prospective tax-exempt accounts, including pension, profit-sharing, and endowment accounts, to Lewis Brothers. In return, Lewis Brothers makes available to Brady Securities on a regular basis the security recommendations and reports of its research staff, which registered representatives of Brady Securities use in serving customers. In addition, Lewis Brothers conducts monthly economic and market reviews for Brady Securities personnel and directs all stock commission business generated by referral accounts to Brady Securities. White, a partner in Lewis Brothers, calculates that the incremental costs involved in functioning as the research department of Brady Securities amount to $20,000 annually. Referrals from Brady

Securities last year resulted in fee income of $200,000, and directing all stock trades through Brady Securities resulted in additional costs to Lewis Brothers clients of $10,000.

Ross, the chief financial officer of Maxwell, contacts White and says that she is seeking an investment manager for Maxwell's profit-sharing plan. She adds, "My friend Hill at Brady Securities recommended your firm without qualification, and that's good enough for me. Do we have a deal?" White accepts the new account but does not disclose his firm's referral arrangement with Brady Securities.

> *Comment*: White violated Standard IV(B.8) by failing to inform the prospective customer of the referral fee payable in services and commissions for an indefinite period to Brady Securities. Such disclosure could have caused Ross to reassess Hill's recommendation and make a more critical evaluation of Lewis Brothers' services.

Example 2. Hanley works for the Trust Department of Central Trust Bank. He receives compensation for each referral he makes to Central Trust's brokerage and personal financial management department that results in a sale. He refers several of his clients to the personal financial management department but does not disclose the arrangement within Central Trust to his clients.

> *Comment*: Hanley has violated Standard IV(B.8) by not disclosing the referral arrangement at Central Trust Bank to his clients. He would be required to disclose, at the time of referral, any referral fee agreement in place between Central Trust Bank's departments. The disclosure should include the nature of the benefit and the value of the benefit and should be made in writing.

Procedures for Compliance

Members should carry out the following practices to stay compliant with Standard IV(B.8):

- Disclose all agreements. Members should disclose, in writing, the existence and terms of any referral fee agreement to any client or prospective client as soon as the member learns that the client or prospective client has been referred by a firm receiving a referral fee.
- Describe in the disclosure the nature of the consideration and the estimated dollar value of the consideration.
- Consult a supervisor and legal counsel concerning any prospective arrangement regarding referral fees.

Standard V: Relationships with and Responsibilities to the Investing Public

Standard V(A)—Prohibition against Use of Material Nonpublic Information

Members who possess material nonpublic information related to the value of a security shall not trade or cause others to trade in that security if such trading would breach a duty or if the information was misappropriated or relates to a tender offer. If members receive material nonpublic information in confidence, they shall not breach that confidence by trading or causing others to trade in securities to which such information relates. Members shall make reasonable efforts to achieve public dissemination of material nonpublic information disclosed in breach of a duty.

Purpose and Scope of the Standard

The purpose of Standard V(A) is to state the responsibilities of AIMR members, holders of the Chartered Financial Analyst designation, and candidates in the CFA Program when they are dealing with the receipt and disclosure of material nonpublic information. Standard V(A) prohibits a member from taking investment action on the basis of information that the member knows or has reason to know was disclosed by the person conveying the information (the "tipper") in violation of a confidence or in breach of a duty. Furthermore, even if no duty is breached, a member violates Standard V(A) by taking investment action or communicating material nonpublic information that the member knows or should have known has been misappropriated or illegally obtained. In addition, in no instance may a member trade or cause others to trade in a security while the member possesses material nonpublic information relating to a tender offer regarding that security. Mere possession of material nonpublic information triggers these trading restrictions. (For detailed discussion of U.S. insider trading law, please refer to the topical study titled "Insider Trading.")

Information is "material" if its disclosure would be likely to have an impact on the price of a security or if reasonable investors would want to know the information before making an investment decision. In other words, information is material if it would significantly alter the total mix of information currently available regarding a security. Information is "nonpublic" until it has been disseminated to the marketplace in general (as opposed to a select group of investors) and investors have had an opportunity to react to the information.

The specificity of the information, the extent of its difference from public information, its nature, and its reliability are key factors in determining whether a particular piece of information fits the definition of material and nonpublic. For example, material information may include the following:

- A company made a rich ore find.
- A company will cut its dividend.
- A company sustained an unexpected substantial loss or profit.
- Earnings projections for a company show a substantial increase or decrease.
- A tender offer is to be made for a company's securities.

Persons who are particularly likely to encounter material nonpublic information include research analysts, portfolio managers, venture capitalists, pension sponsors, investor relations executives, rating agencies, those in commercial loan departments of banks or in underwriting departments of investment banks, trust officers, and others who make or recommend investment decisions. The prohibition against using material nonpublic information applies to recipients who are not directly or indirectly associated with the firm the material nonpublic information is about.

In general, the test for determining if a tipper is breaching a fiduciary duty is whether the tipper personally benefits directly or indirectly from the disclosure. There are generally three types of personal benefits: (1) pecuniary benefit or a reputational benefit that will translate into future earnings for the tipper, (2) a relationship between the insider and the recipient that suggests a quid pro quo from the recipient or an intention to benefit the recipient, and (3) a gift of confidential information to, for example, a relative. An insider who selectively discloses material nonpublic information without a legitimate business purpose for such selective disclosure may be found to have breached a fiduciary duty.

Although a fiduciary duty can be breached by giving a person confidential information and a member can breach a fiduciary duty by using information obtained in confidence, a fiduciary duty cannot be imposed unilaterally by entrusting a person with confidential information. Investment professionals are frequently exposed to nonpublic information, through their contacts with corporate management and others, relating to an issuer and the market for its securities. The free flow of information facilitates market analysis. Therefore, imposing a duty to disclose solely because an individual receives and acts upon material nonpublic information obtained from a corporate insider could undermine the valuable function analysts serve in disseminating information in the marketplace. Members are at risk, however, when they receive material nonpublic information on a selective basis from an insider and then trade.

Similarly, a good analyst can predict a corporate action or event based on a perceptive analysis of material public information or nonmaterial nonpublic information. An analyst may use such information to arrive at conclusions that become material only after the pieces are assembled. Securities professionals must be able to profit from their research efforts. A member should evaluate the materiality of any nonpublic information received to determine whether the disclosure of that information violates the communicator's fiduciary duty. If the member determines that the information is material and has been disclosed in breach of a duty, the member should make reasonable efforts to achieve public dissemination of the information. This effort usually means encouraging the issuer company to make the information public. If public dissemination is not possible, the member should communicate the information only to designated supervisory and compliance personnel within the member's firm and should take no investment action on the basis of the information.

Application of the Standard

Example 1. Barnes, the president and controlling shareholder of the SmartTown clothing chain, decides to accept a proposed tender offer and sell the family business at a price almost double the market price of its shares. He describes this decision to his sister (SmartTown's treasurer), who conveys it to her daughter (who owns no stock in the family company at present), who tells her husband, Staple. Staple, however, tells his stockbroker, Halsey, who immediately buys SmartTown stock for himself.

> *Comment*: No fiduciary relationship, or its functional equivalent, existed between Staple and the Barnes family. Staple was not a member of the inner family circle that ran the SmartTown business; nor was he an employee or a confidant of the controlling faction. Staple's relationship with his wife did not exhibit the necessary influence and reliance to establish that Staple breached a fiduciary duty or similar duty of trust by reporting the information to Halsey. Staple is an outsider, and the information was gratuitously communicated to him.
>
> Because the information involved a tender offer, however, Standard V(A) prohibits Halsey from trading or causing others to trade on the information regardless of how it was obtained. Therefore, Halsey violated Standard V(A).

Example 2. Walsh is riding an elevator up to her office when she overhears the chief financial officer (CFO) for the Swan Furniture Company tell the president of Swan that he has just calculated the company's earnings for the past quarter and they have unexpectedly and significantly dropped. The CFO adds that this drop will not be released to the public until next week. Walsh immediately calls her broker on her cellular phone and tells her to sell Walsh's Swan stock.

> *Comment*: Walsh has not violated Standard V(A) by trading on information she accidentally overheard because no duty was breached when the CFO of Swan discussed the earnings report with the company president and the information was not misappropriated.

Example 3. Walsh is riding back down the elevator on her way home when she hears a cleaning woman tell her companion that, while in the offices of Swan Furniture Company, she looked in a folder marked CONFIDENTIAL and saw that Swan was about to be bought out by another company looking to get into the furniture business. "The company wrote that they will pay four times the market price for Swan's stock!" she whispers. Walsh immediately calls her broker on her cellular phone and tells her to buy back all her Swan stock plus 5,000 more shares.

> *Comment*: In this instance, Walsh has violated Standard V(A) by trading on information that involves a tender offer and that she knows has been misappropriated.

Example 4. Peter, an analyst with Scotland and Pierce Incorporated, is assisting his firm with an IPO for Bright Ideas Lamp Company. Peter participates, via telephone conference call, in a meeting with Scotland and Pierce investment banking employees and Bright Ideas' CEO. Peter is advised that the company's earnings projections for the next year have significantly dropped. Throughout the telephone conference call, several Scotland and Pierce salespersons and portfolio managers walk in and out of Peter's office, where the telephone call is taking place. As a result, they are aware of the drop in projected earnings for Bright Ideas. Before the conference call is concluded, the salespersons trade the stock of the company on behalf of the firm's clients and other firm personnel trade the stock in a firm proprietary account and in employee personal accounts.

> *Comment*: Peter violated Standard V(A) because of his lack of adequate procedures to protect the material nonpublic information he came to possess on the basis of a confidential relationship. His failure to prevent the transfer and misuse of that information caused others to come into possession of the information who eventually traded in the security. Peter's firm should have adopted information barriers,

commonly called "fire walls," to prevent the communication of nonpublic information between departments of the firm.

Example 5. Madison & Lambeau, a well-respected broker/dealer, submits a weekly column to *Securities Weekly* magazine. Once published, the column usually affects the value of the stocks discussed. George, an employee of Madison & Lambeau, knows that *Securities Weekly* is published by Ziegler Publishing, for which his nephew is the night foreman. George's nephew faxes him an advance copy of the magazine before it is printed. In exchange for receiving an advance copy of the magazine, George pays his nephew's rent each month. George regularly trades in the securities mentioned in the Madison & Lambeau column prior to its distribution, and to date, he has realized a personal profit of $42,000 as well as significant profits for his clients.

Comment: George has violated Standard V(A) by trading on information that has been misappropriated.

Example 6. Newman, a CFA charterholder, and his wife volunteer at a local charitable organization to deliver meals to the elderly. One morning, Newman's wife receives a telephone call from Betsy Sterling, another volunteer, who asks if Newman and his wife can fill in for them that afternoon. Mrs. Sterling indicates that her husband is busy at work because his company has just fired their chief financial officer for misappropriation of funds. Mrs. Newman agrees to perform the volunteer work for the Sterlings and advises her husband of the situation. Newman knows that Mr. Sterling is the CEO at O'Hara Brothers Incorporated. Newman determines that this information is not public, then sells his entire holding of 3,000 shares of O'Hara Brothers. Three days later, the firing is announced and the O'Hara Brothers stock drops in value.

Comment: While the information is material and nonpublic, the Sterlings owed no duty to O'Hara Brothers to maintain the confidentiality of the information regarding the CFO. In addition, the information was not misappropriated because it did not involve a tender offer. Mr. Newman thus did not violate Standard V(A) by trading on this information.

Procedures for Compliance

To comply with Standard V(A), members and their firms should establish, maintain, and enforce written compliance policies and procedures designed to prevent the misuse of material nonpublic information. Members who receive material nonpublic information from an issuer should generally consult their supervisor or legal counsel before trading (or causing others to trade) while in possession of that information. **Exhibit 4** diagrams the decisions necessary to ensure compliance with Standard V(A).

The most common and widespread approach to prevent insider trading by employees is the "Fire Wall." The purpose of this information barrier is to prevent communication of material nonpublic information and other sensitive information from one department of a firm to other departments. The minimum elements are

- substantial control (preferably by the compliance department) of relevant interdepartmental communications;
- review of employee trading through effective maintenance of some combination of "watch," "restricted," and "rumor" lists;
- heightened review or restriction of proprietary trading while the firm is in possession of material nonpublic information.

For example, the investment banking and corporate finance departments of a brokerage firm should be segregated from the sales and research departments. The segregation usually means that there should be no overlap of personnel. If possible, even the supervisor or compliance officer who approves communication of information to the research and brokerage departments should not be a member of those departments. The primary objective is to establish a reporting system within a department in which authorized persons review and approve communications between departments. A bank's commercial lending department should be similarly segregated from its trust department and its research operation.

Additional procedures, used typically in conjunction with an information barrier, include

- restricting or prohibiting personal and proprietary employee trading;
- careful monitoring of firm and personal employee trading;
- placing securities on a restricted list when the firm has or may have material nonpublic information (unless the placing of a security on a restricted list would itself tend to reveal outside the firm that the firm is engaged in a nonpublic engagement relating to the security);
- using a stock watch list known only to a limited number of people when the firm has or may have material nonpublic information to monitor transactions in specified securities;
- confining the dissemination of material nonpublic information to persons who have a need to know the information in order to carry out their responsibilities;
- designating a supervisor or compliance officer who will have the specific authority and responsibility to decide whether information is sufficiently public or is sufficiently lacking in materiality that it may

be used as a basis for investment recommendations or decisions.

Firms should circulate written policies and guidelines to all employees. The policies and guidelines should be coupled with a program of seminars and refresher courses for employees.

Other basic components of typical compliance guidelines are the following:

Require communication. Guidelines should require that anyone who receives information that is known or reasonably believed to be material nonpublic information should communicate that information to a designated supervisor or compliance officer without discussing the information with co-workers. The recipient should then be required to refrain from trading on the information or from discussing the information inside or outside the firm until a supervisor decides the information either is not material or has been made public. Separate procedures should be adopted and implemented for safeguarding information received in a special or confidential relationship.

Establish training and compliance procedures. Establish extensive and intensive training and continuing education programs for employees to develop their ability to recognize material nonpublic information and to promote the firm's efforts to prevent misuse of such information.

Review accounts. Require regular review of customer or client accounts and investigation of patterns of heavy trading in particular securities by any employee or firm member. A pattern of trading on inside information can be more easily detected if employees and firm members are required to make periodic reports of their transactions on their own behalf or on behalf of members of their families.

Keep all research. A record of research allows the firm to recreate, after the fact, the thought process leading to a particular investment.

Exhibit 4. Use of Information under Standard V(A)

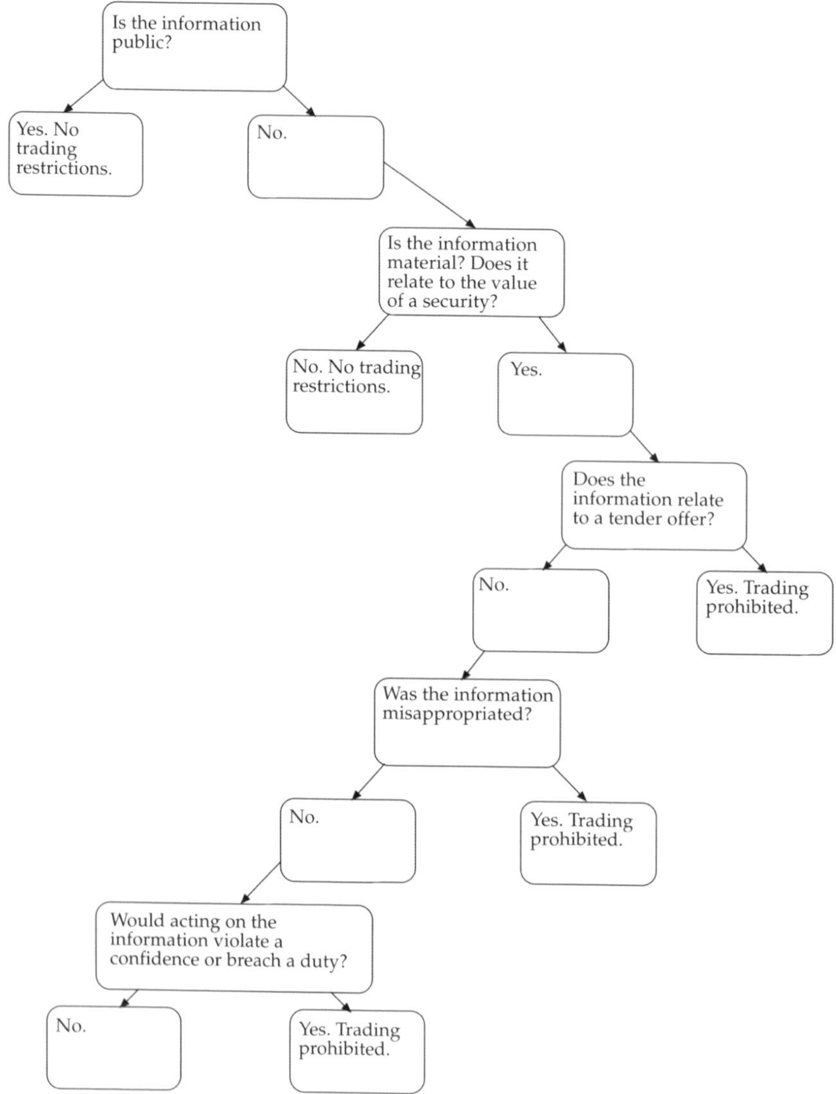

Standard V: Relationship and Responsibility to the Investing Public

Standard V(B)—Performance Presentation

1. Members shall not make any statements, orally or in writing, that misrepresent the investment performance that they or their firm have accomplished or can reasonably be expected to achieve.
2. If members communicate individual or firm performance information directly or indirectly to clients or prospective clients, or in a manner intended to be received by clients or prospective clients, members shall make every reasonable effort to assure that such performance information is a fair, accurate, and complete presentation of such performance.

Purpose and Scope of the Standard

The purpose of Standard V(B) is to state the responsibility of AIMR members, CFA charterholders, and candidates in the CFA Program to avoid misrepresentation of the investment performance of the member or the member's firm. Standard V(B) encourages full disclosure of investment performance data to clients and client prospects.

Standard V(B) addresses any practice that would lead to misrepresentation of a member's performance record, whether the practice involves performance presentation or performance measurement. A member must give a fair and complete presentation of performance information whenever communicating data with respect to the performance history of individual accounts, composites of groups of accounts, or composites of an analyst's or a firm's performance results. Accordingly, misrepresentations of past performance or reasonably expected performance are prohibited.

Performance Presentation Standards: The AIMR Performance Presentation Standards and Global Investment Performance Standards. Historically, investors seeking to hire an investment manager have had difficulty obtaining truly meaningful comparisons of accurate performance numbers. Several practices hindered comparability and accuracy of performance:

- Representative accounts. Managers chose only their best-performing portfolio to portray investment results without presenting the overall performance of the firm.
- Survivorship biases. Managers presented an "average" performance

history that excluded accounts whose poor performance was weak enough to result in termination.

- Portability of investment results. Managers presented performance that was not the record of the firm claiming the performance, but rather the manager's record from a previous employer.
- Varying time periods. Managers presented performance for a selected time period during which the fund produced excellent returns or outperformed its benchmark.

AIMR developed the AIMR Performance Presentation Standards (AIMR-PPS[SM]) and the Global Investment Performance Standards (GIPS[SM]) to address these issues and satisfy the investment community's need for a common, accepted set of standards for the calculation and presentation of investment firms' performance results. The AIMR-PPS standards and GIPS are the manifestation of the guiding ethical principles of fair representation and full disclosure and provide a yardstick for evaluating fairness and accuracy of investment performance presentation. AIMR designed the AIMR-PPS standards and GIPS to

- achieve greater uniformity and comparability among such presentations,
- improve the service offered to investment management clients,
- enhance the professionalism of the industry, and
- bolster the notion of self-regulation.

AIMR adopted and promotes the AIMR-PPS standards and GIPS to achieve the goal of industrywide uniformity in the presentation of performance information, which will enable investors to make direct comparisons among investment managers. Members and their firms are encouraged to adopt either the AIMR-PPS standards or GIPS for reporting historical investment results. Members are not required to be in compliance with either standard to be in compliance with Standard V(B).

The AIMR Performance Presentation Standards. The AIMR-PPS standards are voluntary. Firms are not required but are encouraged by AIMR to comply with the Standards. Nevertheless, clients and potential clients are increasingly asking managers if their results adhere to AIMR Performance Presentation Standards. Consultants are also adding that question to their list of screening criteria used in recommending prospective investment managers to clients. The AIMR-PPS standards have become widely recognized by the investment community as the most effective method for ensuring fair and accurate reporting of investment performance. A manager's claim of compliance with the AIMR-PPS standards, however, does not obviate the need for clients or prospective clients to do the due diligence necessary to evaluate performance data.

The AIMR-PPS standards are divided into four sections that reflect the basic elements of presenting performance information: Construction and Maintenance of Composites, Calculation of Returns, Presentation of Investment Results, and Disclosures.

- Construction and Maintenance of Composites. A composite is an aggregation of a number of portfolios into a single group that is representative of a particular investment objective or strategy. The Standards require all actual, fee-paying discretionary portfolios to be included in at least one *composite* that contains other accounts with a similar strategy or investment objective. The composite return is the asset-weighted average of the performance results of all the portfolios in the composite. Creating meaningful, asset-weighted composites is critical to the fair presentation, consistency, and comparability of results over time and among firms.
- Calculation of Returns. Achieving comparability among investment management firms' performance presentations requires uniformity in methods used to calculate returns. The Standards mandate the use of a certain calculation methodology (e.g., performance must be calculated using a time-weighted total rate of return).
- Presentation of Investment Results. Once a firm has constructed the composites, gathered the input data, and calculated returns, the firm incorporates this information into presentations based on the guidelines set out in the AIMR-PPS standards for presenting the investment performance results. No finite set of guidelines can cover all potential situations or anticipate future developments in the investment industry structure, technology, products, or practices. When appropriate, in order to maintain compliance with the Standards, firms may have the responsibility to include information in their presentations that is not covered by the Standards.
- Disclosures. Disclosures allow firms to elaborate on the raw numbers provided in the presentation and give the end user of the presentation the proper context in which to understand the performance results. To comply with the AIMR-PPS standards, firms must disclose certain information about their performance presentations and the calculation methodology adopted by the firm. Some disclosures are required of all firms, but others are specific to each circumstance and may not be applicable in all situations.

The AIMR-PPS standards for each section are divided between requirements and recommendations. The required elements are those a firm must follow in order to claim compliance with the Standards. Firms are strongly encouraged to adopt and implement the recommendations to ensure that they fully adhere to the spirit and intent of the AIMR-PPS standards.

To claim compliance with the AIMR-PPS standards, the firm must comply on a firmwide basis. Compliance cannot be achieved for particular composites or products. Members or firms can claim compliance only if their presentations fully satisfy the Standards in all material respects. To claim compliance with the Standards without meeting the mandatory requirements is a violation of Standard V(B).

Global Investment Performance Standards. Compliance with the AIMR-PPS standards has not been easy, particularly for global firms. The problems include nonavailability of information, the variety of accounting systems used in different parts of the world, changes in client composition and mandates, and changes in firms' own personnel and investment strategies.

Encouraged by the widespread acceptance of the AIMR-PPS standards as the industry standard in North America, AIMR formed the Global Investment Performance Standards Committee to develop and implement a globally accepted, uniform set of ethical principles to ensure fair representation and full disclosure in the presentation of performance results. GIPS adopts most of the concepts and provisions of the AIMR-PPS standards. The major differences from the AIMR-PPS standards are the relaxation of required historical performance results from 10 years to 5 years and the elimination of requirements for alternative asset classes.

Global adoption of common standards will facilitate the comparison of investment performance results worldwide and result in greater uniformity among such presentations. The establishment of a globally recognized set of performance presentation standards will improve services offered to investment management clients of multinational firms, continue to enhance the professionalism of the industry, and bolster the notion of self-regulation. The GIPS Committee found uniform agreement throughout the world on the need for a single global standard that will serve as a minimum set of requirements.

Application of the Standard

Example 1. Noting the performance of its common trust fund in the past two years, Taylor of Taylor Trust Company states in a brochure sent to his potential clients that "You can expect steady 25 percent annual compound growth of the value of your investments over the year." Although Taylor Trust's common trust fund increased at the rate of 25 percent per annum for one year in which the entire market increased by about that amount, the fund never averaged that growth for more than one year, and the average rate of growth of all of its trust accounts for five years was 5 percent per annum.

Comment: Taylor Trust Company's brochure is in violation of Standard V(B). Taylor should have disclosed that 25 percent growth occurred only in one year. Additionally, Taylor did not include client accounts other than those in the firm's common trust fund. He should have supplied additional details about the performance of both categories of accounts.

By stating that clients can expect a steady 25 percent annual compound growth rate, Taylor also violated Standard IV(B.6), which prohibits statements of assurances or guarantees regarding an investment. Taylor's statement was materially misleading and may also be in violation of Standard IV(B.2).

Example 2. Judd, a senior partner of Allison Capital Management, circulates a performance sheet listing performance figures for capital appreciation accounts for the years 1988 through 1995. Returns are calculated in accordance with AIMR standards except that the composites are not asset weighted, which is a violation of the AIMR-PPS standards.

Comment: Judd is in violation of Standard V(B). When claiming compliance with the AIMR-PPS standards, firms must meet all the requirements and mandatory disclosures and any other additional requirements or disclosures necessary to that firm's specific situation.

Example 3. Leonard is vice president and managing partner of the equity investment group of Mastermind Financial Advisors, a new business. Mastermind recruited Leonard because he had a proven six-year track record with G&P Financial. In developing Mastermind's advertising and marketing campaign, Leonard prepared an advertisement that included the equity investment performance he achieved at G&P Financial. The advertisement for Mastermind did not identify the equity performance as being earned while at G&P. The advertisement was distributed to existing clients and prospective clients of Mastermind.

Comment: Leonard violated Standard V(B) by distributing an advertisement that contained material misrepresentations regarding the historical performance of Mastermind. Standard V(B) requires that members make every reasonable effort to ensure that performance information is a fair, accurate, and complete representation of an individual or firm's performance. If Leonard chooses to use his past performance from G&P in Mastermind's advertising, he should make full disclosure as to the source of the historical performance.

Example 4. Davis developed a mutual fund selection product based on historical information from the 1985–88 period. Davis tested his methodology by applying it retroactively to data from the 1989–97 period, thus producing simulated performance results for those years. In January 1998, Davis' employer decided to offer the product and began promoting it through trade journal advertisements and direct dissemination to clients. The advertisements included the performance results for the 1989–97 period but did not indicate that the results were simulated.

> *Comment*: Davis violated Standard V(B) by failing to clearly identify simulated performance results. Standard V(B) prohibits members from making any statements that misrepresent the performance achieved by them or their firms and requires members to make every reasonable effort to ensure that performance information presented to clients is fair, accurate, and complete. Use of the simulated results should be accompanied by full disclosure as to the source of the performance data, including the fact that the results from 1989 through 1997 were the result of applying the model retroactively to that time period.

Example 5. In a presentation prepared for prospective clients, Jorge Kilmer purported to show the rates of return realized over a five-year period by a "composite" of his firm's discretionary accounts with a balanced objective. This "composite," however, consisted of only a few of the accounts that met the balanced criteria set by the firm, excluded accounts under a certain asset level without disclosing the fact of their exclusion, and included nonbalanced accounts that would boost investment results. In addition, to achieve better results, Kilmer manipulated the narrow range of accounts included in the composite by changing the accounts that made up the composite over time.

> *Comment*: Kilmer violated Standard V(B) by misrepresenting the facts in the promotional material sent to prospective clients, distorting his firm's performance record, and failing to include disclosure that would have clarified the presentation.

Procedures for Compliance

Compliance with the AIMR-PPS standards or GIPS is the best method to avoid violations of Standard V(B), and members should encourage their firms to adhere to either standard or a comparable standard sponsored by a local or regional investment association.

Members can also avoid violations of Standard V(B) by

- considering the knowledge and sophistication of the audience to whom a performance presentation is addressed,
- considering the types of disclosures that would fully explain the

performance results being reported (for example, stating, when appropriate, that results are simulated when model results are used and clearly indicating when the performance record is that of a prior entity),
- maintaining the data and records used to calculate the performance being presented.

Topical Study:
Corporate Governance

Corporate governance can be generally defined as the system by which corporations are directed and controlled. Common stock shareholders have the power through voting rights to influence the management of a corporation. Actively exercising these rights through corporate governance may be an effective way of enhancing portfolio value. Not exercising these rights ignores a valuable ownership right that could be managed for the benefit of the portfolio and, in certain accounts, may constitute a dereliction of legal and fiduciary responsibilities to clients.

In many instances, security holders and account owners delegate their right to vote proxies to professionals who manage their investments. Investment managers must, therefore, adopt procedures to ensure that proxy issues are sufficiently noted, analyzed, and considered to meet the managers' fiduciary duty to their clients. Investment managers have an incumbent responsibility to be thoroughly familiar with the issues that arise in proxies. The recommendations in this study are designed to help professional investors establish and implement a proxy voting policy.

Background

Generally, the owners of a corporation have their interests designated through the issuance of equity shares, with the number of shares representing the proportionate ownership interest. Ownership of these shares entitles the holder to certain rights in the management of the corporation delineated in fundamental corporate documents (e.g., the bylaws of the firm), as well as in laws and practices of the local capital markets.

In practice, the extent of these rights and the practical ability to actively exercise them vary widely. The degree to which the government controls corporate activity and the extent to which allied interests control large ownership blocks affect the ability of individual and institutional investors to exercise these rights effectively.

The globalization of investing and the desire of companies to raise capital in many markets have been powerful incentives to standardize the conditions of equity ownership. With the standardization of accounting practices, the value of shareholder corporate governance rights and the ability to exercise these rights will continue to increase as an important element of security ownership and portfolio management.

Corporate Governance Structure

The "standard" corporate governance structure typically calls for the designation of a board of directors to act as the oversight body of a company. The board has the power to employ and strategically direct company management and the responsibility to ensure that the company is managed in such a way that the shareholders receive a fair return.

The corporate board of directors acts as the direct representative of the shareholders and, in theory, controls the company through their actions in developing and approving a strategic plan of operation and hiring the management of the company. The board has the responsibility of evaluating the performance of company management, overseeing company performance, and making strategic changes necessary to enhance shareholder value. Regardless of the extent of knowledge and actual involvement of a particular board of directors, the directors have legal and fiduciary responsibilities to the shareholders, even though these interests may run counter to the personal interests of management.

In many cases, common shareholders are able to vote for and elect directors to ensure that their rights are adequately addressed. In addition, shareholders may have the ability to vote directly on certain actions, such as the sale or merger of the company, that affect fundamental corporate operating conditions. Although shareholder rights of this type generally accrue only to the common stockholder, under certain conditions, preferred stockholders, bondholders, and other creditors might be able to obtain similar rights or equity shares (for example, in the event of bankruptcy or other types of reorganization).

Role of Investors in the Management of a Company

The ability to participate in or the effectiveness of active involvement in the corporate governance process depends, to a great extent, on the characteristics and objectives of the shareholder. In some cases, an investor with a minor position or a short investment time horizon may be best served by avoiding positions in companies that the investor considers to be poorly governed.

Historically, major investors did not take much interest in corporate governance. In deciding to buy or sell stock, they attempted to achieve their target performance by relying on their judgement of the valuation of company stock. Investors evaluated governance as any other element of the company in arriving at the ultimate security evaluation. The primary analytical factor of "management" may have encompassed the effectiveness of a firm's corporate governance structure.

Investors who were dissatisfied with the management of a particular company followed the "Wall Street Walk" (or "Wall Street Rule") and turned to Wall Street for a solution by selling their shares and investing in a business with better management. Institutional shareholders tended not to vote their shares regularly and intervened directly with company management only in circumstances of crisis.

Following the Wall Street Walk assumes that the manager has the ability to sell the stock. In some cases, the proportion of shares that an investor owns increases the difficulty of selling shares without adversely affecting the market. Investment options for some institutional investors seeking to maintain liquidity may be limited to those companies that have large capitalizations. Maintaining exposure to a desired asset sector may require investing in a company with less than optimal management. In other cases, an investor may adopt a passive management style, such as attempting to match an index such as the S&P 500, as an alternative to an active trading strategy. In these circumstances, investors may have limited investing options and cannot simply "vote with their feet" by moving their investment every time they disagree with management. As a result of these factors and in the absence of major problems, institutional investors may attempt to change the company through negotiations with company management or through exercise of the rights of corporate governance.

Voting Proxies

To meet their fiduciary duty with regard to corporate governance, managers must follow adequate procedures concerning the voting of proxies. Whether proxies are voted by trustees in fiduciary accounts or by individuals for their own accounts, managers must ensure that the necessary information and forms are received and distributed in a timely fashion. When managers are given the responsibility to vote proxies, they must adopt procedures to ensure that issues are noted, analyzed, and considered before voting. Managers of ERISA accounts may have additional responsibilities or guidelines that are imposed by a plan's trustee. Investment managers must be thoroughly familiar with the issues that arise in proxies. Proxies have economic value and must be voted in the interest of the ultimate shareholder or plan beneficiary. Institutional investors cannot simply vote without adequate examination of the underlying issues.

This topical study lists the issues that arise in proxy voting and recommends ways of approaching and analyzing a number of these issues. Although each firm must establish policies and procedures appropriate to its own circumstances, the methods and approaches outlined should be helpful in establishing a formal, written proxy policy.

The skills and experience of the professional investment community, particularly the research and analytic skills, can be used effectively in corporate governance issues, which will ultimately benefit corporations and shareholders alike and enhance the competitiveness of business in global markets. Good corporate governance and good investment decisions go hand in hand.

Obstacles to Effective Proxy Voting. Numerous obstacles exist to establishing an effective proxy voting policy. Some of the more significant ones include the following:

- The lack of a clear policy and support from the management of the investment firm. In particular, many firms have not devised a method for applying in-house investment skills to the proxy process.
- The perception that proxies are "routine." Although this perception may be true in some instances, firms should develop systems to separate routine from high-impact or controversial proxies. Staffs should be trained to handle routine issues according to clear guidelines, thus leaving investment professionals free to handle more complex questions.
- Uncertainty about voting responsibilities for stocks underlying index or "passively managed" funds. A decision to invest entails a responsibility to vote, whether the investment is active or passive.
- Overzealous company management that attempts to influence shareholders. By communicating to their clients a clear, written policy on proxy voting responsibilities, investment advisors can partially insulate themselves from, or have a ready response to, undue pressures by company management.
- The rise of global investment. This trend raises new obstacles to effective proxy voting. Differing disclosure policies and delays in timely receipt of material often plague investment managers. Investment professionals should ascertain the firm's communication policies regarding shareholders and proxy voting.
- Delegation of proxy voting responsibilities. Delegation can be mistakenly seen as a complete "answer" as investment advisors turn to specialized consulting firms for assistance. Using a consultant may make sense but does not relieve firms of their responsibility. Monitoring is necessary to make sure that standards of prudence, care, and diligence are met and that those who do the voting are qualified to make informed decisions.
- Delays in relaying the material from issuer to intermediary to investor. Such delays can make proxy voting difficult. Investment advisors should maintain contact with intermediaries, such as brokers, banks, and custodians, to ensure timely reception of material and to update names and addresses.

Basic Elements of a Proxy Voting Policy

I. Creation of a Proxy Policy

A. Designate a policy-making body (the board, managing directors, or a committee) or an individual to recommend proxy policy and to monitor implementation. ERISA account managers must be certain to clarify whether they will exercise voting discretion or will act at the direction of the plan trustee. If a plan trustee has retained authority to set guidelines concerning the voting of plan proxies, the manager is obligated to adhere to those guidelines unless doing so would be imprudent or otherwise would violate ERISA. The same body or individual should:

1. Develop initial, specific guidelines and institute a regular review process, including review of new or controversial proxy issues.
2. Verify that any decision about how to vote is in accord with the investment interests, stated objectives, and particular preferences, if stated or known, of the investor, participants, or beneficiaries of an account.
3. Discuss the issues involved with those who do the voting and decide whether additional action is necessary (i.e., to initiate and/or cosign shareholder proposals).
4. Provide a review mechanism for any unusual proposals, such as an opposition slate of directors, corporate restructuring related to hostile takeovers, or any proposals that appear not to be in the best interests of shareholders.
5. Consider applying to proxy decisions internal financial ratios or other criteria for evaluating corporate performance. Such applications, for instance, might show such outstanding economic performance over a business cycle that investor confidence in a board and management would outweigh a proposal to classify the board.
6. Provide a process for deciding whether a vote against management should be preceded or followed by a letter, telephone call, in-person discussion with corporate personnel, and/or action to be taken with other concerned firms and organizations.
7. Decide under what conditions those who hold a concentration of stock in their own names or have other vested interest in the corporations in which stock is held should be excluded from participating in the voting.
8. Decide how and when to report to clients and sponsors the positions taken during the proxy season.

B. Identify major proxy issues by particular accounts. Note should be taken of preferences stated by beneficiaries, participants, or individuals for whom funds are held in trust. A manager of a pooled account that maintains ERISA assets may be subject to conflicting proxy voting guidelines from the plans contained in the account. In that instance, the manager must reconcile, to the extent possible, the proxy voting policies of the various plans. To the extent that reconciliation is not possible, the manager should consider voting the securities in proportion to the plan's respective interests in the pooled account. The major proxy-related issues generally fall within five categories: corporate governance, takeover defenses, compensation plans, capital structure, and social responsibility. These categories may include the following:

1. Corporate governance.
   - Confidentiality of voting.
   - Annual election of directors.
   - Composition of board.
   - Equal access to proxy statements.
   - Indemnification of management or directors or both against negligent, imprudent, or unreasonable action.
   - Removal of directors from office only for cause or by a supermajority vote.
   - Cumulative voting.
   - "Sweeteners" to attract support for proposals.
   - Unequal voting rights proposals (superstock).
   - Supermajority proposals.
   - Limitation of shareholder rights to remove directors, amend bylaws, fill board vacancies, call special meetings, nominate directors, and act by written consent—or other actions to limit or abolish shareholder rights to act independently.
   - Proposals to permit management discretion to issue "blank check" stock without prior shareholder approval.
   - Proposals to vote unmarked proxies in favor of management
   - Pre-emptive rights.
2. Takeover defense and related actions.
   - Proposals involving tender offers and mergers.
   - Fair price provisions.
   - Some increases in authorized shares and/or creation of new classes of common or preferred stock.
   - Proposals to introduce or eliminate greenmail provisions.
   - Proposals to reevaluate in-place "shark repellents."
   - Shareholder rights plans (poison pills).
3. Compensation plans.
   - Stock option plans and/or stock-appreciation plans.

- Profit incentive plans and employee stock purchase plans.
- Extension of stock option grants to outside directors.
- Stock option plans and other stock bonus plans, including plans permitting issuance of loans to management or selected employees with authority to sell stock purchased by the loan without immediate repayment, or plans that are overly generous (below market price or with appreciation rights paying the difference between option price and the stock, or allowing the directors to lower the purchase price of outstanding options).
- Incentive plans that become effective in the event of hostile takeovers or mergers (golden and tin parachutes).
- Proposals that create an unusually favorable compensation structure in advance of sale of the company.
- Proposals that fail to link executive compensation to management performance (including golden handcuffs).

4. Capital structure, classes of stock, and recapitalizations.
   - Dual class recapitalizations.
   - Proposals to reincorporate or reorganize into a holding company.
   - Proposals designed to discourage mergers and acquisitions in advance.
   - Proposals to change state of incorporation to a state less favorable to shareholder interests.
5. Social responsibility.
   - Human rights.
   - Environment, such as endorsing the CERES principles.
   - Nuclear weapons and energy-generating facilities.
   - McBride Principles (Northern Ireland).
   - Equal employment and diversity.
   - Community-related economic growth.
   - Anti-addiction (such as alcohol or gambling).

C. A useful proxy policy format might be to (1) state the pros and cons of issues and (2) evaluate specific proxy proposals against the history and productivity of current management as well as the conceptual reasons for or against the proposal.

II. Administration

A. Define responsibility for proxy voting.

1. Externally. In the case of ERISA accounts, or ERISA-type accounts, the plan documents should state who has authority and responsibility to vote all proxies. In other instances, the portfolio

management contract should include such a statement.

2. Internally. Determine the responsibilities of staff and/or committees for following voting guidelines.

B. Develop a system to monitor any delegation of proxy voting responsibility to others.

C. Provide for record keeping.
   1. Maintain a record of stock held.
   2. Reconcile proxies received with the stock held on the record date.
   3. Develop a system to trace missing proxies expeditiously.
   4. Keep a record of how proxies are voted and why:
      - Note any deviations from any stated policy relating to specific issues.
      - Note any contacts from plan sponsors or issuers with staff related to the proxy voting function and the actions taken.
      - Note any apparent conflicts of interest and how they are handled.

D. Provide for a process to monitor performance of a custodian, or its agent, to ensure timely receipt of proxies; the process should include delegation of responsibility to an individual staff member.

E. Avoid or minimize conflicts of interest. Parties vulnerable to conflicts of interest include corporate directors and managers who may also serve on the boards of public and private funds, plan sponsors, analysts and investment management staff who may invest in stock also held in management accounts, and others with direct interest in the outcome of voting (investment banking, credit or loan obligations, corporate finance). When possible, consider implementing "Fire Wall" techniques similar to those used to prevent the flow of material nonpublic information to portfolio managers and analysts.

F. Educate and train staff.
   1. Provide opportunities for staff members to understand the firm's proxy voting policy. Each person related to voting proxies should have a copy of the policy and/or guidelines and an opportunity to discuss them with supervisory staff.
   2. Designate specific staff members to receive all proxies, reconcile receipt with holdings list, distribute proxies to those who do the actual voting, and trace missing proxies in a timely fashion. Make certain all staff members know who does what.
   3. Train staff to separate nonroutine proxies—that is, those involving shareholder rights and the economics of a

corporation—from those that are routine, as the firm guidelines define the categories.

4. Train staff to vote noncontroversial proxies under supervision of a compliance officer, committee, or other designated persons.
5. Provide periodic review sessions at least annually to
   - reacquaint staff handling or voting proxies with the overall policy,
   - reevaluate any previous decisions that deviate from guidelines,
   - discuss current proxy issues, and
   - recommend action on any current "hot issues" or unusual proposals.

Topical Study:
Ethical Practices Involving Client Brokerage—AIMR Soft Dollar Standards

The AIMR Soft Dollar Standards provide guidance to investment professionals worldwide through the articulation of high ethical standards for AIMR Members dealing with "soft dollar" issues. Soft dollar practices involve the use of client brokerage by an investment manager to obtain certain products and services to aid the manager in its investment decision-making process. The practice of using client brokerage to purchase research has become extremely complex, exceeding in large part the usefulness of the existing guidance as currently set forth in the AIMR Standards of Professional Conduct. The AIMR Soft Dollar Standards are consistent with and complement the existing AIMR Standards of Professional Conduct that all AIMR Members and Candidates in the CFA Program are required to follow.

The purposes of the Standards are to define "soft dollars," identify what is "allowable" research, establish standards for soft dollar use, create model disclosure guidelines, and provide guidance for client-directed brokerage arrangements.

The Soft Dollar Standards are *voluntary* standards for Members. If an AIMR Member claims compliance with the Standards, then certain of these Standards are mandatory (i.e., they *must* be followed to claim compliance) and others are recommended (i.e., they *should* be followed). AIMR strongly encourages Members to adopt the required and recommended Standards. If the Soft Dollar Standards are adopted, compliance will not supplant the responsibility to comply with applicable law.[1] AIMR Members should comply at all times with the relevant laws of the countries in which they do business. In situations in which these Standards impose a higher degree of responsibility or disclosure than, but do not conflict with, local law, the Member is held to the mandatory provisions of these Standards.

AIMR recognizes that guidance in this area is not static and will require future refinements to respond to ongoing developments in technology, the law, and the investment management industry. The Standards will be revised and interpreted as necessary to remain current but will continue to

---

[1]For example, in the United States, the Securities Exchange Act of 1934, Investment Company Act of 1940, and Investment Advisers Act of 1940 all address the use of client commissions in soft dollar arrangements. The U.S. Department of Labor also provides regulations regarding directed brokerage practices concerning ERISA-covered pension plans.

honor the overriding fiduciary principles that form the cornerstone of the Soft Dollar Standards.

Background

In 1975, the U.S. Congress created a "safe harbor" under Section 28(e) of the Securities and Exchange Act of 1934 to protect investment managers from claims that they had breached their fiduciary duties by using their client commissions to pay a higher commission to acquire investment research than they might have paid for "execution" services. According to Securities and Exchange Commission (SEC) Staff, the protection of Section 28(e) is available only for securities transactions conducted on an agency basis.[2] Since that time, the soft dollar area has undergone considerable expansion, both in terms of actual usage and the types of products and services for which safe harbor protection is claimed. The complexity of these practices, including technologically sophisticated research tools and the existence of "mixed-use" products, has resulted in a fair amount of legitimate confusion surrounding the appropriate use of soft dollars.

AIMR seeks to provide ethical standards for AIMR Members and those in the industry that engage in soft dollar practices and also emphasizes the paramount duty of the investment manager, as a fiduciary, to place the interests of clients before those of the investment manager. In particular, the Soft Dollar Standards focus on six key areas:

- Definitions—to enable all parties dealing with soft dollar practices to have a common understanding of all of the different aspects of soft dollars.
- Research—to give clear guidance to investment managers on what products and services are appropriate for a manager to purchase with client brokerage.
- Mixed-Use Products—to clarify the manager's duty to clearly justify the use of client brokerage to pay a portion of a mixed-use product.
- Disclosure—to obligate investment managers to clearly disclose their soft dollar practices and give detailed information to each client when requested.
- Record keeping—to ensure that the client can (1) receive assurances that what the investment manager is doing with the client's brokerage

[2]According to the SEC staff, securities transactions conducted on a principal basis cannot claim Section 28(e) "safe harbor" protection. Both principal transactions and those agency transactions unable to qualify for "safe harbor" protection are not necessarily illegal but are evaluated based on the existence of full disclosure, informed client consent, and other fundamental fiduciary principles, including placing the client's interests first.

can be supported in an "audit," and (2) receive important information on request.

- Client-Directed Brokerage—to clarify the manager's role and fiduciary responsibilities with respect to clients.

Overview

The AIMR Soft Dollar Standards focus on the Member's obligations to its clients. Although the Standards primarily focus on the obligations of the Member as investment manager, they may be applicable to other parties involved in soft dollar practices, including brokers, plan sponsors, and trustees. Each of these parties, however, has its own set of obligations that should be considered prior to participating in any soft dollar arrangement.

The AIMR Soft Dollar Standards are ethical principles intended to ensure

- full and fair disclosure of an investment manager's use of a client's brokerage[3];
- consistent presentation of information so that the client, broker, and other applicable parties can clearly understand an investment manager's brokerage practices;
- uniform disclosure and record keeping to enable an investment manager's client to have a clear understanding of how the investment manager is using the client's brokerage; and
- high standards of ethical practices within the investment industry.

No finite set of standards can cover all potential situations or anticipated future developments concerning the types of investment research available to investment managers. However, meeting the objective of full and fair disclosure and ensuring that the "client comes first" obligates an investment manager to disclose fully and clearly to its client the investment manager's practice when addressing any potential conflict concerning the payment methods for investment research.

The AIMR Soft Dollar Standards are based on the following set of fundamental principles that an investment manager should consider when attempting to comply:

- An investment manager is a fiduciary and, as such, must disclose all relevant aspects concerning any benefit the manager receives through a client's brokerage;
- Proprietary research and third-party research are to be treated the same in evaluating soft dollar arrangements, because the research that an investment manager receives from each is paid for with client brokerage;

[3] The term "Brokerage" is described in the definitions section of the Standards.

- Research should be purchased with client brokerage only if the primary use of the research, whether a product or a service, directly assists the investment manager in its investment decision-making process and not in the management of the investment firm; and
- When in doubt, the research should be paid for with investment manager assets, not client brokerage.

Comparison with Current Practices

The AIMR Soft Dollar Standards seek to clarify certain areas of brokerage practices that have been a source of confusion for AIMR Members. By emphasizing the basic fiduciary responsibilities of AIMR Members with respect to their client's assets, the Soft Dollar Standards are intended to illuminate the line between permissible and impermissible uses of client brokerage. In this respect, the Standards do not create "new law" but address well-established principles applicable to the investment manager–client relationship.

In other respects, a reiteration of the current "soft dollar" practices would fail to adequately address the issues raised by the complexity of current brokerage practices faced by AIMR Members. The Soft Dollar Standards, therefore, depart from certain well-established practices in the soft dollar area and address practices beyond those that currently claim Section 28(e) safe harbor protection.

The Soft Dollar Standards are not to be read as in any way changing the scope of activities that the SEC determines to fall within the safe harbor. Instead they are separate, ethical standards applicable to a variety of practices implicated in Soft Dollar Arrangements. Thus, these Standards will impose higher standards of conduct in certain areas on AIMR Members that voluntarily elect to comply with the Standards, as follows:

1. Definition of Soft Dollar Arrangements

a. *Proprietary, in addition to third-party, research.* Traditionally, soft dollar arrangements are understood to address those products or services provided to the investment manager by someone other than the executing broker, products or services that are commonly known as "third-party" research. Such an approach is deficient in light of the range of products and services provided by both third-party research providers and "in-house" research departments of brokerage firms. Thus, any meaningful Standards must also recognize the importance of research provided by the executing broker, commonly known as "proprietary" or "in-house" research.

For purposes of the Soft Dollar Standards, "soft dollar arrangements" include proprietary, as well as third-party, research arrangements and seek to treat both categories the same. Although these Standards do *not* suggest an "unbundling" of proprietary research, they do require the investment manager to provide certain basic information regarding the types of research obtained with client brokerage through proprietary research arrangements. Moreover, these Standards should not be read to require research obtained either through third-party or proprietary arrangements to be attributed on an account-by-account basis or otherwise to require a "tracing" of products or services.

b. *Principal, in addition to agency, trades.* Traditionally, the term "soft dollars" refers to commissions generated by trades conducted on an agency basis.[4] However, such an approach fails to recognize that research may be obtained through the use of "spreads" or "discounts" generated by trades conducted on a principal basis. For the purposes of the Soft Dollar Standards, soft dollar arrangements include transactions conducted on an agency *or* principal basis.

2. Definition of Research

Traditionally, "allowable" research in the soft dollar context is evaluated by whether it provides lawful and appropriate assistance to an investment manager in the investment decision-making process. This approach, however, leaves AIMR Members with inadequate guidance. Consequently, the Soft Dollar Standards embrace a definition of research that requires the primary use of the soft dollar product or service to directly assist the investment manager in its investment decision-making process and not in the management of the investment firm.

In many cases, this determination may not lend itself to absolute precision, but an investment manager must use its best judgment as a fiduciary to justify the use of client brokerage to pay for a product or service. The Standards suggest the use of a three-tiered analysis to aid AIMR Members in determining whether a product or service is research. Such an approach is intended to provide needed guidance for AIMR Members in determining when it is appropriate to use client brokerage to purchase a product or service.

---

[4]As noted above, the "safe harbor" provided by Section 28(e) of the Securities Exchange Act of 1934, as interpreted by the SEC staff, applies only to those transactions conducted on an agency, not principal, basis.

3. **Enhanced Disclosure**

Disclosure of an AIMR Member's brokerage practices will provide the Member's client with a means of evaluating the Member's soft dollar practices and how client brokerage is used. Under the Soft Dollar Standards, the AIMR Member must disclose to its clients certain information, the majority of which the Member is already required under current law to disclose, or to maintain, in order to meet federal disclosure requirements. Moreover, although the Soft Dollar Standards require the AIMR Member to disclose the *availability* of additional information, this information does not actually have to be provided, unless it is specifically requested by the client.

4. **Compliance Statement**

Finally, the Soft Dollar Standards contemplate the use of a voluntary statement of compliance. Only a claim of compliance with these Standards requires an investment manager to comply with all of the mandatory provisions of these Standards and only as to the client brokerage that its compliance statement relates. Thus, an investment manager that claims compliance with the Soft Dollar Standards must provide the client with a statement that any brokerage arrangement with respect to *that* client's account comports with the mandatory provisions of these Standards. Such a compliance statement will help to ensure the continued integrity of the Standards and provide clients with additional assurance with respect to how their brokerage is used by their investment manager.

Definitions

For purposes of the AIMR Soft Dollar Standards, the following terms apply:

Agency Trade refers to a transaction involving the payment of a commission.

Best Execution refers to executing Client transactions so that the Client's *total cost* is the most favorable under the particular circumstances at that time.

Broker refers to any person or entity that provides securities execution services.

Brokerage refers to the amount on any trade retained by a Broker to be used directly or indirectly as payment for execution services and, when applicable, Research supplied to the Investment Manager or its Client in connection with Soft Dollar Arrangements or for benefits provided to the Client in Client-Directed Brokerage Arrangements. For these purposes, trades may be conducted on an agency *or* principal basis.

Brokerage Arrangement refers to an arrangement whereby a Broker provides services or products that are in addition to execution. Brokerage Arrangements include Investment Manager-Directed and Client-Directed Brokerage Arrangements.

Brokerage and Research Services refers to services and/or products provided by a Broker to an Investment Manager through a Brokerage Arrangement.

Client refers to the entity, including a natural person, investment fund, or separate account, designated to receive the benefits, including income, from the Brokerage generated through Securities Transactions. A Client may be represented by a trustee or other Fiduciary, who may or may not have Investment Discretion.

Client-Directed Brokerage Arrangement refers to an arrangement whereby a Client directs that trades for its account be executed through a specific Broker in exchange for which the Client receives a benefit in addition to execution services. Client-Directed Brokerage Arrangements include rebates, commission banking, and commission recapture programs through which the Broker provides the Client with cash or services or pays certain obligations of the Client. A Client may also direct the use of limited lists of brokers—not for the purpose of reducing Brokerage costs but to effect various other goals (e.g., increased diversity by using minority-owned brokers) or geographical concentration.

Commission refers to the amount paid to the Broker in addition to the price of the security and applicable regulatory fees on an Agency Trade.

Fiduciary refers to any entity, or a natural person, including an AIMR Member, that has discretionary authority or responsibility for the management of a Client's assets or other relationships of special trust.

Investment Decision-Making Process refers to the quantitative and qualitative processes and related tools used by the Investment Manager in rendering investment advice to its Clients, including financial analysis, trading and risk analysis, securities selection, broker selection, asset allocation, and suitability analysis.

Investment Discretion refers to the sole or shared authority (whether or not exercised) to determine what securities or other assets to purchase or sell on behalf of a Client.

Investment Manager refers to any entity, or a natural person, including an AIMR Member, that serves in the capacity of asset manager to a Client. The Investment Manager may have sole, shared, or no Investment Discretion over an account.

Investment Manager-Directed Brokerage Arrangement refers to Proprietary and Third-Party Research Arrangements.

Member refers to any individual who is required to comply with the AIMR Code of Ethics and Standards of Professional Conduct in accordance with the AIMR Bylaws.

Mixed-Use refers to services and/or products, provided to an Investment Manager by a Broker through a Brokerage Arrangement, that have the capacity to be used for both the Investment Decision-Making Process *and* management of the investment firm.

Principal Trade refers to a transaction involving a "discount" or a "spread."

Proprietary Research Arrangement refers to an arrangement whereby the Investment Manager directs a Broker to effect Securities Transactions for Client accounts in exchange for which the Investment Manager receives Research from, and/or access to, the "in-house" staffs of the brokerage firms.

Provided by a Broker refers to (1) in Proprietary Research Arrangements, Research developed by the Broker and (2) in Third-Party Research Arrangements, Research for which the obligation to pay is between the Broker and Third-Party Research Provider, not between the Investment Manager and Third-Party Research Provider.

Research refers to services and/or products provided by a Broker, the primary use of which must directly assist the Investment Manager in its Investment Decision-Making Process and not in the management of the investment firm.

Section 28(e) Safe Harbor refers to the "safe harbor" set forth in Section 28(e) of the U.S. Securities Exchange Act of 1934, which provides that an Investment Manager that has Investment Discretion over a Client account is not in breach of its fiduciary duty when paying more than the lowest Commission rate available if it determines in good faith that the rate paid is commensurate with the value of Brokerage and Research Services provided by the Broker.

Securities Transactions refers to any transactions involving a Broker, whether conducted on an agency basis or principal basis.

Soft Dollar Arrangement refers to an arrangement whereby the Investment Manager directs transactions to a Broker, in exchange for which the Broker provides Brokerage and Research Services to the Investment Manager. Soft Dollar Arrangements include Proprietary and Third-Party Research Arrangements but do *not* include Client-Directed Brokerage Arrangements. Soft Dollar Arrangements are sometimes referred to herein as Investment Manager-Directed Brokerage Arrangements, where applicable.

Third-Party Research Arrangement refers to an arrangement whereby the Investment Manager directs a Broker to effect Securities Transactions for Client accounts in exchange for which the Investment Manager receives Research provided by the Broker, which has been generated by an entity *other than* the executing Broker.

AIMR Soft Dollar Standards

I. General

Principles

A. These Soft Dollar Standards apply to all AIMR Members' Proprietary and Third-Party Research Arrangements, with or without Commissions, and recognize two fundamental principles:
   1. Brokerage is the property of the Client.
   2. The Investment Manager has an ongoing duty to ensure the quality of transactions effected on behalf of its Client, including
      a. seeking to obtain Best Execution,
      b. minimizing transaction costs, and
      c. using Client Brokerage to benefit Clients.

Required

B. An Investment Manager in Soft Dollar Arrangements must always act for the benefit of its Clients and place Clients' interests before its own.

C. An Investment Manager may not allocate a Client's Brokerage based on the amount of Client referrals the Investment Manager receives from a Broker.

   Clarification: With respect to mutual funds, the Investment Manager's Client is the fund. However, in this context, the fund's board, not the fund, establishes the policies with respect to the use of certain brokers.

II. Relationships with Clients

Required

A. The Investment Manager must disclose to the Client that it may engage in Soft Dollar Arrangements prior to engaging in such Arrangements involving that Client's account.

Recommended

B. The Investment Manager should assure that, over time, all Clients receive the benefits of Research purchased with Client Brokerage.
   1. *Agency Trades.* While it is permissible for the Investment Manager to use a Client's Brokerage derived from Agency Trades to obtain Research that may not directly benefit that particular Client at that particular time, the Investment

Manager should endeavor to ensure that, over a reasonable period of time, the Client receives the benefit of Research purchased with other Clients' Brokerage.

2. *Principal Trades.* The Investment Manager should determine if the particular Principal Trade is subject to certain fiduciary requirements (e.g., ERISA, Investment Company Act of 1940) which require that Client Brokerage derived from Principal Trades must benefit the Client account generating the Brokerage. If such requirements do not apply, it is permissible to use Client Brokerage derived from Principal Trades to benefit Client accounts other than the account generating the Brokerage if the Investment Manager discloses this practice and obtains prior consent from the Client.

   Clarification: Certain fiduciary statutes require that brokerage derived from a Principal Trade must directly benefit the Client account generating the Trade. In such situations, even consent by the Client will not waive this legal requirement. Compliance with the Soft Dollar Standards should not be read to, in any way, absolve one's responsibilities to comply fully with the applicable law regarding Principal Trades.

III. Selection of Brokers

Principle

A. Selecting Brokers to execute Clients' Securities Transactions is a key component of the Investment Manager's ability to add value to its Client portfolios. The failure to obtain Best Execution may result in impaired performance for the Client.

Required

B. In selecting Brokers, the Investment Manager must consider the capabilities of the Broker to provide Best Execution.

Recommended

C. In evaluating the Broker's capability to provide Best Execution, the Investment Manager should consider the Broker's financial responsibility, the Broker's responsiveness to the Investment Manager, the Commission rate or spread involved, and the range of services offered by the Broker.

   Clarification: These criteria are relevant components to the Broker's ability to obtain the most favorable total cost under the particular circumstances at that time.

IV. Evaluation of Research

Required

A. In determining whether to use Client Brokerage to pay for Research, the Investment Manager must use the following criteria:
   1. Whether the Research under consideration meets the definition of Research contained in these Standards.
   2. Whether the Research benefits the Investment Manager's Client(s).
   3. Whether the Investment Manager is able to document the basis for the determinations.
   4. Whether under certain fiduciary regulations (e.g., ERISA, the Investment Company Act of 1940) for Principal Trades, the Research directly benefits the Client account generating the trade. If the Principal Trades are not subject to such regulations, the Research may benefit Client accounts other than those generating the trade if the Investment Manager has made disclosure and obtained prior Client consent.

B. The inability to decide and document that the Research meets the above criteria requires that the Investment Manager *not* pay for such Research with Client Brokerage.

C. In determining the portion of Mixed-Use Research to be paid with Client Brokerage, the Investment Manager must:
   1. Be able to make a reasonable, justifiable, and documentable allocation of the cost of the Research according to its expected usage.
   2. Pay with Client Brokerage only the portion of the Research that is actually used by the Investment Manager in the Investment Decision-Making Process.
   3. Reevaluate the Mixed-Use Research allocation at least annually.

V. Client-Directed Brokerage

Principle

A. Because Brokerage is an asset of the Client, not the Investment Manager, the practice of Client-Directed Brokerage does not violate any investment manager duty per se.

B. In a Client-Directed Brokerage Arrangement:

Required

   1. The Investment Manager must not use Brokerage from another Client account to pay for a product or service

purchased under the Client-Directed Brokerage Arrangement.

Recommended

2. The Investment Manager should disclose to the Client:
   a. the Investment Manager's duty to continue to seek to obtain Best Execution, and
   b. that arrangements that require the Investment Manager to commit a certain percentage of Brokerage may affect the Investment Manager's ability to (i) seek to obtain Best Execution and (ii) obtain adequate Research.
3. The Investment Manager should attempt to structure the Client-Directed Brokerage Arrangement in a manner that comports with Appendix A to the Soft Dollar Standards (Exhibit A to this Topical Study).

VI. Disclosure

In addition to disclosure required elsewhere in the Soft Dollar Standards:

Required

A. An Investment Manager must clearly disclose, with specificity and in "plain language," its policies with respect to all Soft Dollar Arrangements, including:
   1. *To Clients and potential Clients.* An Investment Manager must disclose whether it may use the Research to benefit Clients other than those whose trades generated the Brokerage. This disclosure must address whether the trades generating the Brokerage involved transactions conducted on a principal basis.
   2. *To Clients.* An Investment Manager must disclose (i) the types of Research received through Proprietary or Third-Party Research Arrangements; (ii) the extent of use; and (iii) whether any affiliated Broker is involved.

      Clarification: Description of the types and use of Research should be appropriate to the type of Research Arrangement involved. The disclosures required or recommended in the Soft Dollar Standards do not contemplate an "unbundling" of Proprietary Research Arrangements. Instead, the description of Research should, in the judgment of the Investment Manager, provide Clients with the ability to understand the type of Research involved *in the degree of detail* appropriate to the source of the Research.

B. To claim compliance with these Standards for any Client account, an Investment Manager must provide the Client with a statement that any Soft Dollar Arrangements with respect to the particular Client account comport with the AIMR Soft Dollar Standards. This statement must be provided at least annually.

   Clarification: This statement is required only if the Investment Manager is claiming compliance with the Soft Dollar Standards. If applicable, the statement is to be provided to the individual Client to which the claim is being made.

C. An Investment Manager must prominently disclose in writing to its Client that additional information in accordance with the AIMR Soft Dollar Standards concerning the Investment Manager's Soft Dollar Arrangements is available on request. Such additional information should include the following on at least an annual basis:

   Clarification: Although certain additional information is suggested, the Soft Dollar Standards are intended to preserve the ability of the Client and Investment Manager to determine what other information may be relevant in light of particular Client needs or types of accounts.

   1. *On a firmwide basis.* A description of the products and services that were received from Brokers pursuant to a Soft Dollar Arrangement, regardless of whether the product or service derives from Proprietary or Third-Party Research Arrangements, detailed by Broker.
   2. *For a specific Client account*:
      a. the total amount of Commissions generated for that Client through a Soft Dollar Arrangement, detailed by Broker; and
      b. the total amount of Brokerage directed by that Client through Directed Brokerage Arrangements.

      Clarification: The disclosure required in this section is intended to provide the requesting Client with certain basic items of information: a description of what the entire firm obtained through Soft Dollar Arrangements, the identity of brokers providing those products and services, the total amount of Directed Brokerage attributable to the Client, and the total amount of Commissions generated for the requesting Client's account.
   3. The aggregate percentage of the Investment Manager's Brokerage derived from Client-Directed Brokerage

Arrangements and the amount of that Client's Directed Brokerage, as a percentage of that aggregate.

a. The Investment Manager is not obligated to report amounts of Client-Directed Brokerage that constitute less than 10 percent of the Manager's aggregate amount of Client-Directed Brokerage.

Recommended

When requested by a Client:

D. The Investment Manager should provide a description of the product or service obtained through Brokerage generated from the Client's account.

E. The Investment Manager should provide the aggregate dollar amount of Brokerage paid from all accounts over which the Manager has Investment Discretion.

VII. Record Keeping

Required

The Investment Manager must maintain, when applicable, all records that

A. are required by applicable law;

B. are necessary to supply Clients on a timely basis with the information required by Soft Dollar Standard VI;

C. document arrangements, oral or written, obligating the Investment Manager to generate a specific amount of Brokerage;

D. document arrangements with Clients pertaining to Soft Dollar or Client-Directed Brokerage Arrangements;

E. document any agreements with Brokers pertaining to Soft Dollar Arrangements;

F. document transactions with Brokers involving Soft Dollar Arrangements, including (1) a list of Proprietary or Third-Party Research providers and (2) a description of the service or product obtained from the provider;

G. document the bases of allocation in determining to use Client Brokerage to pay for any portion of a Mixed-Use service or product;

H. indicate how the services and products obtained through Soft Dollar Arrangements directly assist the Investment Manager in the Investment Decision-Making Process;

I. show compliance with the AIMR Soft Dollar Standards, including the identity of the Investment Manager personnel responsible for determining such compliance.

J. copies of all Client disclosures and authorizations.

Exhibit A: Recommended Practices for Client-Directed Brokerage Arrangements

In Client-Directed Brokerage Arrangements:

A. When directed by a Fiduciary, the Investment Manager should receive written assurance from the Fiduciary that the Client-Directed Brokerage Arrangement will solely benefit the Client's account.

B. The Investment Manager should attempt to structure Client-Directed Brokerage Arrangements so that
   1. they do not require the commitment of a certain portion of Brokerage to a single Broker, and
   2. Commissions are negotiated and seeking to obtain Best Execution is still relevant.

C. The Investment Manager should request from its Client in any Client-Directed Brokerage Arrangement written instructions that
   1. restate the Investment Manager's continuing responsibility for seeking to obtain Best Execution,
   2. list the eligible Brokers,
   3. specify the approximate target percentage or dollar amount of transactions to be directed, and
   4. state procedures for monitoring the Arrangements.

D. The Investment Manager should regularly communicate with the Client for the purpose of jointly evaluating the Client-Directed Brokerage Arrangement, including
   1. the potential for achieving Best Execution,
   2. the list of Brokers and their trading skills,
   3. the target percentage of transactions to be directed to the selected Brokers, and
   4. the Investment Manager's trading style and liquidity needs.

Exhibit B: Permissible Research Guidance

Central to whether a product or service constitutes "Research" that can be paid for with Client Brokerage is whether the product or service provides lawful and appropriate assistance to the Investment Manager in carrying out its investment decision-making responsibilities. This determination pivots on whether the product or service aids the Investment Decision-Making Process instead of the general operation of the firm.

The AIMR Soft Dollar Standards add guidance by requiring that the primary use of the Research must directly assist the Investment Manager in its Investment Decision-Making Process and not in the management of the investment firm.

Formulating what is allowable Research is not subject to hard and fast rules. Rather, the context in which something is used and the particulars of an Investment Manager's business form the framework for this determination. In evaluating a practice, the substance of *actual* usage will prevail over the *form* of some possible usage.

Three-Level Analysis

The AIMR Soft Dollar Standards assist the Investment Manager in making this determination by setting forth a three-level analysis to assist the Investment Manager in determining whether a product or service is Research. In the vast majority of cases, if the criteria of all three levels are satisfied, the Investment Manager can then feel comfortable in using Client Brokerage to pay for the Research. When conducting the analysis, the Investment Manager must consider the ethical framework of the Soft Dollar Standards. In conjunction with the Soft Dollar Standards' Client disclosure requirements, an Investment Manager must be able to explain to its Client how the Research—and when applicable, its component parts—assists in the Investment Decision-Making Process. Stated another way, the Investment Manager should only obtain Research with Client Brokerage if the Manager would feel comfortable disclosing and explaining the decision in a face-to-face meeting with the Client.

Level I—Define the Product or Service. The first step is for the Investment Manager to define the product or service to be purchased with Client Brokerage. In most instances, the product or service is clearly defined (e.g., an industry report). However, many products and services consist of different components that are related only to the ability of the product or service to assist the Investment Manager in its Investment Decision-Making Process (e.g., a computer work station that runs Research software). For such multicomponent products or services, the Investment

Manager, consistent with the Soft Dollar Standards' ethical framework, must narrowly construe the component parts that are necessary for the products or services to directly assist the Investment Manager in the Investment Decision-Making Process.

For example, the computer work station could be considered a closely related component of the product or service that constitutes the "Research." The electricity needed to run the computer, however, is not closely related and, if paid with Client Brokerage, would violate the ethical principles of the Soft Dollar Standards.

Level II—Determine Usage. The second step is for the Investment Manager to determine that the primary use of the product or service, as defined by the Investment Manager in the Level I analysis, will directly assist the Investment Manager in its Investment Decision-Making Process.

For example, an Investment Manager subscribes to the Bloomberg Service and uses this service only to enable all persons visiting the Investment Manager's offices to look up the price of securities and analyze market trends. Under the Level I analysis, the Investment Manager defines the service as the market data received from Bloomberg, plus the Bloomberg supplied terminal and the dedicated line necessary to receive the Bloomberg service in the Investment Manager's offices. However, under the Level II analysis, the Investment Manager does not use the Bloomberg service to directly assist it in its Investment Decision-Making Process. To the contrary, the Investment Manager subscribes to the Bloomberg Service as a benefit to the firm. The Bloomberg Service, therefore, cannot be paid for with Client Brokerage.

Level III—Mixed-Use Analysis. The third step occurs only after the Investment Manager determines that the product or service is Research by completing the Level I and Level II analysis above. The Investment Manager must then determine what portion of the Research is used by the Investment Manager to directly assist it in the Investment Decision-Making Process. If less than 100 percent of the Research is used for assistance in its Investment Decision-Making Process, the Investment Manager must consider the Research as Mixed-Use Research. With Mixed-Use Research, the Investment Manager can use Client Brokerage to pay for only that portion of the Research used by the Investment Manager in the Investment Decision-Making Process and not in the management of the investment firm.

For example, if the Bloomberg service discussed in the Level III analysis was actually used 50 percent of the time to determine market and industry trends as part of the Investment Manager's Investment Decision-Making Process, the Investment Manager could pay for 50 percent of the Bloomberg service with Client Brokerage.

Conclusion

The Investment Manager can establish that the product or service is Research that can be purchased with Client Brokerage only after the Investment Manager has taken two steps. First, the Investment Manager must have defined the product or service (Level I analysis). Second, the Investment Manager must have determined that the primary use of the product or service will directly assist the Investment Manager in the Investment Decision-Making Process rather than in the management of the investment firm (Level II analysis). The final step is for the Investment Manager to determine what portion of the Research will be used by the Investment Manager in the Investment Decision-Making Process and pay only for that portion with Client Brokerage (Level III analysis).

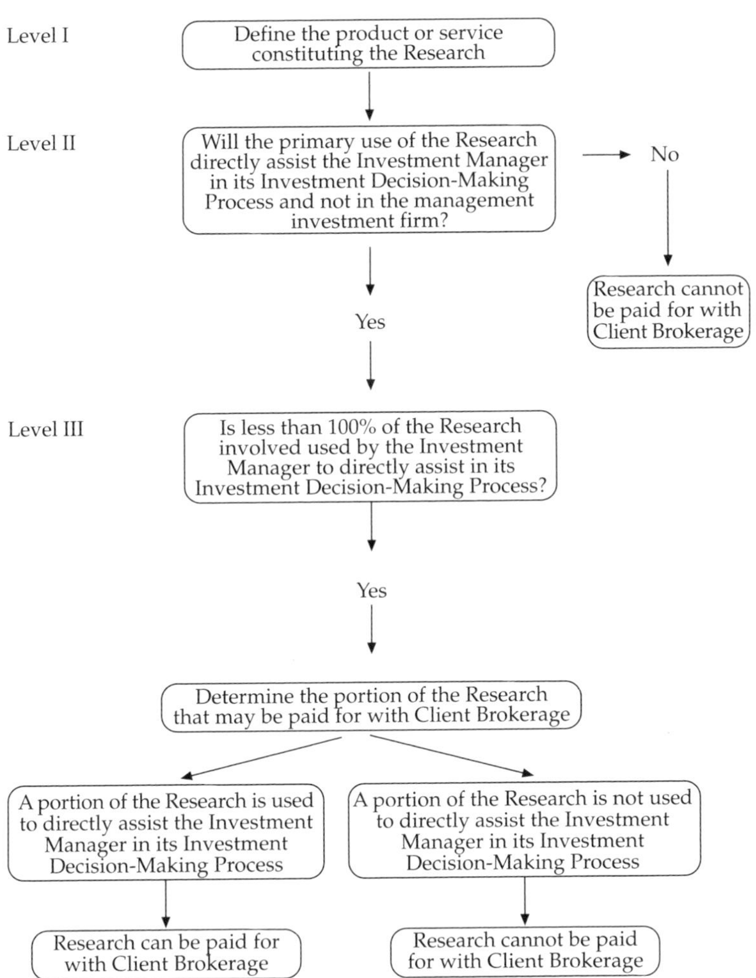
Level I
Define the product or service constituting the Research
Level II
Will the primary use of the Research directly assist the Investment Manager in its Investment Decision-Making Process and not in the management investment firm?
No
Research cannot be paid for with Client Brokerage
Yes
Level III
Is less than 100% of the Research involved used by the Investment Manager to directly assist in its Investment Decision-Making Process?
Yes
Determine the portion of the Research that may be paid for with Client Brokerage
A portion of the Research is used to directly assist the Investment Manager in its Investment Decision-Making Process
A portion of the Research is not used to directly assist the Investment Manager in its Investment Decision-Making Process
Research can be paid for with Client Brokerage
Research cannot be paid for with Client Brokerage

Exhibit C: Case Study under the AIMR Soft Dollar Standards

XYZ Firm is an Investment Manager that seeks to comply with the AIMR Soft Dollar Standards and claim such compliance. XYZ, a Member of AIMR, manages a variety of accounts: separate accounts, including accounts of employee benefit plans subject to ERISA, accounts of non-ERISA institutional investors, and accounts of wealthy individuals; several collective investment vehicles, including a group trust for employee benefit plans subject to ERISA and/or governmental plans; a "hedge fund" for institutional and other "sophisticated" individual investors; and three SEC-registered investment companies, including an equity fund, a fixed-income fund, and a money market fund.

XYZ executes trades for its Client accounts with several broker–dealers who conduct trades for XYZ on both a principal and agency basis. Some of the broker–dealers have offered to provide XYZ with the following products and/or services for XYZ's own use, to be paid for with XYZ's Client Brokerage business: (1) desks and office equipment; (2) trading room television sets that receive the Financial News Network and other financial news services supplied by cable and satellite television services; (3) the Bloomberg Service, which includes a Bloomberg terminal; and (4) software that will assist XYZ in analyzing economic trends in industries followed by the Firm, as well as a widely available computer work station on which to install and operate the software. In addition, XYZ has received the following requests from Clients: (5) a pension fund Client subject to ERISA has requested that XYZ direct a portion of its Brokerage from its separate account to Broker ABC to obtain research information to be provided to the plan trustees; (6) a public pension plan has requested that XYZ direct a portion of its Brokerage to Broker ABC in return for cash credits to be paid to the Plan; (7) a non-ERISA institutional investor in XYZ's hedge fund has requested that XYZ direct a portion of the hedge fund's brokerage to Broker ABC to compensate Broker ABC for research services provided to the institutional investor; and, (8) the SEC-registered investment companies have requested that XYZ direct a portion of the equity fund's Brokerage to Broker ABC in return for credits to be used to reduce or eliminate all of the registered investment companies' custodian fees.

What steps or other actions must or should XYZ take to comply with the Soft Dollar Standards and/or other AIMR Standards of Professional Conduct?

Discussion

XYZ Firm is facing a set of decisions that typically confronts Investment

Managers in connection with their use of Client Brokerage. XYZ should approach these decisions in a logical and systematic fashion to identify all relevant issues and ensure compliance with applicable law and AIMR Soft Dollar Standards. As an initial matter, XYZ should clearly isolate and identify the proposed transactions contemplated. Then, in order to determine compliance with applicable law and AIMR Soft Dollar Standards, XYZ should (1) consider fundamental principles that apply to the conduct of AIMR Members, (2) identify applicable laws and regulations and analyze the proposed transactions in light of those laws and regulations, and (3) identify the AIMR Soft Dollar Standards and analyze the proposed transactions in light of those Standards. XYZ may pursue the proposed transactions only after satisfying itself that the transactions pass this systematic, multilevel analysis.

Isolate and Define the Proposed Transactions. One of the benefits of the AIMR Soft Dollar Standards is that they help Investment Managers to clearly define their practices as they relate to their Clients' Brokerage. By referring to the definitions contained in the Soft Dollar Standards, XYZ should determine that the broker–dealers' offer to provide the products and services in Transactions 1–4 described in the "Facts" section possibly constitutes a Soft Dollar Arrangement. Because XYZ is contemplating directing transactions to the broker–dealers to receive execution on trades and to receive products and services that will benefit XYZ directly, this offer may meet the AIMR Soft Dollar Standards definition of a Soft Dollar Arrangement. An additional measure of whether Transactions 1–4 qualify as Soft Dollar Arrangements under the AIMR Soft Dollar Standards is whether the products and services received by XYZ qualify as Research as defined in the Soft Dollar Standards. Transactions 5–8 may constitute Client-Directed Brokerage Arrangements, as defined in the AIMR Soft Dollar Standards, if XYZ determines that the *clients* are directing that their trades be routed through specific broker–dealers in order that the *clients* may receive benefits *in addition to* execution services.

Fundamental Principles. In considering the transactions that have been proposed, XYZ should adhere to a set of fundamental principles contained in three of the AIMR Standards that generally govern a Member's conduct in this area. Standard I (Fundamental Responsibilities) of the AIMR Standards of Professional Conduct requires that a Member be familiar and comply with all applicable laws governing their professional activities. XYZ is thus charged with a duty to know and apply the provisions of law that are implicated by the proposed transactions. Even if XYZ has adopted the AIMR Soft Dollar Standards, compliance with these Standards does not absolve XYZ of the responsibility to comply with applicable law. For situations in which the AIMR Standards impose a higher degree of responsibility or disclosure than, but do not conflict with, applicable law, XYZ must adhere to the provisions of the AIMR Standards *in addition to* any provisions of applicable law.

Moreover, Standard I of the AIMR Soft Dollar Standards contains fundamental principles that govern any of XYZ's activities involving Soft Dollar Arrangements. Standard I states that (1) Brokerage is the property of the Client and (2) XYZ has an ongoing duty to ensure the quality of transactions effected on behalf of its Clients, which includes

- seeking to obtain Best Execution,
- minimizing transactions costs, and
- using Client Brokerage to benefit Clients.

These principles are reflected in the AIMR Soft Dollar Standards' requirement that XYZ, in considering a Soft Dollar Arrangement, must act for the benefit of its Clients and place its Clients' interests before its own.

Finally, Standard V of the AIMR Soft Dollar Standards, governing Client-Directed Brokerage Arrangements, requires that XYZ must not use Brokerage from another Client account to pay for a product or service purchased under the Client-Directed Brokerage Arrangement.

Applicable Laws and Regulations. Members are expected at all times to comply with the applicable laws of the countries in which they do business. For example, in the United States, the Securities Exchange Act of 1934, Investment Company Act of 1940, Investment Advisers Act of 1940, and Employment Retirement Income Security Act of 1974 would govern certain or possibly all of the transactions that XYZ is considering. Regardless of the country in which XYZ is doing business, as a threshold matter, it must analyze each transaction for compliance with applicable law. Only those transactions that comply with local laws are eligible for subsequent analysis under the AIMR Soft Dollar Standards.

Applicable Relevant Standards. Assuming each of the proposed transactions has "survived" the first two stages of analysis, they must still comply with provisions of the AIMR Soft Dollar Standards in order for XYZ to pursue them. Because XYZ has previously determined that each of the transactions qualifies as a possible Soft Dollar Arrangement (depending on whether the products or services qualify as Research under the AIMR Soft Dollar Standards) or a Client-Directed Brokerage Arrangement (depending on whether XYZ's Client is directing its trades to receive a benefit), XYZ must satisfy the following three broad requirements to claim compliance with the Soft Dollar Standards:

- Determine that each arrangement is permitted by the AIMR Soft Dollar Standards.
- Disclose the Investment Manger's Soft Dollar policies to its Clients.
- Maintain the specified records.

A. Determinations of Eligibility. Standard III of the AIMR Soft Dollar Standards requires that, as an initial matter in selecting any broker, XYZ must consider the capabilities of the broker to provide Best Execution. Once XYZ has satisfied itself that a particular broker will provide Best Execution, XYZ must next evaluate any additional research provided by the broker under the following four criteria specified in Soft Dollar Standard IV:

- The research under consideration must meet the definition of Research contained in the Soft Dollar Standards.
- The Research must benefit XYZ's clients.
- XYZ must be able to document the basis for its determination.
- Under certain fiduciary regulations (i.e., ERISA, the Investment Company Act of 1940), for trades conducted on a principal basis, the Research must directly benefit the Client account generating the trade. If not so limited by such regulations, the Research must directly benefit the Client account generating the trade, unless XYZ has made disclosure and obtained prior Client consent.

The meaning of the term "Research" is crucial to XYZ's evaluation under Soft Dollar Standard IV. "Research" is defined in the AIMR Soft Dollar Standards to mean services and/or products the primary use of which must directly assist the Investment Manager in its Investment Decision-Making Process and not in the management of the investment firm.

Transaction 1—Use of Client Brokerage to Pay for Desks and Office Equipment. Transaction 1 would not qualify for Research as defined in the Soft Dollar Standards because desks and office equipment would not satisfy the Soft Dollar Standards' definition of Research. Although XYZ should be able to determine that desks and office equipment do not qualify as Research based on the plain terms of the definition, the result becomes clear when XYZ applies the three-level analysis. Under that analysis, XYZ would first define the products or services that it desires to purchase with Client Brokerage. The desks are a discrete and simple product that can be clearly identified. Although office equipment is a somewhat general term, XYZ should also be able to clearly identify the office equipment being offered (e.g., photocopier, fax machine, etc.). XYZ next would analyze the primary use of these products to determine whether they will directly assist XYZ's Investment Decision-Making Process. At this point, XYZ clearly should understand that desks and most office equipment cannot be considered to aid directly in the Investment Decision-Making Process and hence do not qualify as Research under the

AIMR Soft Dollar Standards. Because the Soft Dollar Standards only permit XYZ to receive Research as defined in the AIMR Soft Dollar Standards, XYZ could not engage in Transaction 1 and claim compliance with the AIMR Soft Dollar Standards.

Transaction 2—Use of Client Brokerage to Pay for Trading Room Television Sets. Transaction 2 involves a service that is more difficult than office equipment to analyze under the definition of Research contained in the Soft Dollar Standards. The service that XYZ desires to purchase is really a composite of products and services that may or may not qualify as Research under the definition provided in the Soft Dollar Standards. XYZ's first task is to define the service under the first level of analysis. Accordingly, XYZ should narrowly construe the component parts that are *necessary* for the service at issue in this example (i.e., financial news networks) to assist XYZ in its Investment Decision-Making Process. In this situation, XYZ could reasonably conclude that the component parts (i.e., television sets, individual financial news services, and cable or satellite providers) are necessary for the total service to assist XYZ in its Investment Decision-Making Process. Thus, the service is potentially eligible to be paid for with client brokerage, *provided* that the total service satisfies the next level of analysis.

Applying the next level of analysis would allow XYZ to conclude that the service may qualify as Research if the primary use of the service is to directly aid the Investment Manager in its Investment Decision-Making Process. Even if financial news services have a broader use than to provide data to Investment Managers for purposes of making investment decisions, it would be consistent with the Soft Dollar Standards for XYZ to conclude that such services meet the primary use analysis—if based on actual use.

Transaction 3—Use of Client Brokerage to Pay for the Bloomberg Service. Transaction 3 involves a similar analysis under the definition of Research contained in the AIMR Soft Dollar Standards. As with Transaction 2, XYZ's first step is to define the products or services that XYZ proposes to purchase with Client Brokerage. Again, XYZ should narrowly construe the component parts and could reasonably conclude that the Bloomberg terminal is a necessary component to receive the Bloomberg Service.

In applying the next level of analysis, XYZ may also reasonably conclude that the primary use of the Bloomberg Service, with its specific focus on real-time market news and analysis, does directly aid in the Investment Decision-Making Process. The service, therefore, may satisfy the first two levels of analyzing the definition of Research contained in the

Soft Dollar Standards. However, if XYZ uses the Bloomberg Service and terminal to allow Clients to access financial information, the primary use of the service would not be to assist XYZ in its Investment Decision-Making Process, and the service would not qualify as Research under the AIMR Soft Dollar Standards. If XYZ uses the Bloomberg Service and terminal both in its own Investment Decision-Making Process and for Client purposes, at the third level of analysis, XYZ must make a good faith determination as to what portion of the service is actually used in the Investment Decision-Making Process. Only this portion may be paid for with Client Brokerage. XYZ must reevaluate this allocation on an annual basis.

Transaction 4—Use of Client Brokerage to Pay for Software and Computer Work Stations. At this point, XYZ should be comfortable applying the three-level analysis required to define Research under the Soft Dollar Standards. Transaction 4 involves the same analysis that confronted XYZ in the first three transactions. In defining the product in Transaction 4 (i.e., the research software), XYZ might reasonably determine that each of the component parts (the software and workstation) is necessary for the product to assist in the Investment Decision-Making Process.

Furthermore, XYZ might reasonably conclude under the second level of analysis that the software (and its component parts) will directly aid XYZ's Investment Decision-Making Process. If the primary use of the software is to directly assist XYZ in its Investment Decision-Making Process (as indicated by Level II analysis), XYZ may purchase the software using Client Brokerage. However, as with Transaction 3, only that portion actually used by XYZ in its Investment Decision-Making Process (as determined by Level III analysis) may be paid for with Client Brokerage, and any mixed-use allocation must be reevaluated annually.

Client-Directed Transactions. The eligibility of Transactions 5–8 must be determined under the portions of the AIMR Soft Dollar Standards related to Client-Directed Brokerage Arrangements. Standard V of the AIMR Soft Dollar Standards requires that, in considering Transactions 5–8, XYZ must not use Brokerage from another Client account to pay for a product or service purchased under the Client-Directed Brokerage Arrangement. Standard V also recommends that XYZ attempt to structure the Client-Directed Brokerage Arrangement in accordance with certain recommended practices under the AIMR Soft Dollar Standards.

Transaction 5—Directing of Brokerage by ERISA Client to Benefit Plan Trustees. In considering Transaction 5, XYZ must be particularly cognizant of the definition of Client contained in the Soft Dollar Standards.

The Standards define Client to refer to "the entity, including a natural person, investment fund, or separate account, designated to receive the benefits, including income, from the Brokerage generated through Securities Transactions."

Although this definition of Client also recognizes that a Client may be represented by a trustee or other Fiduciary, XYZ must be sensitive to the fundamental principle contained in Standard I of the AIMR Soft Dollar Standards that stresses that Brokerage is the property of the *Client*, not the trustee or Fiduciary representing the Client. XYZ should immediately question whether Transaction 5 qualifies as a Client-Directed Brokerage Arrangement because the additional benefit flows not to the Client but to the Client's trustees. Because Transaction 5 likely does not qualify as a proper Client-Directed Brokerage Arrangement, if XYZ were to pursue it, XYZ would be violating the fundamental principle that requires the use of Client Brokerage to benefit Clients. XYZ should, therefore, decline to pursue Transaction 5.

Transaction 6—Directing of Brokerage by Public Pension Plan to Obtain Cash Credits for the Plan. Transaction 6, however, would be a permissible Client-Directed Brokerage Arrangement under the Soft Dollar Standards because Client Brokerage would be used to generate cash credits that solely benefit the Client. XYZ should attempt to structure the arrangement in conformity with the recommended practices for Client-Directed Brokerage Arrangements that are contained in the Soft Dollar Standards, which would require XYZ to:

- Disclose to the Client XYZ's duty to continue to seek to obtain Best Execution.
- Disclose to the Client that committing a certain percentage of the Client's Brokerage to a particular broker–dealer may affect XYZ's ability to seek to obtain Best Execution and purchase adequate Research.
- XYZ should receive written assurance from the plan trustees that the Client-Directed Brokerage Arrangement will solely benefit plan beneficiaries.
- XYZ should attempt to structure the Client-Directed Brokerage Arrangement so that it does not require the commitment of a certain portion of Brokerage to a single broker and so that commissions are negotiated and seeking to obtain Best Execution is still relevant.
- XYZ should request from the Client written instructions that (1) restate XYZ's continuing responsibility for seeking to obtain Best Execution, (2) list eligible brokers; (3) specify the target percentage of transactions to be directed, and (4) state procedures for monitoring the arrangement.

- XYZ should regularly communicate with the Client for the purpose of jointly evaluating the Client-Directed Brokerage Arrangement, including (1) the potential for achieving Best Execution, (2) the list of brokers and their trading skills, (3) the target percentage of transactions to be directed to selected brokers, (4) XYZ's trading style and liquidity needs, and (5) other factors identified by the Client as relevant to the selection of brokers.

Transaction 7—Directing of Brokerage by Institutional Investor in Hedge Fund to Compensate Broker for Research Provided to Investor. Transaction 7 raises issues under Standard V of the AIMR Soft Dollar Standards because Standard V requires that XYZ not use Brokerage from another Client account to pay for a product or service purchased under the Client-Directed Brokerage Arrangement. In Transaction 7, XYZ's hedge fund is a commingled pool containing numerous investors. The AIMR Soft Dollar Standards define Client to refer to the beneficiaries of an *entity*, including, as in this case, *all* of the beneficiaries of an investment fund. However, the product or service purchased under this particular Client-Directed Brokerage Arrangement has benefited *only* the institutional investor in the hedge fund, not all of the Client's underlying investors and thus may be construed to violate the principles in Standard V of the AIMR Soft Dollar Standards. XYZ, therefore, should not pursue Transaction 7.

Transaction 8—Directing of a Portion of One Fund's Brokerage by Three Investment Companies to Benefit All Three Companies. Transaction 8 raises similar concerns as Transactions 5 and 7. XYZ is apparently directed by three distinct Clients (each of the three registered funds) to direct brokerage of one Client (i.e., the equity fund) to benefit all three Clients. XYZ should not pursue this arrangement because it would violate the principle in Standard V of the AIMR Soft Dollar Standards, which states that brokerage from another Client account should not be used to pay for a product or service purchased under a Client-Directed Brokerage Arrangement.

B. <u>Disclosure</u>. In order to claim compliance with the AIMR Soft Dollar Standards, XYZ must also meet specific disclosure obligations relating to its Brokerage practices. In addition to XYZ's disclosure obligations described above in the discussion of the transactions, XYZ must clearly disclose the following information relating to its Soft Dollar and Client-Directed Brokerage Arrangements:

- XYZ must disclose to Clients and potential Clients whether XYZ may use the Research to benefit Clients other than those whose trades generated the Brokerage and whether the trades generating the Brokerage involved transactions conducted on a principal basis.

- XYZ must disclose to Clients (1) a description of the types of Research received through the arrangements, (2) the extent of its use, and (3) whether any broker affiliate of XYZ was involved.
- XYZ must provide each Client with a statement that any Soft Dollar or Client-Directed Brokerage Arrangements with respect to its account comport with the AIMR Soft Dollar Standards (this statement must be provided at least annually).
- XYZ must disclose in writing to its Clients that additional information in accordance with the AIMR Soft Dollar Standards concerning XYZ's Soft Dollar and Client-Directed Brokerage Arrangements is available on request. Such additional information should include (1) a firmwide description of the products and services that were received from each broker pursuant to a Soft Dollar Arrangement, including the identity of those Brokers; (2) for a specific Client account, the total amount of Commissions generated for the Client through Soft Dollar Arrangements, detailed by Broker and reporting the amount of Brokerage directed by the Client to specific brokers; and (3) the aggregate percentage of XYZ Brokerage derived from Client-Directed Brokerage Arrangements and the amount of the particular Client's Directed Brokerage as a percentage of the aggregate, subject to a 10 percent *de minimis* amount.

C. Record Keeping. In addition to the eligibility determinations and disclosure obligations, in order to claim compliance with the AIMR Soft Dollar Standards, XYZ must also maintain, when applicable, all records that

- are required by applicable law;
- are necessary to supply Clients on a timely basis with the information required by Soft Dollar Standard VI;
- document arrangements, oral or written, obligating the Investment Manager to generate a specific amount of Brokerage;
- document arrangements with Clients pertaining to Soft Dollar or Client-Directed Brokerage Arrangements;
- document any agreements with Brokers pertaining to Soft Dollar Arrangements;
- document transactions with Brokers involving Soft Dollar Arrangements, including (1) a list of Proprietary or Third-Party Research providers and (2) a description of the service or product obtained from the provider;
- document the bases of allocation in determining to use Client Brokerage to pay for any portion of a Mixed-Use service or product;
- indicate how the services and products obtained through Soft Dollar

Arrangements directly assist XYZ in the Investment Decision-Making Process;

- show compliance with the AIMR Soft Dollar Standards, including the identity of XYZ personnel responsible for determining such compliance;
- are copies of all Client disclosures and authorizations.

Exhibit D: Analysis of Proposed Transactions under Applicable U.S. Law

Section 28(e) of the U.S. Securities Exchange Act of 1934 provides a "safe harbor" for investment managers from claims that they breached a fiduciary duty owed to a client by causing a client to pay higher commission costs in return for receipt of "brokerage and research services" that benefit the investment manager.[5] Regulations under the U.S. Investment Advisers Act of 1940 require investment managers who are registered with the U.S. Securities and Exchange Commission to provide disclosure to clients regarding their allocation of client brokerage, including whether the receipt of research that benefits the manager is a consideration in allocating brokerage. In addition, provisions of the U.S. Investment Company Act of 1940 govern transactions that apply to investment company assets, and provisions of the U.S. Employee Retirement Income Security Act (ERISA) of 1974 will apply to any transaction that involves the assets of a "plan" as the term is defined in ERISA. Assuming XYZ is doing business in the United States, XYZ is charged with the responsibility under AIMR's Standards of Practice of knowing and complying with the relevant provisions of these laws.

Transactions 1–4. XYZ must first consider whether Transactions 1–4 would satisfy the SEC's definition of permissible research for purposes of Section 28(e). Research or brokerage products or services are the only products or services that are covered by the Section 28(e) safe harbor. Thus, XYZ will only be protected from potential legal challenges based on its paying a higher commission rate if the goods or services offered in the proposed transactions qualify as research as defined by the SEC. With the exception of Transaction 1, each of the proposed transactions would probably satisfy the SEC's definition of "research," which is that the product or service provides lawful assistance to XYZ in making investment decisions. Because Transaction 1 would likely *not* satisfy this standard, it would not qualify for the protection of the Section 28(e) safe harbor and would need to be analyzed in light of any restrictions imposed by other applicable laws. Transaction 1 quite possibly would raise best execution concerns under existing SEC interpretations and, if connected with investment company brokerage, would raise additional concerns under provisions of the Investment Company Act that restrict affiliates of a mutual fund from receiving compensation as an agent for the sale of the fund's

[5]As a "safe harbor," Section 28(e) cannot be violated but offers protection from violations that might otherwise be deemed to occur under relevant laws.

property. Moreover, if Transaction 1 involved plan assets as defined in ERISA, it would raise concerns under provisions of ERISA that require fiduciaries (including XYZ) to act solely in the interest of the plan's beneficiaries and for the exclusive purpose of providing benefits to the plan's beneficiaries.

Transactions 5–8. Transactions 5–8 would *not* fall within the Section 28(e) safe harbor because Section 28(e) requires that the person *selecting* the broker–dealer be the person exercising investment discretion over the account. In XYZ's case, because the *client* is selecting the broker–dealer, Transactions 5–8 would not fall within the Section 28(e) safe harbor.

Nevertheless, because brokerage is an asset of the client, such arrangements may still be accomplished, provided they do not violate other relevant provisions of U.S. law. Transaction 5 should raise immediate concerns for XYZ because the benefit of the research information is flowing to the plan's trustees and in-house staff, and is not used for the *exclusive benefit* of the plan beneficiaries. XYZ should conclude that to follow client instructions in Transaction 5 would likely result in a violation by XYZ of the substantive prohibitions of ERISA. Similarly, Transaction 8 should raise immediate concerns for XYZ under provisions of the Investment Company Act because brokerage of the equity fund is being used to reduce custody expenses of *all* three registered investment companies. Such an arrangement is likely prohibited by sections of the Investment Company Act that affirmatively prohibit joint transactions among affiliated funds. XYZ should, therefore, also determine that Transaction 8 is prohibited by the Investment Company Act.

Summary. Transactions 1, 5, and 8 do not qualify for the safe harbor protection of Section 28(e). Transaction 1 may be permissible under existing law if XYZ provides full disclosure and obtains informed client consent, provided that the transaction does not involve investment company or benefit plan assets. Because Transaction 5 clearly involves plan brokerage, it would be prohibited by ERISA. Similarly, Transaction 8 is prohibited by provisions of the Investment Company Act. Transaction 5 and Transaction 8, therefore, do not survive XYZ's initial analysis under applicable U.S. law.

Exhibit E: Analysis of Proposed Transactions under Applicable Canadian Law

The Ontario Securities Commission (the OSC) and the Commission des Valeurs Mobiliers du Quebec (the CVMQ) have respectively adopted OSC Policy Statement 1.9 and CVMQ Policy Statement No. Q-20, (the Soft Dollar Policies). The other securities administrators have not released formal policies with respect to soft dollars. The Soft Dollar Policies govern the use by dealers of commissions on brokerage transactions as payment for goods or services other than order execution services,[6] services directly related to order execution, or investment decision-making services.[7] The negotiation of commissions on brokerage transactions executed on behalf of a manager[8] of a portfolio or fund of securities is governed by the general obligation of the manager to act in the best interests of the beneficiaries of the portfolio or fund. Accordingly, such commissions must be used only as payment for goods or services that are for the benefit of the beneficiaries and should not be used as payment for goods or services that are for the benefit of the manager.

The Soft Dollar Policies provide that a dealer may not use any portion of the commissions earned on brokerage transactions executed on behalf of the manager as payment for goods or services provided to the manager, other than order execution services or investment decision-making services. It also provides that a manager may not direct brokerage transactions to a dealer as payment for goods or services provided to the manager, other than order execution services or investment decision-making services. As there is concern about widening the categories of permissible soft dollar transactions, the OSC has decided that staff should only grant exemptions on a case-by-case basis because they are contemplated by the OSC Policy 1.9.

---

[6]"Order execution services" means (1) order execution and (2) services directly related to order execution, such as clearance, settlement, and custody, whether the services are provided by a dealer directly or by a third party.

[7]"Investment decision-making services" means (1) advice as to the value of securities and the advisability of effecting transactions and securities, (2) analysis and reports concerning securities, portfolio strategy, performance, issuers, industries, or economic or political factors and trends, and (3) databases or software to the extent they are designed mainly to support the services referred to in (1) and (2), whether the services are provided by a dealer directly or by a third party.

[8]A manager is a person or company entrusted with the management of a portfolio or fund on behalf of third-party beneficiaries.

Disclosure. On request, managers must disclose to the relevant commission, beneficiary, or trustee of a portfolio or fund the names of the persons or companies that have provided any investment decision-making services to the manager and a summary of the nature of those services that were paid for by commissions on brokerage transactions.

Dealer as Principal. When transacting as principal, a dealer may not buy securities from or sell securities to a manager if the price of the securities has been adjusted to compensate the dealer for goods or services provided to the manager, other than order execution services or investment decision-making services.

Mutual Funds. Similarly, mutual fund managers may not pay dealers for the distribution of shares or units of the mutual fund by directing brokerage transactions to the dealer or, at the request of the dealer, to a third party, unless the commission rates charged are equivalent to those which would have been normally charged by the dealer if the dealer did not distribute shares or units of the mutual fund and if certain disclosure requirements are met. In addition, such payments cannot be made as inducement or reward for the dealer or the principal distributor selling or having sold securities of the mutual fund or maintaining or having maintained particular levels of securities of the mutual fund in accounts of clients. Furthermore, all brokerage must be directed through representatives designated as the institutional representatives of the dealer, as opposed to retail representatives.

The offering documents of a mutual fund must disclose the actual use of commission dollars, including the names of the persons or companies who have provided any investment decision-making services to the mutual fund, a summary of the nature of those services, and a best estimate of the aggregate amount of any commissions on brokerage transactions that were directed to dealers since the date of the last offering documents for which the commissions were linked to the distribution of shares or units of the mutual fund by the dealers.

Transactions. Assuming XYZ is doing business in Canada, XYZ is charged with the responsibility under AIMR's Standards of Professional Conduct of knowing and complying with the relevant provisions of these laws.

Transaction 1—Use of Client Brokerage to Pay for Desks and Office Equipment. The use of client brokerage to pay for desks and office equipment would not qualify as "investment decision-making services" or "order execution services" as these terms are defined by the Soft Dollar Policies. Thus, this transaction would be prohibited.

Transactions 2–4. Each of the proposed transactions would likely satisfy the OSC's definition of "investment decision-making services."

Transaction 2—Use of Client Brokerage to Pay for Trading Room Television Sets (Including Individual Financial News Services and Cable or Satellite Providers). These services provide an analysis of industries or economic or political factors and trends. Therefore the services fit within the definition of investment decision-making services.

Transaction 3—Use of Client Brokerage to Pay for the Bloomberg Service. The Bloomberg Service focuses on real-time market news and analysis. Thus, the service fits within the definition of investment decision-making services.

Transaction 4—Use of Client Brokerage to Pay for Software and Computer Work Stations. The definition of investment decision-making services specifically includes databases or software to services such as analysis and reports concerning economic trends. The software is designed to analyze economic trends in industries followed by the firm. Accordingly, this part of Transaction 4 would be allowed. Although the work station is not specifically included in the definition of investment decision-making services, it is required to support the software and would be allowed by implication.

Transaction 5—Directing of Brokerage by ERISA Client to Benefit Plan Trustees. In Canada, a private pension plan governed by provincial pension benefits standards legislation or the federal Pension Benefits Standards Act would be the approximate equivalent of an ERISA plan under U.S. law. The Ontario Pension Benefits Act provides that the administrator of a pension plan is not entitled to any benefit from the pension plan other than pension benefits, ancillary benefits, or a refund of contributions and fees and expenses related to the administration of the pension plan and permitted by the common law or provided for in the pension plan.

Because Transaction 5 confers a benefit on the trustee of the pension fund, rather than on the beneficiaries or members of the pension plan, and a specific benefit is not being conferred on the administrator of the pension plan, this transaction would be prohibited.

Of interest is the Canadian securities administrators' concern regarding the practice whereby a pension plan sponsor requires the pension plan manager to direct brokerage transactions to a particular dealer who will use a portion of the commission income from this transaction to provide the sponsor with goods or services.

Transaction 6—Directing of Brokerage by Public Pension Plan to Obtain Cash Credits for the Plan. No direct parallel exists in Canada to a

U.S. "public pension plan" concept wherein the plan is not subject to some form of provincial or federal pension standards legislation (i.e., most public sector plans are subject to pension benefit standards legislation).

Transaction 6 would not violate Canadian legislation. Because the goods and services contemplated in Transaction 6 would not be provided to the manager from the dealer, the Soft Dollar Policy would not be violated and the manager would not be in violation of the manager's general obligation to benefit beneficiaries.

Transaction 7—Directing of Brokerage by an Institutional Investor in a Hedge Fund to Compensate the Broker for Research Provided to the Investor. The term "hedge fund" is not defined under Canadian securities law; the marketplace uses this term to refer to funds that leverage their assets through the use of derivative contracts.

In this transaction, the dealer is not receiving payment for goods or services provided to the manager. Nevertheless, the manager has a general obligation to act in the best interests of the beneficiaries of the fund, including the requirement to satisfy "best execution" obligations when directing brokerage. Consequently, commissions may only be used as payment for goods and services that are for the benefit of the beneficiaries. Directing brokerage at the request of one investor will not satisfy these obligations.

Transaction 8—Directing of a Portion of One Fund's Brokerage by Three Investment Companies to Benefit All Three Companies. As in Transaction 7, the manager must act to the benefit of the beneficiaries. Because this transaction appears to benefit the beneficiaries, the transaction would not be prohibited.

Summary. Transactions 1, 5, and 7 are prohibited by the Soft Dollar Policies. Transaction 1 provides the manager with a good that does not qualify as an "investment decision-making service." Transaction 5 provides the plan trustee with a benefit that the trustee is not entitled to receive under pension benefits standards legislation. Similarly, Transaction 7 uses brokerage commissions in a manner that is not in the best interests of the beneficiaries of the fund. These transactions, therefore, do not "survive" XYZ's initial analysis under applicable Canadian law.

Sample Reports

The following sample reports are intended to clarify the disclosure obligations contemplated under Standard VI, which imposes on an Investment Manager the duty to provide certain information on Client request. Where relevant, reference is provided to the applicable Standard.

Sample Report A

Client Name: Date of Report:
Investment Firm:
Time Period Covered (12 months):

1. Total Dollar Amount of Commissions Generated from Client Account, Detailed by Broker [C.2.a.]

Broker X:	$230,000
Broker Y:	$650,000
Broker Z:	$120,000
Total Amount:	$1,000,000

2. Total Dollar Amount of Brokerage Directed by Client [C.2.b.] $267,000

Sample Report B

Client Name: Date of Report:
Investment Firm:
Time Period Covered (12 months):

Description of Research Purchased through Soft Dollar Arrangements on a Firmwide Basis, Detailed by Broker [C.1]

Broker A
- Access to health care analysts
- Access to biotech analysts

Broker B
- Bloomberg services
- Reuters services
- Oil industry reports and analyses

Broker C
- Market analysis of fixed-income instruments

Topical Study:
Fiduciary Duty

The concept of fiduciary duty is central to legal thought and applies directly to many fields. The term has no comprehensive or clear definition, however. To hold someone to a fiduciary duty generally means to hold them to a higher standard of loyalty and care than the standard to which most people are held. Persons are held to a fiduciary duty when they are responsible for the care of the assets of others, as in the case of portfolio managers, or when they are responsible for the personal affairs of others, as in the case of lawyers. The extent of a fiduciary's duty depends on each particular relationship.

The fiduciary must always act prudently and with discretion regarding the assets of others. A fiduciary is charged with having more knowledge than the average person. Conflicts of interest may arise between the fiduciary's self-interest and the interests the fiduciary is charged with protecting. Imposition of a fiduciary duty attempts to eliminate any conflicts or improprieties by imposing a high standard of loyalty and care on the fiduciary.

AIMR members, entrusted with assets that belong to others, are charged with a fiduciary duty. This topical study highlights the issues that fiduciaries should address, but members should consult an attorney for expert advice on specific situations.

Fiduciary Duties around the World

This study addresses fiduciary responsibilities primarily in the United States, but the concept of fiduciary duty is not exclusive to the United States. Because everyday business affairs always involve relationships of trust and confidence, many countries have developed the concept of fiduciary duty. AIMR members are expected to follow any fiduciary duties imposed on them by their country or province. In the absence of any law, AIMR members' activities should be governed by the Code of Ethics and Standards of Professional Conduct. Members should always follow fiduciary principles of discretion, loyalty, and care and must always act in the client's best interest.

Trust Management

Trust management is the area that generated the concept of fiduciary duty and sets the standard for all laws regarding fiduciaries. In the landmark Massachusetts Supreme Court case, *Harvard v. Amory*, the court instructed the trustee, as fiduciary,

> to observe how men of prudence, discretion and intelligence manage their own affairs, not in regard to speculation, but in regard to the permanent disposition of their funds, considering the probable income, as well as the probable safety of the capital to be invested.

This instruction became known as the Prudent Man Rule.

In general, the Prudent Man Rule has been construed as a directive to preserve capital and avoid risk, but the interpretations of this directive have evolved over the years. Earlier this century, the courts in the United States sought to force trustees to preserve capital and avoid risk by allowing trustees to invest only in certain assets. The legal list statutes that were created detailed the assets that were suitable for investment of trust monies. The lists were usually brief because they allowed investment in only low-risk instruments, such as certificates of deposit, savings bonds, and Treasury bills. All other types of investments were automatically considered imprudent. Although this approach mitigated some types of risk, it did not take into account the effects of inflation and other factors that affect the portfolio.

Most U.S. jurisdictions have adopted some form of the Prudent Man Rule that directs a fiduciary, in the absence of provisions in the trust or other statutes to the contrary, to make only such investments as a prudent person would make in pursuit of the preservation of capital and regularity of income. Some investments are restricted; for example, the purchase of securities for purposes of speculation, the purchase of securities in new and untried enterprises, and the purchase of land for resale are all deemed improper.

Only recently have the U.S. courts begun to acknowledge that the legal list statutes and the narrow directive to preserve capital and avoid risk constrain trustees' ability to help the trusts they administer outpace inflation. Modern portfolio theory (MPT) dictates that trustees consider a portfolio in its entirety, and not just on an investment-by-investment basis, because a single investment standing alone may seem risky, but when it is placed in the context of the overall portfolio, it can actually help to mitigate the portfolio's overall risk. Courts in the United States are increasingly acknowledging the value of MPT and the desirability of looking at each investment as composing part of a whole portfolio rather than standing alone. This view is articulated in the Prudent Investor Rule, under which, the trustee as fiduciary must:

- adhere to fundamental fiduciary duties of loyalty, impartiality, and prudence;
- maintain overall portfolio risk at a reasonable level. That is, risk and return objectives must be reasonable and suitable to the trust. The trade-

off between risk and return is the fiduciary's central concern;

- provide for the reasonable diversification of trust investments. The Prudent Investor Rule places no limits on the types of investments; the trustee can invest in any asset as long as it plays an appropriate role in achieving the risk–return objectives of the trust and meets the other requirements of prudent investing;
- act with prudence in deciding whether and how to delegate authority to experts and in selecting and supervising agents. This part of the rule is a radical departure from earlier law that frowned on any delegation by fiduciaries;
- be cost conscious when investing. The trustee should incur only costs that are reasonable in amount and appropriate to the investment responsibilities of the trusteeship. The duty to be cost conscious has been interpreted as limiting the trustee to those expenses that are necessary or appropriate to carry out the purposes of the trust and are authorized by the terms of the trust. Cost-conscious administration should take account of market efficiency and should compare transaction costs resulting from a particular strategy with the strategy's reasonably expected returns.

The Prudent Investor Rule is on its way to being adopted in almost every U.S. jurisdiction. Its main principles are already reflected in statutory language dealing with the management of various types of charitable, pension, and public funds.

Trustees recognize that a conflict of interests often exists between the primary or current beneficiaries of a trust and the remaindermen (secondary or later beneficiaries of the trust). Current life-income beneficiaries would prefer to receive a high rate of current income; remaindermen would rather have growth and stability of principal. Trustees have a duty to exercise their best skill and care to serve all beneficiaries impartially and with equal consideration of their needs. The trustee must usually invest to produce income without risking loss of principal.

Management of a trust's assets raises many other issues for consideration. One important consideration is the effect of taxes on the trust's assets. If not properly planned for, taxes can significantly reduce a portfolio's actual returns. The advice of an accountant or tax attorney may prove invaluable in evaluating a trust's management. Another consideration is the applicability of legal requirements in the daily administration of the trust. For example, in order to keep a check on the trustee's management of the trust, some states require trustees to submit a periodic accounting of trust assets to the court. Trustees should check with their attorney for the details of this requirement.

ERISA and Fiduciary Duty

The Employee Retirement Income Security Act (ERISA), enacted in the United States in 1974, has become a major force in fiduciary duty law. The principles and procedures that are required of fiduciaries under ERISA are excellent guidelines for any trustee or fiduciary. The ERISA laws are remarkably complex, however. Members are strongly urged to consult an attorney who specializes in ERISA law for any specific situations that may arise.

ERISA governs every qualified private employee benefit plan in the United States. The trustee of an employee stock-option plan is subject to the same fiduciary duties as an ERISA trustee and must follow the plan's directions. It does not govern church plans, governmental plans, plans only for officers of a corporation, or plans to establish compliance with worker's compensation, unemployment compensation, or disability insurance laws.

ERISA requires that every person who is a fiduciary to the plan must carry out his or her duties in accordance with the plan documents and laws governing the plan and according to ERISA's definition of fiduciary duty. Under ERISA, a person is a fiduciary if he or she

- exercises any discretionary authority or discretionary control with respect to the management of the plan or exercises any authority or control with respect to the management or disposition of plan assets;
- renders investment advice for a fee or other compensation, direct or indirect, with respect to any plan asset or has any authority or responsibility to do so;
- has discretionary authority or discretionary responsibility in the administration of the plan.

A person or entity can also be named a fiduciary by the plan instrument, appointed pursuant to plan provisions, or identified as a fiduciary by a person who is an employer or employee organization of the plan, acting alone or together.

ERISA trustees cannot delegate their fiduciary duties. A fiduciary can delegate investment management responsibilities to a qualified investment manager as long as the investment manager accepts such appointment and acknowledges that the manager is a plan fiduciary. The fiduciary should select an investment manager prudently, have prudent benchmarks or guidelines for the manager, and monitor the manager's performance. If a fiduciary or named fiduciary delegates his or her fiduciary responsibility, the fiduciary may still be liable for a breach of fiduciary duty under certain circumstances.

Fiduciary responsibilities under ERISA are clear. Fiduciaries must discharge their duties with respect to the plan

- solely in the interest of plan participants and beneficiaries;
- for the exclusive purpose of providing benefits to participants and their beneficiaries and defraying reasonable plan expenses;
- with the care, skill, prudence, and diligence under the circumstances then prevailing that a prudent person acting in like capacity and familiar with such matters would use in the conduct of an enterprise of a like character and with like aims (the Prudent Expert Rule);
- by diversifying the investments of the plan so as to minimize the risk of large losses, unless doing so is clearly not prudent under the circumstances;
- in accordance with the governing plan documents, as long as they are consistent with ERISA.

The ERISA fiduciary needs to be as prudent as the average expert, not simply as the average person. The fiduciary must act solely in the best interest of plan participants and beneficiaries and use all available care, skill, prudence, and diligence.

The duty to act with prudence pertains not only to the substance of a fiduciary's decisions but also to the procedures that an ERISA fiduciary must follow. ERISA fiduciaries must adhere to the following prudent procedures:

- establish a written investment policy for the plan;
- diversify plan assets;
- make investment decisions with the skill and care of a prudent expert;
- monitor investment performance;
- control investment expenses;
- avoid prohibited transactions.

Although the ERISA fiduciary duty allows for a fairly broad range of investments, it does prohibit certain transactions. An ERISA fiduciary can never

- deal with plan assets in his or her own interest or for his or her own account (self-dealing);
- act in a transaction involving the plan on behalf of a party with interests adverse to the plan (conflict of interest);
- receive any compensation for his or her own personal account from any party dealing with the plan in connection with a transaction involving plan assets (kickbacks).

Some transactions between a plan and a party in interest are generally prohibited. A party in interest is generally any person or entity who is or may be able to influence the plan or whose transactions with the plan could constitute a conflict of interest. With some narrow exceptions, a fiduciary cannot cause the plan to engage in a transaction that constitutes a direct or indirect

- sale, exchange, or leasing of any property between the plan and a party in interest;
- lending of money or other extension of credit between the plan and a party in interest;
- furnishing of goods, services, or facilities between the plan and a party in interest;
- transfer of any assets of the plan or the use of any assets of the plan to a party in interest;
- acquisition on behalf of the plan of any security or real property of the fiduciary's employer in violation of ERISA guidelines [406(a)(1)(E)].

However, under ERISA, a fiduciary may

- receive a benefit to which he or she is entitled as a participant or beneficiary, as long as it is computed and paid consistently with the plan terms;
- receive reasonable compensation for services rendered and reimbursement for expenses incurred;
- be an officer, employee, agent, or representative of a party in interest.

One common type of pension plan governed by ERISA is the defined-contribution plan, in which the beneficiary exercises control over the assets in his or her account. If a beneficiary does, in fact, exert meaningful, independent control over the assets in his or her account, then the fiduciary of the plan will not be liable for the loss or breach of fiduciary duty that is the result of the beneficiary's exercise of control. The fiduciary must still adhere to the fiduciary duties as applicable to the plan, however, and all AIMR members who manage assets of defined-contribution plans must follow the tenets of the Code and Standards.

Investment in an employee pension or benefit plan is probably the most important investment that the average employee makes. Employees' present and future quality of life depend on their investments in, or contributions to, the pension or employee benefit plan and how the plan is managed. ERISA-covered employee pension or benefit plans are complex in nature, and because of their importance in the employee's life, an employee may ask for advice or guidance on the pension or benefit plan. Therefore, members should take note that the rendering of investment advice to a plan can cause the person giving the advice to become a fiduciary under ERISA and expose that person to liability as a fiduciary under ERISA. A person gives investment advice under ERISA if he or she, for a fee or other compensation,

- gives advice about the value of plan assets or makes recommendations as to the advisability of investment in, purchasing, or selling assets and, either directly or indirectly,

- has discretionary authority or control with respect to purchasing plan assets or
- gives such advice on a regular basis—under a mutual agreement, arrangement, or understanding—that the advice will serve as the primary basis for investment decisions and that the advice will be individualized on the basis of the particular needs of the plan regarding such matters as, among other things, investment policies or strategy, overall portfolio composition, or diversification of plan assets.

Note that "for a fee or other compensation" is interpreted rather broadly. Fees do not need to be stated explicitly; all fees involved in the transaction are available for scrutiny as possible fees or other compensation.

Public Pension Plans

Trustees or sponsors of public pension plans are subject to many of the same requirements as fiduciaries of trusts and private pension plans. Most jurisdictions in the United States have adopted laws or guidelines for public pension plans that closely follow ERISA mandates, although the laws vary widely among jurisdictions. A member who holds a fiduciary position for a public pension plan must scrutinize any laws and state statutes governing the public organization to determine what type of duty is owed and to whom the duty is owed. A member who is a fiduciary for a public pension plan must also follow the guidelines set out by the governing organization for the management of its pension assets. In the absence of specific direction, the fiduciary of this type of plan should follow the basic tenet of fiduciary laws: loyalty, impartiality, and prudence when making decisions involving plan assets.

Generally, fiduciaries of public pension plans have two broad duties. First and foremost, fiduciaries of public pension plans must always act with loyalty to fund participants and their beneficiaries. Second, they must administer the funds in a prudent manner—by following any specific restrictions on investments and by adhering to general trust law regarding acceptable standards for investment conduct.

The statutes that govern public funds differ greatly from state to state. Many states prohibit any conflicts of interest, but some state statutes explicitly allow the governing body of the fund to specify investment actions that may result in conflicts. For example, a state may allow a tax-exempt employee pension fund to invest in tax-exempt bonds issued by its representative local government. When making investments, however, fiduciaries of such public funds should always weigh the available net total returns from taxable issues against the tax-exempt municipal bonds.

Moreover, such transactions may be detrimental to the interest of the public employees who are beneficiaries of the plan if the plan receives the lower rate of interest typically paid by tax-exempt bonds while local citizens are gaining from collateral benefits municipal bonds provide, such as improved services, new jobs, lower taxes, or increased job security for public employees.

To bolster the local economy, state or local governments may also allow, or even require, retirement plans under their jurisdiction to invest in local projects or through local businesses. Such investments may sometimes seem imprudent; they can result in less competent plan management or the assumption of higher risk. Some argue that this perception is not justified because the investments provide collateral benefits to the plan participants. Others argue that collateral benefits cannot justify imprudent investments: The plan participants cannot choose the investment, and participants should not forfeit a portion of their future retirement income for nebulous current collateral returns that may not directly benefit them.

Although state statutes may allow for certain conflicts of interest, AIMR members should note that they are subject to the high standards of the Code and Standards. Therefore, when acting as fiduciaries to public plans being operated under specifications and guidelines that may result in investment conflicts, AIMR members must be aware of the potential conflicts, establish the legality of directions and restrictions (by independent counsel if necessary), and remain faithful to the personal and professional conduct specified under the Code and Standards.

Money Management

Investment managers and advisors of funds, whether mutual funds or separately managed accounts, are also held to a fiduciary duty. Such advisors have a fiduciary duty to the fund's investors or the beneficiaries of the separate accounts. The U.S. Investment Advisers Act of 1940 (Advisers Act) states that advisors cannot

- employ any device or scheme to defraud any client or prospective client;
- engage in any transaction or course of business that may operate as a fraud or deceit upon any client or prospective client;
- engage in transactions as a principal or as an agent in a client's account without first disclosing the transaction to the client and receiving the client's consent;
- engage in any act or course of business that is fraudulent, deceptive, or manipulative.

In *SEC v. Capital Gains Research Bureau*, the Supreme Court of the United States stated that the Advisers Act reflects a Congressional recognition of the "delicate" fiduciary nature of an investment advisory relationship, and the intent to eliminate, or at least to expose, all conflicts of interest.

The advisor as fiduciary has an affirmative duty of honesty and good faith as well as a duty to use reasonable care to avoid misrepresentations. The advisor as fiduciary must act solely in the best interests of the client and must make full and fair disclosure of all material facts, particularly when the advisor's interests may conflict with the client's interests.

In keeping with the principles espoused in the Code and Standards, the member investment advisor must always

- have a reasonable and independent basis for investment advice;
- obtain best execution for clients' securities transactions when the advisor is in a position to direct brokerage transactions;
- ensure that investment advice and actions are suitable to the client's objectives, needs, and circumstances;
- avoid all misrepresentations;
- remain loyal to the client and put the client first in all dealings;
- disclose all material facts and real or potential conflicts of interest.

Brokers and Dealers

Brokers and dealers are also held to a higher standard of care than the average person. Although this standard of care has not been expressly articulated as a fiduciary duty, broker/dealers are liable for knowingly or recklessly engaging in excessive trading in customers' accounts (churning), for accepting funds when they are insolvent, for manipulating the market, and for fraud under the "shingle theory." The shingle theory states that broker/dealers should be subject to strict standards because they are "hanging out their shingles" (advertising themselves) as market professionals. The theory states that inherent in the relationships between broker/dealers and their clients is the representation that the customer will be dealt with fairly. Broker/dealers are in a position to exploit their customers' trust and ignorance, and therefore, they are held to a higher duty of care.

AIMR's Code and Standards do not make distinctions among brokers, dealers, and investment advisors when it comes to fiduciary duties toward customers. All members must comply with the conduct required of them by the Code and Standards or applicable law, whichever is higher.

Analysts

Although analysts may not have as much client contact as other investment professionals or as many advisory responsibilities as investment advisors, as fiduciaries, they still have basic responsibilities to their employer and their employer's clients. They owe the same duty of independent judgment, adequate disclosure, and fair dealing as investment professionals with client contact. Members who are financial analysts should strive to maintain independence and objectivity when undertaking their analyses.

Charitable Organizations and UMIFA

Directors and officers of charitable organizations and managers of charitable fund assets are fiduciaries. Fiduciaries for charitable organizations around the world must follow any spending and investment policies that their organization has adopted. Some organizations have strict investment policies that limit investment options to certain types or classes of investments; for example, some charitable organizations encourage "social investing"; other organizations do not take social factors into consideration when making investment decisions. Some organizations have aggressive policies that, rather than prohibiting investments by type, look to the portfolio's total risk and return. Many organizations have spending policies that dictate the amount the charitable organization can spend. As charitable organizations have grown in size and importance to the economy, government regulation of them has increased.

When serving as fiduciaries for charitable organizations, whether in the United States or not, members must first look to applicable law for guidance as to their duties. In addition, members must always follow any spending and investment policies that the organization has adopted. Finally, members also must follow the general principles of fiduciary duty: discretion, loyalty, and care.

Fiduciaries of charitable organizations based in the United States may be bound by the Uniform Management of Institutional Funds Act (UMIFA). The general principles of UMIFA conform to the principles of fiduciary duty espoused by MPT. Charities governed by UMIFA are able to invest in a wide variety of assets and are not restricted by legal list statutes.

Under UMIFA, fiduciaries are held to a standard of ordinary business care and prudence under the facts and circumstances prevailing at the time of the actions or decision. UMIFA drafters intended the standard to be broad enough to allow trustees to adapt to rapidly changing economic climates. The standard of ordinary business care is generally comparable to that of a director of a corporation rather than the stricter standard to which a private trustee is held. The ordinary business care standard does not dictate that the fiduciary act as a prudent man or prudent investor would but, rather, requires only that directors exercise ordinary and reasonable care in their duties and act with honesty and good faith. Fiduciaries must consider the long- and short-term institutional needs and resources of the charity in carrying out its purpose—the charity's present and anticipated financial requirements, expected total return on its investments, price-level trends, and general economic conditions. However, states that have adopted UMIFA do not interpret the ordinary business care standard in a uniform manner, so fiduciaries should consult an attorney for relevant law in their state.

A governing board of trustees in a state that has adopted UMIFA can delegate the management of its endowment to investment professionals, but the trustees retain the duty to formulate investment policy. Courts that have decided cases under UMIFA have also found a duty to properly supervise the investment professionals and the investments that they make. Trustees should take an active role in overseeing fund managers and reviewing investments to ensure that the objectives of the funds are met.

Social Investing, Relationship Investing, and the Fiduciary

Fiduciaries often feel pressure from various constituencies to engage in social investing—investing with a view toward the social or political statements made by such an investment. For example, some fund participants may want managers to invest only in those organizations that are "green" or "environmentally conscious"; other constituencies may ask for investing only in companies or countries that meet certain social or political criteria; still other constituencies may want to avoid certain products, such as tobacco or firearms. Members should keep in mind that the fiduciary duty of prudence is paramount and dictates that trustees judge investments according to the following criteria: risk and return, asset diversification, and cost-conscious investing. These principles should come first when making an investment decision.

ERISA guidelines address the issue of social investing directly. ERISA guidelines issued by the U.S. Department of Labor state that the ERISA prudence standard requires a fiduciary to make investment decisions first on grounds of economic and investment merit. Consideration of social factors may be an incidental, but never primary, consideration of investments that are equal in economic and financial terms.

Public pension funds may feel pressure to screen investments for social attributes. They must first adhere to fiduciary duties, however, and any specific investment guidelines stated for them in their governing statutes and plan documents.

Relationship investing considers the potential of a company to produce greater returns if the fund takes an active approach in influencing the management of the company's affairs, either through the size of the fund's ownership position on its own or through combining its position with other ownership positions. Again, fiduciaries should consider the economic benefits of such an investment before engaging in relationship investing.

This consideration should include the costs associated with the approach, such as costs for attending shareholder meetings and actively monitoring the company affairs. Also, the level of investment necessary to establish influence in a corporation's affairs may be antithetical to the requirement for diversification of overall plan assets.

Relationship investing is allowed under ERISA. An investment strategy that attempts to influence a company's management is consistent with ERISA fiduciary duty if the fiduciary concludes that there is a reasonable expectation that such attempts are likely to enhance the value of the plan's investment in the corporation. ERISA fiduciaries should check ERISA guidelines for the voting of proxies, which are plan assets.

Another important consideration in relationship investing is the conflict of interest that may arise when a fiduciary of a fund that holds a large block of a corporation's stock also serves as a trustee or director of that corporation. The director's duty is to the shareholders in general; the fund fiduciary, as trustee/shareholder, desires to help his or her fund specifically. Fiduciaries should take special care to ensure that both interests are given due consideration.

Glossary of Important Terms

ERISA: Employee Retirement Income Security Act, enacted in 1974. ERISA governs all qualified private employee benefit plans in the United States. The U.S. Department of Labor decides ERISA fiduciary issues. Because ERISA affects many persons and plans controlling millions of dollars in assets, decisions on and interpretations of fiduciary law under ERISA influence all aspects of fiduciary duties.

Fiduciary: One who holds a relationship of trust or confidence. A person who has a fiduciary duty to another must act in the other's best interest, must maintain the other's trust and confidences, and must act with discretion. A fiduciary is charged with a higher standard of care and a higher degree of knowledge than the average person.

Legal List Statute: A statute that enumerates what particular types or classes of investment are acceptable and what types or classes of investment are prohibited. For example, a statute may state that government bonds are acceptable investments for a fiduciary but that corporate bonds are unacceptable.

Modern Portfolio Theory: Increasingly popular theory of trust investment and portfolio management that looks more toward the portfolio as a whole and less toward the prudence of a single investment in the portfolio.

Ordinary Business Care: Standard that requires fiduciaries to exercise ordinary and reasonable care in their duties, use honesty and good faith, and act with prudence in light of the facts and circumstances prevailing at the time of the action or decision. This standard does not require the fiduciary to act as a prudent man or prudent investor would act. The standard is interpreted differently by states that have enacted UMIFA.

Prudent Expert Rule: Rule by which ERISA fiduciaries are governed: They must act with the care, skill, prudence, and diligence under the circumstances then prevailing that a prudent person acting in a like capacity and familiar with such matters would use in the conduct of an enterprise of a like character and with like aims. The Prudent Expert Rule holds the fiduciary to the standard of a person familiar with the relevant matters, not simply a prudent person in general. This standard applies to fiduciaries managing investments under ERISA.

Prudent Investor Rule: Modern conception of the Prudent Man Rule that requires a trustee to act prudently and with caution, discretion, loyalty, and care but does not restrict the assets in which a trustee can invest. The Prudent Investor Rule makes heavy use of Modern Portfolio Theory and applies the standard of prudence to the entire portfolio rather than to individual investments. It identifies the fiduciary's central consideration as the trade-off between risk and return. The Prudent Investor Rule is fast becoming the standard for fiduciaries.

Prudent Man Rule: The baseline standard used in determining fiduciary duty. Under this rule, first espoused in *Harvard v. Amory*, the fiduciary has an obligation to manage the assets entrusted to him or her with the same care and discretion that a prudent person would. How prudent people would manage their affairs has been the subject of much debate. Generally, however, the duty has been defined as avoidance of undue risk, preservation of capital, and acting in the best interests of the beneficiaries of the trust.

Relationship Investing: Investing with the goal of influencing the management of the company in which the investment is made.

Shingle Theory: Legal theory embraced by U.S. courts that once a broker or dealer "hangs out a shingle" or depicts himself or herself to the public as capable of providing brokerage/securities dealing services, the implication is that he or she has the back-office and other capabilities to perform the duties of an investment professional and thus should be held to a higher standard of care.

Topical Study:
Insider Trading

AIMR members, CFA charterholders, and candidates in the CFA Program are required to comply with the laws governing the use of material nonpublic information and the activity commonly known as insider trading or insider dealing. Because investment professionals have frequent contact with corporate insiders who have information relating to issuers and their securities, their potential exposure to nonpublic information is great. Investment professionals must, therefore, be aware of and understand the laws governing their conduct in dealing with such information.

What Is Inside Information?

"Inside information" is generally defined as information about a company that is both material and nonpublic. Under the securities laws of the United States, information is material if a reasonable investor is likely to consider it significant in making an investment decision or if the information is reasonably certain to have a substantial impact on the market price of a company's securities. Information is nonpublic if it has not been generally disclosed to the marketplace. To become public, information must be disseminated so that it is reasonably available to investors generally. The disclosure of information by a corporate insider to a select group of analysts is not sufficient to make that information public under the U.S. securities laws.

In practice, materiality is broadly defined. A party is unlikely to successfully defend an insider trading accusation on the grounds that the information at issue was not material. In the context of publicly traded securities, market price impact is a widely used test of materiality; if the disclosure of a fact is reasonably certain to have a substantial effect on the market price of the security, the fact is material. With respect to face-to-face dealings in securities that have no open and developed market, the test is whether the party on the opposite side of the transaction would have considered the information significant to his or her investment decision.

Information regarding the following topics should be considered material in the insider trading context:

- a forthcoming dividend declaration or omission;
- corporate reorganizations or takeovers;
- the acquisition or loss of a major contract;
- a major purchase or sale of company assets;
- an event of default;
- knowledge of forthcoming press coverage of a company's affairs,

whether positive or negative;

- substantial increases or decreases in earnings projections;
- substantial mineral finds by a mining company, regulatory approvals of a product (for example, U.S. Federal Drug Administration approval of a pharmaceutical product), and issuance or denial of patents (to technology or software companies, for example).

Other types of information have also formed the basis for insider trading accusations.

The sanctions for violations of insider trading rules can be severe. Therefore, any investment professional who comes into possession of information about a company that may meet the definition of inside information should consult with a supervisor, compliance officer, or counsel before engaging in transactions in that company's securities.

Liability for Insider Trading

No statutory definition of insider trading exists in the United States. Instead, the Securities and Exchange Commission (SEC) and the courts have developed theories of insider trading liability under the general antifraud provisions of Section 10(b) and Rule 10b-5. These theories have evolved in a series of cases spanning nearly 30 years.

Although this topical study focuses on the law of the United States, nearly every country with developed securities markets has enacted legislation prohibiting insider dealing. Given the considerable variations in the laws of different jurisdictions, consulting counsel in the countries where one is trading securities is advisable to ensure compliance with the insider dealing laws. Note also that the jurisdictional reach of the SEC and courts has been expanding, so even parties who believe that their trading activities are outside the United States may be subject to sanctions under U.S. laws when those activities have an impact on U.S. markets.

The Traditional Theory in the United States. Prior to 1980, nearly everyone who was in possession of inside information was prohibited from trading on it or communicating it to anyone. After the 1980 U.S. Supreme Court decision in *Chiarella v. United States*, a securities trader cannot be held guilty of fraud for failing to disclose material nonpublic information in his or her possession prior to the consummation of a transaction unless the trader has a duty to disclose that information. The mere possession of material nonpublic information does not give rise to a duty to disclose that information. The duty to disclose information or abstain from trading on the basis of that information arises only when a fiduciary relationship or a similar relationship of trust and confidence is involved between parties to a transaction. The classic example of a relationship resulting in the duty to "disclose or abstain" is that between corporate officers and directors, on one side, and the shareholders of the corporation, on the other.

Under the traditional theory, liability may extend to parties who are not typical insiders of a corporation when those parties obtain access to corporate information by virtue of their special confidential relationships with the corporation. Such parties are sometimes called "temporary insiders." Typical temporary insiders are lawyers, accountants, investment bankers, financial consultants, and financial analysts working for rating agencies or as underwriter representatives in securities offerings, who are given access to confidential information solely for corporate purposes and with the expectation that they will not disclose that information. Insider trading cases against such parties often arise in connection with mergers and acquisitions but are not limited to that context.

Liability under the traditional theory was extended to "tippees" by the Supreme Court's decision in *Dirks v. Securities and Exchange Commission*. A tippee can be any person, including a financial analyst, who learns material nonpublic information from a corporate insider. Tippee liability derives from the liability of the insider; the tippee is sometimes said to "inherit" the insider's fiduciary duty. Liability can be imposed on a tippee only when an insider breaches a fiduciary duty to shareholders by disclosing information to the tippee and when the tippee knows, or should know, that the insider is acting improperly by disclosing the information. Thus, under this theory, an analyst can be held liable for insider trading only when the source of information is breaching a fiduciary duty to the corporation's shareholders by sharing the information with the analyst.

To determine whether an insider has breached a fiduciary duty, U.S. courts have examined whether the insider "tipped" the information with an improper purpose—that is, with the expectation of some personal benefit from the disclosure. The personal benefit to the insider is often financial, but a breach of duty may also be found in the following circumstances:

- the tipper's reputation in the financial community is enhanced by the disclosure;
- a relationship exists between the insider and the tippee that suggests a quid pro quo from the insider to the tippee;
- the insider makes a "gift" of confidential information to a relative or friend.

In 1980, the SEC adopted Rule 14e-3 under the Securities and Exchange Act of 1934, which specifically prohibits trading on or communicating material nonpublic information relating to proposed tender offers. Although U.S. courts disagree somewhat about the proper limits of

Rule 14e-3, the prevailing view is that a breach of fiduciary duty by an insider need not occur for insider trading liability to result under Rule 14e-3. Investment professionals should take particular care when dealing with information about tender offers, as the potential for liability for insider trading is even greater under Rule 14e-3 than under Rule 10b-5. In *United States v. Chestman*, for example, the defendant was convicted of insider trading under Rule 14e-3 whereas his convictions under Rule 10b-5 were overturned.

The Misappropriation Theory. Under the traditional theory in the United States, insider trading liability can arise only when the person trading has (or, in the case of a tippee, inherits) a duty to the company whose securities are traded and breaches that duty. Other than situations involving tippee liability, the traditional theory does not reach trading by individuals who have no duties to a securities issuer, even if those individuals are trading on the basis of material nonpublic information. The U.S. Supreme Court has adopted the "misappropriation theory" of insider trading liability to reach the conduct of such individuals in the case of *U.S. v. O'Hagan*.

Under the misappropriation theory, a person commits securities fraud when he or she misappropriates material nonpublic information in breach of a duty owed to an employer or any other person who is not the securities issuer and uses that information in a securities transaction or communicates it to others. Unlike the traditional theory, securities fraud may be found even if the violator does not owe any duty to the shareholders of the issuing corporation or have any relationship at all to those shareholders. Under the misappropriation theory, any person who trades on the basis of material nonpublic information misappropriated from another person can be guilty of insider trading.

In the O'Hagan case, an attorney working on a hostile tender offer was convicted of insider trading under the misappropriation theory. O'Hagan used information entrusted to him to purchase securities for his personal account. O'Hagan was not an insider of the target company, but his situation satisfied the two elements of misappropriation: (1) deception of the person from whom he received the inside information; and (2) the deception was "in connection with the purchase or sale of a security."

Liability under the misappropriation theory extends to the conduct of any person who uses material nonpublic information in breach of a duty to another party, such as his or her employer. Before the U.S. Supreme Court affirmed the misappropriation theory, several lower courts were using it to prosecute many non-insiders. In *United States v. Newman*, for example, investment bankers and the manager of the over-the-counter trading department of a brokerage firm were indicted on insider trading charges under the misappropriation theory. The investment bankers breached the trust and confidence placed in them by their employers and their employers' clients by misappropriating confidential information about mergers and acquisitions from clients of their firms and conveying it to Newman, who used the information in securities transactions. Similarly, in *SEC v. Willis*, a broker was charged with insider trading for using confidential information conveyed to him by a psychiatrist, who had misappropriated it from one of his patients.

The misappropriation theory has also been used to convict individuals such as financial printers, journalists, and employees of law firms and investment banks of insider trading. For example, in *United States v. Carpenter*, employees of the *Wall Street Journal* were convicted of insider trading in a scheme in which the author of the "Heard on the Street" column leaked information to others who executed trades based on the information. Employees of the *Journal* had no duty to the shareholders of the corporations at issue; liability was premised on the misappropriation of the information in violation of the *Journal*'s policy of maintaining the confidentiality of prepublication news. An equally divided U.S. Supreme Court affirmed the convictions in Carpenter but did not issue an opinion addressing the misappropriation theory.

Similarly, employees of financial printers who discover the identities of potential merger targets and trade in the securities of those corporations are liable for insider trading under the misappropriation theory. In *SEC v. Materia*, a financial printer was convicted under the misappropriation theory. The conviction was premised on the employee's breach of a duty to his employer, and his employer's customers, to maintain the confidentiality of information. Under the same rationale, the office services manager of a law firm was found guilty in *SEC v. Musella* for trading on the basis of information about the firm's clients learned in the course of his employment.

Several U.S. courts have extended the reach of the misappropriation theory. For example, a psychiatrist who traded on inside information learned during confidential sessions with a patient has been held liable for insider trading. In a recent case, *United States v. Cooper*, a psychotherapist pled guilty to insider trading charges based on his purchase of Lockheed call options just in advance of the Lockheed–Martin Marietta merger. He learned of the impending merger in sessions with a patient, a high-level Lockheed executive to whom he was providing marriage counseling. In a related case, *U.S. v. Rottenberg*, a friend who received a tip on the Lockheed merger from the same psychiatrist also pled guilty to insider trading charges.

In *SEC v. Taylor*, the wife of a director of MidSouth Corporation and her two brothers settled charges brought by the SEC in connection with their purchases of MidSouth securities in advance of a merger announcement. The SEC charged that the woman misappropriated information about the merger from her husband's office in their home. Note, however, that marriage and other family relationships are not necessarily relationships of confidence sufficient to create liability under the misappropriation theory. In Chestman, the leading case addressing the misappropriation theory, the defendant broker's conviction was overturned because the court found that the source of his information had not breached a duty by sharing the information. The source, Kenneth Loeb, had learned information about a tender offer for the shares of Waldbaum's supermarket from his wife, a member of the Waldbaum family. Because he was not consulted on family business matters, Loeb did not owe any duty to the Waldbaum family; nor did he owe a duty to his wife to maintain the confidentiality of the information she shared. In addition, under Chestman, one party cannot unilaterally impose a relationship of confidence on another merely by sharing nonpublic information. In the court's view, Loeb was a "gratuitous" recipient of the information and had no duty to maintain the confidentiality of the information.

By endorsing the use of the misappropriation theory, the U.S. Supreme Court defined the fundamental limitations of the theory's reach. The theory's legal application, however, remains uncertain. Therefore, members should continue to exercise caution when buying or selling securities of companies for which they have access to inside information. Members should exercise special care when making personal trades based on information gained through "selective disclosure"—that is, when a company tells information to a certain group of securities analysts before it tells the public. Members that trade on this type of information may violate Standard V(A).

In general, members who misappropriate material nonpublic information and use that information in a securities recommendation or transaction violate Standard V(A). Such a violation occurs whether or not the member owes a duty to the shareholders of the company, the member's employer, or any other person or entity.

Defenses to Claims of Insider Trading: The Mosaic Theory

Securities analysts and investment managers function in a variety of contexts in the securities industry through their work for broker/dealers, banks, investment advisors, mutual fund complexes, insurance companies, pension funds, and other employers. A financial analyst must gather and interpret large quantities of information from many sources. A financial analyst may use significant conclusions derived from the analysis of public and nonmaterial nonpublic information as the basis for investment recommendations and decisions even if those conclusions would have been material inside information had they been communicated directly to the analyst by a company. Under the "mosaic theory," financial analysts are free to act on this "mosaic" of information without risking liability.

The practice of financial analysis depends on the free flow of information. For the fair and efficient operation of the capital markets, analysts and investors must have the greatest amount of information possible to facilitate well-informed investment decisions about how and where to invest capital. Accurate, timely, and intelligible disclosures are essential if analysts and investors are to obtain the data needed to make informed decisions about how and where to invest capital. These disclosures must go beyond the information mandated by the reporting requirements of the federal securities laws and should include specific business information about items used to guide a company's future growth, such as new products, capital projects and the competitive environment. Analysts seek and use such information to compare and contrast investment alternatives.

Much of the information used by analysts comes directly from companies. Analysts often receive such information through contacts with corporate insiders, especially investor relations and finance officers. Information may be disseminated in the form of press releases, through oral presentations by company executives in analysts' meetings or conference calls, or during analysts' visits to company premises. In seeking to develop the most accurate and complete picture of a company, analysts also reach beyond contacts with companies themselves and collect information from such sources as customers, contractors, suppliers, and companies' competitors.

U.S. courts and the SEC have recognized the importance of the role of financial analysts in facilitating the flow of information in the marketplace and have sought to strike a balance between the preservation of that role and the enforcement of insider trading prohibitions. The United States Supreme Court recognized the value of the analytical function in its 1983 opinion in *Dirks v. Securities and Exchange Commission.* The *Dirks* Court reaffirmed the notion that insider trading liability should not result "merely from one's ability to acquire information because of his position in the market." The Court specifically noted the importance of allowing analysts to use the information they gather:

> Imposing a duty to disclose or abstain solely because a person knowingly receives material nonpublic information from an insider and trades on it could have an inhibiting influence on the role of market analysts, which the SEC itself recognizes it necessary to the preservation of a healthy market. It is commonplace for analysts to 'ferret out and analyze information' . . . and this often is done by meeting with and questioning corporate officers and others who are insiders. And information that analysts obtain normally may be the basis for judgments as to the market worth of a corporation's securities. The analyst's judgment in this respect is made available in market letters or otherwise to clients of the firm. It is the nature of this type of information, and indeed of the markets themselves, that such information cannot be made simultaneously available to all of the corporation's stockholders or to the public generally.

The U.S. SEC has also noted the value of the analyst function:

> [Analysts] are in the business of formulating opinions and insights—not obvious to the general investing public—concerning the attractiveness of particular securities. In the course of their work, analysts actively seek out bits and pieces of corporate information not generally known to the market for the express purpose of analyzing that information and informing their clients who, in turn, can be expected to trade on the basis of the information conveyed. The value to the entire market of these efforts cannot be gainsaid; market efficiency in pricing is significantly enhanced by such initiatives to ferret out and analyze information, and thus the analyst's work redounds to the benefit of all investors.

Accordingly, insider trading violations should not result when a perceptive analyst reaches a conclusion about a corporate action or event through an analysis of public information and items of nonmaterial nonpublic information. Investment professionals should note, however, that although analysts are free to use mosaic information in their research reports, they should save and document all their research. Evidence of the analyst's knowledge of public and nonmaterial nonpublic information about a corporation strengthens the assertion that the analyst reached his or her conclusions solely through legal means of access to information.

Despite the mosaic theory, analysts in possession of material nonpublic information act at their risk in making any investment recommendation or decision. Although an analyst might recommend a specific course of action based on factors apart from the inside information in his or her possession, the analyst's conclusions are likely to be deemed tainted by the knowledge of material nonpublic information. Generally, the existence of an independent reason for an investment decision does not provide a valid defense against charges of insider trading. Thus, the mere possession of material nonpublic information about a security should trigger restrictions on investment actions relating to that security.

Selective Disclosure

Issues of "selective disclosure" raise insider trading concerns. When disclosing information, corporations cannot discriminate among the recipients without risking insider trading liability. Once a corporation determines that information is material and should be made public, it must disclose the information to the marketplace generally, not to a chosen few. Information that is made available to analysts remains nonpublic until it is made available to investors in general.

Companies should develop and follow disclosure policies designed to ensure that information is disseminated to the marketplace in an equitable manner. For example, analysts from small firms should receive the same information and attention from a company as analysts from large firms receive. Similarly, companies should not provide certain information to buy-side analysts but not to sell-side analysts, or vice versa. Furthermore, a company should not discriminate among analysts in the provision of information or blackball particular analysts who have given negative reports on the company in the past.

Issues of selective disclosure often arise when a corporate insider provides material information to analysts in a briefing or conference call before that information is released to the public. Analysts and investor relations professionals must realize that such disclosures can be considered tipping under the insider trading laws and should act accordingly to avoid liability. Corporations should consider issuing press releases prior to analyst meetings and conference calls and scripting those meetings and calls to decrease the chance that further information will be disclosed. If material nonpublic information is disclosed for the first time in an analyst meeting or call, the corporation should promptly issue a press release or otherwise make the information publicly available. Analysts should also be alert to the possibility that they are selectively receiving material nonpublic information when a company provides them with guidance or interpretation of such publicly available information as financial statements or SEC filings or when a company representative reviews and comments on drafts of the analyst's reports.

Analysts must be aware that a disclosure made to a room full of analysts does not necessarily make the disclosed information "public" for purposes of the insider trading laws. Analysts should treat any information selectively disclosed carefully and be mindful of their obligations under the securities laws and the AIMR Standards of Professional Conduct. Specifically, when a member deems selectively disclosed information to be material, the member must encourage the public dissemination of that information and abstain from making investment decisions on the basis of that information unless and until it is broadly disseminated to the marketplace. Moreover, members are not to engage in any conduct that may induce company insiders into disclosing material nonpublic information.

Procedures for Compliance

AIMR has long advocated that members and their firms adopt compliance procedures to prevent the misuse of material nonpublic information. Particularly important is improving compliance in such areas as the review of employee and proprietary trading, documentation of firm procedures, and the supervision of interdepartmental communications in multiservice firms. Compliance procedures should suit the particular characteristics of a firm, including its size and the nature of its business. To ensure their effectiveness, most compliance procedures should contain the following basic provisions.

Fire Walls. An information barrier commonly referred to as a "Fire Wall" is the most widely used approach to preventing insider trading violations by employees and protecting firms from potential liability. A Fire Wall is designed to prevent the communication of material nonpublic information between departments of a firm. It restricts the flow of confidential information to those who need to know the information in order to perform their jobs effectively. The minimum elements of such a system are the following:

- substantial control of relevant interdepartmental communications, preferably through a clearance area within the firm, in either the compliance or legal department;
- review of employee trading through the maintenance of "watch," "restricted," and "rumor" lists;
- documentation of the procedures designed to limit the flow of information between departments and of the enforcement actions taken pursuant to those procedures;
- heightened review or restriction of proprietary trading while a firm is in possession of material nonpublic information.

Although documentation requirements must for practical reasons take into account the differences between the activities of smaller firms and those of large, multiservice firms, firms of all sizes and types benefit by improving the documentation of their internal enforcement of Fire Wall procedures. Therefore, even at small firms, procedures concerning interdepartmental communication, the review of trading activity, and investigation of possible violation should be compiled and formalized—particularly for ensuring compliance with the Insider Trading and Securities Fraud Enforcement Act (ITSFEA). For example, firms should maintain an entry log of securities placed on their watch and restricted lists. Multiservice firms should maintain written records of the communications between various departments. A failure to maintain documentation sufficient to re-create the actions taken to enforce a Fire Wall procedure makes determining the adequacy of that procedure nearly impossible; so the firm cannot rely on that procedure as a defense against charges of insider trading.

Firms should place a high priority on training and should consider instituting comprehensive, interactive training programs, particularly for employees in sensitive areas. At a majority of firms, the most comprehensive training efforts take place during an employee's orientation. These efforts should be supplemented by internal memorandums and/or seminars designed to reinforce existing firm policies and keep employees informed of significant legal, regulatory, and industry developments.

Procedures concerning the restriction or review of a firm's proprietary trading while in the possession of material nonpublic information necessarily vary with the types of proprietary trading in which a firm may engage. A prohibition on all types of proprietary activity when a firm comes into possession of material nonpublic information is not appropriate. For example, when a firm acts as a market maker, a proprietary trading prohibition may be counterproductive to the goals of maintaining both the confidentiality of information and market liquidity. This concern is particularly keen in the relationships between small, regional broker/dealers and small issuers. In many situations, a firm will take a small issuer public with the understanding that the firm will continue to be a market maker in the stock. In these instances, a withdrawal by the firm from market-making acts is a clear tip to outsiders. Firms that continue market-making activity while in the possession of material nonpublic information should, however, instruct their market makers to remain passive to the market—that is, take only the contra side of unsolicited customer trades.

In risk arbitrage trading, the case for a trading prohibition is more compelling: In contrast to market making, the impetus for arbitrage trading is neither passive nor reactive, and the potential for illegal profits is greater.

The most prudent course for firms is to suspend arbitrage activity when a security is placed on the watch list. Those firms that do continue arbitrage activity face a high hurdle in proving the adequacy of their internal procedures and must demonstrate stringent review and documentation of firm trades.

As a practical matter, to the extent possible, firms should consider the physical separation of departments and files to prevent the communication of sensitive information. For example, the investment banking and corporate finance areas of a brokerage firm should be separated from the sales and research departments, and a bank's commercial lending department should be segregated from its trust and research departments. There should be no overlap of personnel between such departments. A single supervisor or compliance officer should have the specific authority and responsibility to decide whether or not information is material and whether it is sufficiently public to be used as the basis for investment decisions. Ideally, the supervisor or compliance officer responsible for communicating information to a firm's research or brokerage area would not be a member of that area.

A primary objective of an effective Fire Wall procedure is to establish a reporting system in which authorized persons review and approve communications between departments.

If an employee behind a Fire Wall believes that he or she needs to share confidential information with someone on the other side of the Wall, the employee should consult a designated compliance officer to determine whether sharing the information is, in fact, necessary and how much information should be shared. If the sharing is necessary, the compliance officer should coordinate the process of "looking over the Wall" so that the necessary information is shared and the integrity of the procedure is maintained.

For a Fire Wall to be effective in a multiservice firm, an employee can be allowed to be on only one side of the Wall at any given time. Inside knowledge may not be limited to information about the specific offering or the current financial condition of the company. Analysts may be exposed to a host of information about the company, including new-product development or future budget projections, that clearly constitutes inside knowledge and thus precludes the analyst from returning to his or her research function. For example, an analyst who follows a particular company may be "brought over the Wall" because of his or her expertise on that company when the firm's investment banking department is involved in a deal with the company. That analyst must then be treated as though he or she were an investment banker; the analyst must remain on the investment banking side of the Wall until any information he or she learns is publicly disclosed. In short, the analyst cannot use any information learned in the course of the project for research purposes and cannot share that information with colleagues in the research department.

Other Procedures. An information barrier is the minimum procedure a firm should have in place to protect itself from liability. Firms should also consider restrictions or prohibitions on personal trading by employees and should carefully monitor both proprietary trading and personal trading by employees (see the topical study titled "Personal Investing"). Firms should require employees to make periodic reports, to the extent that such reporting is not already required by the securities laws, of their own transactions and transactions made for the benefit of family members. Securities should be placed on a restricted list when a firm has or may have material nonpublic information. Of course, the broad distribution of a restricted list often triggers the sort of trading the list was developed to avoid. Therefore, a watch list shown to only the few people responsible for compliance should be used to monitor transactions in specified securities. The use of a watch list in combination with a restricted list is an increasingly common means of ensuring an effective procedure.

Written compliance policies and guidelines should be circulated to all employees of a firm. Compliance procedures that are not documented are nearly worthless in protecting an entity from liability. Policies and guidelines should be used in conjunction with training programs aimed at enabling employees to recognize material nonpublic information. As noted, material nonpublic information is not always clearly identifiable as such. Employees must be given sufficient training to make an informed decision or to consult a supervisor or compliance officer before engaging in questionable transactions.

Obligations under AIMR's Code and Standards

Investment professionals may come into possession of material nonpublic information under two circumstances, and their duties under AIMR Standard V(A) vary with these circumstances. First, members may receive information as a result of their confidential relationships with securities issuers. For example, an analyst may receive information when acting as a financial consultant or as the representative of a rating agency, a lender, or an underwriter for an issuer. When acting in these roles, analysts are likely to be considered temporary insiders of the issuer. In such situations, members can use the information for its intended purpose without encouraging further disclosure of the information. They cannot, however, use the information for any other purpose or share the information with other members of their firms.

Second, members may receive information from an issuer when no confidential relationship exists between them. In this situation, Standard V(A) requires members to evaluate the materiality of the information they receive and consider whether the source of the information is violating a duty by disclosing it. As discussed in the compliance section, these decisions should normally be made in consultation with a compliance officer or supervisor. If the information is deemed material and is thought to be disclosed in breach of a duty, the member should make reasonable efforts to achieve public dissemination of the information. This effort usually means encouraging the corporation to issue a press release or otherwise make the information public. Until the information is publicly disseminated, the member should not take any investment action on the basis of the information. To be fully protected, the investment professional should refrain from taking any action at all in the securities at issue, even if that action can be justified on other grounds. In addition, the information should not be communicated to anyone other than designated supervisory and compliance personnel within the member's firm.

Topical Study:
Personal Investing

Members have a duty to put the interests of their clients, the interests of their firm, and the integrity of the investment profession over and above their own self-interest. They must conduct their investment activities by exercising good judgment to achieve and maintain independence and objectivity that is unaffected by any potential conflict of interest or circumstance that may adversely affect their judgment. The long-term success of the industry depends on public confidence that investment professionals are adhering to the highest possible ethical and professional standards. Policies and procedures designed to prevent potential conflicts of interest, or even the appearance of a conflict of interest, with respect to personal transactions are critical to establishing investor confidence in the securities industry[1].

Fiduciary Responsibilities of Investment Industry Personnel

Investment advisors and money managers are in a position of trust and responsibility and, therefore, owe their customers a duty of loyalty. Advisors must deal fairly with their clients and place their clients' interests ahead of their own when making investment decisions. However, conflicts between the client's interest and an investment professional's personal interest frequently occur. Although conflicts of interest exist, there is nothing inherently unethical about individual managers, advisors, or mutual fund employees making money from personal investments so long as (1) the client is not disadvantaged by the trade, (2) the investment professional does not benefit personally from trades undertaken for clients, and (3) the investment professional complies with applicable regulatory requirements. Although real and perceived conflicts of interest may be inevitable, the primary objective for the investment industry is to develop appropriate methods for resolving the conflicts to ensure that the clients' interests are kept paramount.

Personal Investing and AIMR's Code and Standards

The Code of Ethics and Standards of Professional Conduct that relate to personal investing are designed to prevent potential conflicts of interest and the appearance of conflicts of interest with respect to members' personal

[1]This topical study summarizes AIMR's Personal Investing Task Force Report issued May 1995. A copy of the full text is available from AIMR.

transactions. The Standards require that members conduct their investment activities by exercising good judgment to achieve and maintain independence and objectivity that is unaffected by any potential conflict of interest. Members are required to place their fiduciary obligation to their clients first in all dealings and not benefit from positions that their clients occupy in the marketplace.

All five Standards address, in some manner, the issues that arise from the personal trading of investment company personnel.

Task Force Recommendations

AIMR's Personal Investing Task Force was formed to examine issues related to the personal investing of investment managers. The Task Force recommended specific guidelines for members and firms based on the guiding principles laid down in the Code and Standards.

General Recommendations. The Task Force Report reinforces the basic intent of AIMR's Code and Standards: to advance the integrity of the global investment profession and to build and maintain the public trust. AIMR members are required to conduct their professional activities in compliance with the Code and Standards, including, but not limited to, standards relating to personal investing activities.

One alternative the Task Force considered for addressing conflicts of interest created by personal investing was a ban on all personal investing by money managers or investment advisors. The Task Force decided, however, that a ban might be an easy standard to implement and enforce, but it would discourage talented individuals from entering the industry, which would directly harm the average investor. Short of implementing a complete ban on personal trading, *investment personnel and their firms can eliminate conflicts of interest by establishing adequate review and compliance procedures for governing personal investing activities.*

Paramount to any discussion of appropriate investment practices and compliance procedures is the recognition of the critical role that supervisors play in establishing and implementing ethical and professional standards for their firms. It is the responsibility of supervisors to establish and implement internal compliance procedures. Members who act in supervisory roles are expected to understand what constitutes an adequate compliance system for their firms and to make reasonable efforts to see that appropriate procedures are established, documented, and communicated to relevant personnel and to the legal, compliance, and auditing departments. The member supervisor must make reasonable efforts to detect fraudulent or deliberately misleading statements and practices and other improper or inadequate work or conduct. Supervisors should bring an inadequate compliance system to the attention of senior managers and recommend corrective action. If the investment manager clearly cannot discharge supervisory responsibilities because no compliance system is in place or the system is inadequate, the member should refuse to accept supervisory responsibility until procedures are adopted that permit the exercise of reasonable supervision.

Specific Recommendations. Because investment firms vary greatly in assets under management, types of clients, number of employees, and so on, each firm should establish policies regarding personal investing that are best suited to the firm. The firm should then prominently disclose those policies to clients and prospective clients. For instance, the Task Force recommended a 60-day rule to address short-term trading by investment professionals in their personal accounts. Other measures, such as prohibiting trades in stock based on the company's market capitalization or otherwise establishing restricted categories of securities, might be appropriate for various firms.

The specific provisions of each firm's standards will vary, but all firms should adopt certain basic procedures to address the conflict areas created by personal investing. These include

No participation in equity IPOs.

Recommendation: Restrictions should be placed on participation by investment personnel in an IPO of equity or equity-related securities, but investment personnel should not be prevented from purchasing government issues, such as municipal bonds or other government securities.

Some eagerly awaited IPOs may significantly rise in value shortly after the issue is brought to market. Because the new issue may be highly attractive and sought after, the opportunity to participate in the IPO may be limited. Therefore, purchases of IPOs by investment personnel create conflicts of interest in two principal ways. First, participation in an IPO may have the appearance of appropriating an attractive investment opportunity from clients for personal gain—a clear breach of the duty of loyalty to clients. Second, because opportunities to participate in IPOs are limited, there may be an appearance that the investment opportunity is bestowed as an incentive to make future investment decisions for the benefit of the party making the opportunity available.

Reliable and systematic review procedures should be established to ensure that conflicts relating to IPOs are identified and appropriately dealt with by supervisors. Members should not benefit from the position that their clients occupy in the marketplace—through preferred trading, the allocation of limited offerings, and/or oversubscription.

To address these conflicts, investment personnel should be restricted from participating in equity or equity-related IPOs. Managers should not, however, be prevented from purchasing government issues—municipal bonds and other government securities. Policies should provide for special situations that may not fall neatly into the prescribed definition of an equity or equity-related IPO. These special situations should be examined by a review committee made up of senior firm officials and/or independent parties who will objectively determine whether the manager should act on the security in question.

> *Restrictions on private placements.*
> Recommendation: Strict limits should be placed on investment personnel acquiring securities in private placements, and appropriate supervisory and review procedures should be established to prevent noncompliance.

Firms do not routinely use private placements for clients (e.g., venture capital deals) because of the high risk associated with them. Conflicts relating to private placements are more significant to members who manage large pools of assets or act as plan sponsors; these managers are offered special opportunities, such as private placements, as a reward for or as an enticement to continue to do business with a particular broker.

Participation in private placements raises conflict-of-interest issues that are similar to issues surrounding IPOs. Investment personnel should not be involved in transactions, including (but not limited to) private placements, that could be perceived as favors or gifts designed to influence future judgment or to reward past business deals.

Whether the venture eventually proves to be good or bad, managers have an immediate conflict concerning private placement opportunities: Participants in private placements have an incentive to recommend these investments to clients if and when they go public, regardless of the suitability of the investments for their clients, to increase the value of the participants' personal portfolios.

> *Establish blackout/restricted periods.*
> Recommendation: Investment personnel involved in the investment decision-making process should not initiate trades in a security within the same 24-hour period that their firms have a pending buy or sell order in that same security until the order is executed or canceled.

Individual firms must decide who within the firm should be required to comply with the trading restrictions. At a minimum, all individuals who are involved in the investment decision-making process should be subject to the same restricted period.

Each firm must determine specific requirements relating to blackout and restricted periods that are most relevant to the firm while ensuring that the procedures are governed by the guiding principles set forth in the Code and Standards. Size of firm and type of securities purchased are relevant factors. For example, in a large firm, a blackout requirement is, in effect, a total trading ban because the firm is continually trading in most securities. In a small firm, the blackout period is more likely to prevent the investment manager from front running.

Primary emphasis should be on appropriate review procedures prior to a trade rather than the establishment of post-trade blackout periods. A conflict of interests may be perceived if a manager is not restricted from trading for his or her personal account after trading for his or her firm. Appropriate review and approval procedures address such conflicts for the benefit of the public without unduly restricting a manager.

> *Short-term trading.*
> Recommendation: As a general matter, investment personnel should not engage in short-term transactions (transactions within a 60-day period) to eliminate conflicts presented by potential front-running transactions.

Firms should also, however, establish clearing provisions whereby an independent review committee or senior officer within the firm has authority to clear a personal transaction within a 60-day period for exceptional or unusual circumstances. Firms should also encourage the placement of firm and manager accounts at risk along with the investments of clients.

> *Gifts.*
> Recommendation: To maintain their independence, investment personnel should not accept any gift of more than de minimis value from anyone doing business with their firm.

A corollary of their duty of loyalty to their clients is members' duty to maintain their independence and objectivity when recommending or selecting investment vehicles.

> *Service as directors.*
> Recommendation: Allow investment personnel to serve as directors with prior approval and disclosure.

Although service as a director poses potential conflicts, investment professionals are under considerable pressure today to become involved in corporate governance. Venture capitalist groups, for example, have a vested interest in serving on boards of directors. In addition, a viable strategy for certain investment management organizations is to be close to a limited number of companies. Certain managers are on boards of directors to influence policy. (Organizations should be aware, however, that for a publicly traded company to have a person who is active in the investment process as a director may inhibit investment flexibility over time.)

Members who are investment managers may serve on boards of directors of corporations, but they should seek prior approval from their employer and fully disclose such service to all relevant parties. Members are encouraged to review compensation arrangements and/or other special treatment of board directors and to make certain that these arrangements do not create conflicts of interest. Firms should establish policies outlining the circumstances for which service as a director is appropriate. The type and scope of the policy will depend, in part, on the size of a firm and its investment strategies, expertise, and products. Members must also establish "Fire Walls" to prevent the sharing of material nonpublic information.

> *Reporting requirements.*
> Recommendation: Supervisors should establish reporting procedures for investment personnel, including duplicate confirmations, disclosure of personal holdings/beneficial ownerships, and preclearance procedures.

Once trading restrictions are in place, they must be enforced. The best method for monitoring and enforcing procedures established to eliminate conflicts of interest relating to personal trading is through reporting requirements, including the following:

- Disclosure of holdings in which the employee has a beneficial interest. Disclosure by investment personnel to the firm should be made upon commencement of the employment relationship and at least annually thereafter. To address privacy considerations, disclosure of personal holdings should be handled in a confidential manner by the firm.
- Providing duplicate confirmations of transactions. Investment personnel should be required to direct their brokers to supply duplicate copies or confirmations to their firms of all their personal securities transactions and copies of periodic statements for all securities accounts. Firms should establish additional reporting requirements, including the frequency of such reporting, that emphasize AIMR's intention to promote full and complete disclosure and that explain the role and responsibilities of supervisors. The duplicate confirmation requirement has two purposes: (1) The requirement sends a message that "people are looking" and makes it difficult for an individual to act unethically, and (2) it enables verification of the accounting of the flow of personal investments that cannot be determined from merely looking at transactions or holdings.

- Preclearance procedures. Investment personnel should clear all personal investments to identify possible conflicts prior to the execution of personal trades. Preclearance procedures are designed to identify possible conflicts before a problem arises. Preclearance procedures are consistent with AIMR's Code and Standards and demonstrate that members and their firms place the interest of their clients ahead of their own personal investing interests.

  Disgorgement.
  Recommendation: Investment personnel should "break the trade" made in violation of a firm's personal trading policies and disgorge any profit on such transactions.

The preference is that investment personnel and their firms develop procedures for eliminating conflicts of interest before a personal trade occurs, but remedies are needed for those times when violations do occur. Whether the ultimate result of the transaction is a profit or loss is irrelevant to whether the conflict of interest leading to the opportunity existed. Therefore, when an employee purchases a security in violation of a firm's trading policy, even if inadvertently, the employee should break the trade by immediately reversing the transaction, no matter whether a profit or a loss occurred. Disgorgement provides a mechanism for remedying violations of policies after the fact that result in profit to the employee. Individual firms may determine the most appropriate method for allocating disgorged profits so long as the monies accrued in the event of a personal trading violation do not benefit the individual or the firm.

  Disclosure of policies.
  Recommendation: Members should fully disclose their firm's personal investing policies to investors upon request.

The infusion of information on employees' personal investment activities and policies into the marketplace will foster an atmosphere of full and complete disclosure and calm the public's legitimate concerns about the conflicts of interest posed by the personal trading of investment personnel. The disclosure must be helpful to investors, however, not simply boilerplate language containing some vague admonition that investment personnel are "subject to policies and procedures regarding their personal trading."

AIMR Standards of Practice Exam (with Answers and Analysis)

Standards of Practice Examination

Unless otherwise stated in the question, all individuals in the following questions are AIMR members and, therefore, are subject to the AIMR Code of Ethics and Standards of Professional Conduct.

1. Smith, a research analyst with a brokerage firm, decides to change his recommendation on the common stock of Green Company, Inc., from a buy to a sell. He mails this change in investment advice to all the firm's clients on Wednesday. The day after the mailing, a client calls with a buy order for 500 shares of Green Company. In this circumstance, Smith should:
   a. Accept the order.
   b. Advise the customer of the change in recommendation before accepting the order.
   c. Not accept the order until five days have elapsed after the communication of the change in recommendation.
   d. Not accept the order because it is contrary to the firm's recommendation.

2. All of the following statements about a member's use of clients' brokerage commissions are true *except*:
   a. Client brokerage commissions should be used by the member to ensure that fairness to the client is maintained.
   b. Client brokerage commissions may be used by the member to pay for securities research used in managing the client's portfolio.
   c. Client brokerage commissions should be commensurate with the value of the brokerage and research services received.
   d. Client brokerage commissions may be directed to pay for the investment manager's operating expenses.

3. Sanctions that AIMR may impose on its members include:

   I. Revocation of the member's registration as an investment advisor.
   II. Private censure.
   III. A monetary fine.
   IV. Suspension of membership.

   a. I and III only.
   b. II and IV only.
   c. II, III, and IV only.
   d. I, II, III, and IV.

4. Jamison is a junior research analyst with Howard & Howard, a brokerage and investment banking firm. Howard & Howard's mergers and acquisitions department has represented the Britland Company in all of its acquisitions for the past 20 years. Two of Howard & Howard's senior officers are directors of various Britland subsidiaries. Jamison has been asked to write a research report on Britland. What is the best course of action for her to follow?
   a. Jamison may write the report but must refrain from expressing any opinions because of the special relationships between the two companies.
   b. Jamison may write the report so long as the officers agree not to alter it.
   c. Jamison may write the report if she discloses the special relationships with the company in the report.
   d. Jamison should not write the report because the two Howard officers are constructive insiders.

5. Which of the following statements clearly *conflicts* with the recommended procedures for compliance presented in AIMR's *Standards of Practice Handbook*?
   a. Investment recommendations may be changed by an analyst without prior approval of a supervisory analyst.
   b. Prior approval must be obtained for the personal investment transactions of all employees.
   c. For confidentiality reasons, personal transactions should not be compared with those of clients or the employer unless requested by regulatory organizations.
   d. Personal transactions should be defined as including transactions in securities owned by the employee and members of his or her immediate family and transactions involving securities in which the employee has a beneficial interest.

6. Bronson provides investment advice to the board of trustees of a private university endowment fund. The trustees have provided Bronson with the fund's financial information, including planned expenditures. Bronson receives a phone call on Friday afternoon from Murdock, a prominent alumnus, requesting that Bronson fax him comprehensive financial information about the fund. According to Murdock, he has a potential contributor but needs the information that day to close the deal and cannot contact any of the trustees. Based on AIMR Standards, Bronson should:
   a. Send Murdock the information because disclosure would benefit the client.
   b. Not send Murdock the information to preserve confidentiality.
   c. Send Murdock the information, provided Bronson promptly

notifies the trustees.

d. Send Murdock the information because it is not material nonpublic information.

7. Young, a portfolio manager with Northside Bank, has just been given investment authority for a newly acquired pension account. Client objectives have not yet been established. On the day the account is received, $2 million in bonds, representing 4 percent of the portfolio, mature. Which of the following is Young's *best* course of action on that day?
   a. Contact the client's former investment advisor and take investment action based on previously used guidelines.
   b. Invest the proceeds in accordance with the bank's current asset allocation strategy.
   c. Invest the proceeds in cash equivalents until a meeting can be arranged to establish fund objectives.
   d. Make no decision until client objectives have been established.

8. To fulfill the duty to inform their employer that they must follow AIMR's Code and Standards, members must:
   a. Inform their immediate supervisor in writing.
   b. Inform their immediate supervisor either orally or in writing.
   c. Inform the firm's chief executive officer in writing.
   d. Inform the firm's chief executive officer either orally or in writing.

9. Miller heads the research department of a large brokerage firm. The firm has many analysts, some of whom are subject to the Code and Standards. If Miller delegates some supervisory duties, which statement best describes her responsibilities under the Code and Standards?
   a. Miller's supervisory responsibilities do not apply to those subordinates who are not subject to the Code and Standards.
   b. Miller no longer has supervisory responsibility for those duties delegated to her subordinates.
   c. Miller retains supervisory responsibility for all subordinates despite her delegation of some duties.
   d. AIMR's Standards prevent Miller from delegating supervisory duties to subordinates.

10. Willier is the research analyst responsible for following Company X. All the information he has accumulated and documented suggests that the outlook for the firm's new products is poor, so the stock should be rated a weak hold. During lunch, however, Willier overhears a financial analyst from another firm offer opinions that conflict with Willier's forecasts and expectations. Upon returning to his office, Willier

releases a strong buy recommendation to the public. Willier:

a. Was in full compliance with the Standards.
b. Violated the Standards by failing to distinguish between facts and opinions in his recommendation.
c. Violated the Standards because he did not seek approval of the change from his firm's compliance department.
d. Violated the Standards because he did not have a reasonable and adequate basis for his recommendation.

11. The Standards state that when presenting material to others, members shall not "copy or use, in substantially the same form as the original, material prepared by another without acknowledging and identifying the name of the author, publisher, or source of such material." The analyst may use information from other sources without acknowledgment, however, if the information:

a. Does not include a buy or sell recommendation.
b. Is factual information published in recognized financial and statistical reporting services.
c. Was originally communicated verbally.
d. Is being reported only to the member's employer or associates.

12. An investment management firm has been hired by ETV Corporation to work on an initial public offering for the company. The firm's brokerage unit now has a sell recommendation on ETV, but the head of the investment banking department has asked the head of the brokerage unit to change the recommendation from sell to buy. According to the Standards, the head of the brokerage unit would be permitted to:

a. Increase the recommendation by no more than one increment (in this case, to a hold recommendation).
b. Place the company on a restricted list and give only factual information about the firm.
c. Assign a new analyst to decide if the stock deserves a higher rating.
d. Reassign responsibility for rating the stock to the head of the investment banking unit.

13. Albert and Tye, who recently started their own investment advisory business, have registered to take the Level III CFA examination. Albert's business card reads, "Judy Albert, CFA Candidate." Tye has not put anything about the CFA designation on his business card, but promotional material that he designed for the business describes the CFA requirements and indicates that Tye participates in the CFA Program and has completed Levels I and II. According to the Standards:

a. Albert has violated the Standards but Tye has not.
b. Tye has violated the Standards but Albert has not.
c. Both Albert and Tye have violated the Standards.
d. Neither Albert nor Tye has violated the Standards.

14. Scott works for a regional brokerage firm. He estimates that Walkton Industries will increase its dividend by $1.50 a share during the next year. He realizes that this increase is contingent on pending legislation that would, if enacted, give Walkton a substantial tax break. The U.S. representative for Walkton's home district has told Scott that, although she is lobbying hard for the bill and prospects for passage look good, Congress's concern over the federal deficit could cause the tax bill to be voted down. Walkton has not made any statements regarding a change in dividend policy. Scott writes in his research report, "We expect Walkton's stock price to rise by at least $8.00 a share by the end of the year. Because the dividend will increase by $1.50 a share, the stock price gain will be fueled, in large part, by the increase in the dividend. Investors buying the stock at the current time should expect to realize a total return of at least 15 percent on the stock." Which of the following is/are *true*?

    I. Scott violated the Standards because he used material inside information.
    II. Scott violated the Standards because he failed to separate opinion from fact.
    III. Scott did not violate the Standards.

a. I only.
b. II only.
c. I and II only.
d. III only.

15. Which *one* of the following actions will *not* help to ensure the fair treatment of brokerage firm clients when a new investment recommendation is made?

a. Limit the number of people in the firm who are aware in advance that a recommendation is to be disseminated.
b. Distribute recommendations to institutional clients prior to individual accounts.
c. Minimize elapsed time between the decision and the dissemination of a recommendation.
d. Monitor the trading activities of firm personnel.

16. The mosaic theory holds that an analyst:

a. Violates the Code and Standards if the analyst fails to notify her or his employer of the Code and Standards or fails to have knowledge of and comply with applicable laws.

b. Can use material public information or nonmaterial nonpublic information in the analyst's analysis.
c. Should use all available and relevant information in support of an investment recommendation.
d. Should distinguish between facts and opinions in research reports.

17. Jurgens is a portfolio manager with an investment firm based in New York. One of her firm's clients has told Jurgens that he will compensate her beyond that provided by her firm on the basis of the capital appreciation of his portfolio each year. Jurgens should:
    a. Turn down the additional compensation because it will result in conflicts with the interests of other clients' accounts.
    b. Receive permission from AIMR for the compensation arrangement.
    c. Obtain permission from her employer prior to accepting the compensation arrangement.
    d. Turn down the additional compensation because it will create undue pressure on her to achieve strong short-term performance.

18. One of the discretionary accounts managed by Farnsworth is the Jones Corporation employee profit-sharing plan. Jones, the company president, recently asked Farnsworth to vote the shares in the profit-sharing plan in favor of the company-nominated slate of directors and against the directors sponsored by a dissident stockholder group. Farnsworth does not want to lose this account because he directs all the account's trades to a brokerage firm that provides Farnsworth with useful information about tax-free investments. Although this information is not of value in managing the Jones Corporation account, it does help in managing several other accounts. The brokerage firm providing this information also offers the lowest commissions for trades and best execution. Farnsworth investigates the director issue, concludes that management's slate is better for the long-run performance of the firm than the dissident group's slate, and votes accordingly. Farnsworth:
    a. Violated the Standards in voting the shares in the manner requested by Jones but not in directing trades to the brokerage firm.
    b. Did not violate the Standards in voting the shares in the manner requested by Jones or in directing trades to the brokerage firm.
    c. Violated the Standards in directing trades to the brokerage firm but not in voting the shares as requested by Jones.
    d. Violated the Standards in voting the shares in the manner requested by Jones and in directing trades to the brokerage firm.

19. Brown works for an investment counseling firm. Green, a new client of the firm, is meeting with Brown for the first time. Green used another counseling firm for financial advice for years, but she has switched her account to Brown's firm. After a few minutes of get-acquainted talk, Brown explains to Green that she has discovered a highly undervalued stock that offers large potential gains. She recommends that Green purchase the stock. Brown has committed a violation of the Standards. What should she have done differently?
    a. Brown should have determined Green's needs, objectives, and tolerance for risk before making a recommendation for any type of security.
    b. Brown should have asked Green her reasons for changing counseling firms. If the discovery process indicated that Green had been treated unfairly at the other firm, Brown should have notified AIMR of any violation.
    c. Brown should have thoroughly explained the characteristics of the company to Green, including the characteristics of the industry in which the company operates.
    d. Brown should have explained her qualifications, including her education, training, experience, and the meaning of the CFA designation.

20. Grey recommends the purchase of a mutual fund that invests solely in long-term U.S. Treasury bonds. He makes the following statements to his clients:

    I. "The payment of the bonds is guaranteed by the U.S. government; therefore, the default risk of the bonds is virtually zero."
    II. "If you invest in the mutual fund, you will earn a 15 percent rate of return each year for the next several years."

    Did Grey's statements violate AIMR's Code and Standards?

    a. Statement I and II violated the Code and Standards.
    b. Only statement I violated the Code and Standards.
    c. Only statement II violated the Code and Standards.
    d. Neither statement violated the Code and Standards.

21. Anderb, a portfolio manager for XYZ Investment Management Company—a registered investment organization that advises investment companies and private accounts—was promoted to that position three years ago. Bates, her supervisor, is responsible for reviewing Anderb's portfolio account transactions and her required monthly reports of personal stock transactions. Anderb has been using Jonelli, a broker, almost exclusively for portfolio account brokerage transactions. For securities in which Jonelli's firm makes a market,

Jonelli has been giving Anderb lower prices for personal purchases and higher prices for personal sales than Jonelli gives to Anderb's portfolio accounts and other investors. Anderb has been filing monthly reports with Bates only for those months in which she has no personal transactions, which is about every fourth month. Which of the following applies/apply?

I. Anderb violated the Code and Standards in that she failed to disclose to her employer her personal transactions.
II. Anderb violated the Code and Standards by breaching her fiduciary duty to her clients.
III. Bates violated the Code and Standards by failing to enforce reasonable procedures for supervising and monitoring Anderb in Anderb's trading for her own account.

a. I only.
b. I and II only.
c. II and III only.
d. I, II, and III.

22. Which of the following is/are a correct statement of a member's duty under the Code and Standards?

I. In the absence of specific applicable law or other regulatory requirements, the Code and Standards govern the member's actions.
II. A member is required to comply only with applicable local laws, rules, regulations, or customs even though the AIMR Code and Standards may impose a higher degree of responsibility or a higher duty on the member.
III. A member who trades securities in a foreign securities market where no applicable local laws or stock exchange rules regulate the use of material nonpublic information may take investment action based on material nonpublic information.

a. I only.
b. III only.
c. II and III only.
d. I and II only.

23. Ward is scheduled to visit the corporate headquarters of Evans Industries. Ward expects to use the information obtained to complete his research report on Evans stock. Ward learns that Evans plans to pay all of Ward's expenses for the trip, including costs of meals, hotel room, and air transportation. Which of the following actions would be the *best* course for Ward to take under the Code and Standards?

a. Accept the expense-paid trip and write an objective report.

b. Pay for all travel expenses, including costs of meals and incidental items.
c. Accept the expense-paid trip but disclose the value of the services accepted in the report.
d. Write the report without taking the trip.

24. Which of the following statements is/are correct under the Code and Standards?

    I. AIMR members are prohibited from undertaking independent practice in competition with their employer.
    II. Written consent from the employer is necessary to permit independent practice that could result in compensation or other benefit in competition with a member's employer.
    III. Written consent from the outside prospective client is necessary to permit independent practice that could result in compensation or other benefit in competition with a member's employer.
    IV. Members are prohibited from making arrangements or preparations to go into a competitive business before terminating their relationship with their employer.

    a. I and IV only.
    b. II, III, and IV only.
    c. II and III only.
    d. IV only.

25. Under AIMR Rules of Procedure for the Proceedings Related to Professional Conduct, membership in AIMR and/or the right to use the CFA designation may be summarily suspended by AIMR's Designated Officer for the following misconduct:

    I. Conviction for a crime that is defined as a felony or its equivalent.
    II. Indefinite bar from registration under the securities laws (even though reapplication may be made after a specific period of time).
    III. Failure to complete and return a professional conduct statement for each of two successive years.

    a. I and II only.
    b. II and III only.
    c. I, II, and III.
    d. III only.

26. Smithers is a financial analyst with XYZ Brokerage Company. She is preparing a purchase recommendation on JNI Corporation. Which of the following situations would represent a conflict of interest for Smithers and, therefore, would have to be disclosed?

I. Smith is on retainer as a consultant to JNI.
II. XYZ holds for its own account a substantial common stock position in JNI.
III. Smith has material beneficial ownership of JNI through a family trust.
IV. Smith's brother-in-law is a supplier to JNI.

a. II and III only.
b. I and IV only.
c. I, II, and III only.
d. I, II, and IV only.

27. Michelieu tells a prospective client, "I may not have a long-term track record yet, but I'm sure that you'll be very pleased with my recommendations and service. In the three years that I've been in the business, my equity-oriented clients have averaged a total return of more than 26 percent a year." The statement is true, but Michelieu only has a few clients, and one of his clients took a large position in a penny stock (against Michelieu's advice) and realized a huge gain. This large return caused the average of all of Michelieu's clients to exceed 26 percent a year. Without this one investment, the average gain would have been 8 percent a year. Has Michelieu violated the Standards?

a. Yes, because the statement about return ignores the risk preferences of his clients.
b. No, because Michelieu is not promising that he can earn a 26 percent return in the future.
c. No, because the statement is a true and accurate description of Michelieu's track record.
d. Yes, because the statement misrepresents Michelieu's track record.

28. An investment banking department of a brokerage firm often receives material nonpublic information that could have considerable value if used in advising the firm's brokerage clients. In order to conform to the Code and Standards, which one of the following is the best policy for the brokerage firm?

a. Permanently prohibit both purchase and sell recommendations of the stocks of clients of the investment banking department.
b. Establish physical and informational barriers within the firm to prevent the exchange of information between the investment banking and brokerage operations
c. Prohibit purchase recommendations when the investment banking department has access to material nonpublic information but, in view of the fiduciary obligation to clients, allow sale of current holdings.

d. Monitor the exchange of information between the investment banking department and the brokerage operation.

29. Stewart has been hired by Goodner Industries, Inc., to manage its pension fund. Stewart's fiduciary duty is owed to:

    a. The management of Goodner.
    b. The shareholders of Goodner.
    c. The participants and beneficiaries of Goodner's pension plan.
    d. Each of the above equally.

30. The stated purposes of Standard IV(B)(8), Disclosure of Referral Fees, are to:

    I. Help the customer or client evaluate the full cost of the services.
    II. Help the customer or client evaluate any possible partiality shown in the recommendation of services.
    III. Help the customer or client evaluate potential conflicts of interest as a result of the participation of immediate family in transactions.

    a. I and II only.
    b. II and III only.
    c. I and III only.
    d. I, II, and III.

Exam Answers and Analysis

1. b This question involves Standard IV(B.3), Fair Dealing. Smith disseminated a change in the stock recommendation to his clients but then received a request contrary to that recommendation from a client who had not yet received the recommendation. Prior to executing the order, Smith should take additional steps to ensure that the customer has received the change of recommendation. Answer *a* is incorrect because the client placed the order prior to receiving the recommendation and, therefore, does not have the benefit of Smith's most recent recommendation. Answer *c* is incorrect because it would result in a delay in executing an order requested by the client. Answer *d* is also incorrect; simply because the client request is contrary to the firm's recommendation does not mean a member can override a direct request by a client. After Smith contacts the client to ensure that the client received the changed recommendation, if the client still wants to place a buy order for the shares, Smith is obligated to comply with the client's directive.

2. d This question involves Standard IV(B.1), Fiduciary Duties, and the specific topic of soft dollars. Answer *d* is the correct choice because client brokerage commissions may not be directed to pay for the investment manager's operating expenses. Answer *b* would be an incorrect choice because brokerage commissions may be directed to pay for securities research used in managing a client's portfolio. Answers *a* and *c* outline two criteria by which members should determine how to use brokerage commissions: if the use (1) is fair to and in the best interests of clients and (2) is commensurate with the value of the services provided. Members are obligated in all situations to disclose to clients their practices in the use of client brokerage commissions.

3. b This question involves the disciplinary sanctions available to AIMR's Professional Conduct Program (PCP) as stated in AIMR's Bylaws and Rules of Procedure for Proceedings Related to Professional Conduct. The PCP can suspend membership or impose a private censure on members for violating the Code and Standards or certain requirements of AIMR's Bylaws. AIMR has no authority to revoke a member's registration as an investment advisor or impose a monetary fine.

4. c This question involves Standard IV(B.7), Disclosure of Conflicts to Clients and Prospects. The question establishes a conflict of interest whereby an analyst, Jamison, is asked to write a research report on a company that is a client of Jamison's employer. In addition, two directors of the company are senior officers of Jamison's employer.

Both facts are conflicts of interest and must be disclosed by Jamison in her research report. Answer *d* would be incorrect because an analyst is not prevented from writing a report because of the special relationship the analyst's employer has with the company so long as that relationship is disclosed. Whether or not Jamison expresses any opinions in the report is irrelevant to her duty to disclose a conflict of interest. Not expressing opinions does not relieve the analyst of her responsibility to disclose the special relationship between the two companies. Therefore, answer *a* is incorrect. Answer *b* is also incorrect. Although an employer should not put pressure on an analyst to alter a report in any way and Jamison cannot change the report based on her employer's influence, the conflict of interest that must be disclosed is the relationship between the two companies.

5. c This question asks about compliance procedures relating to personal investments of members. The statement in answer *c* clearly conflicts with the recommended procedures in the *Handbook*. Employers should compare personal transactions of employees with those of clients on a regular basis regardless of the existence of or request by a regulatory organization. Such comparisons ensure that members' personal trades do not conflict with their duty to their clients, and the comparisons can be conducted in a confidential manner. The statement in answer *a* does not necessarily conflict with the procedures in the *Handbook*. Whether analysts can change their recommendations without prior approval of a supervisory analyst is a policy matter to be determined by the firm. Answer *b* is incorrect because firms are encouraged to establish policies whereby employees clear personal transactions prior to making trades. Answer *d* describes the categories of securities that compliance procedures designed to monitor personal transactions should cover.

6. b This question relates to Standard IV(B.1), Fiduciary Duties, and Standard IV(B.5), Preservation of Confidentiality. In this case, the member manages funds of a private endowment. Members owe a fiduciary duty to their clients, who are in this case the trustees of the fund. Bronson cannot disclose confidential financial information to anyone without the permission of the fund, regardless of whether the disclosure may benefit the fund. Therefore, answer *a* is incorrect. Answer *c* is also incorrect because Bronson must notify the fund and obtain the fund's permission before publicizing the information. Answer *d* is incorrect because, even if the information is nonmaterial, the member cannot disclose the information because it is confidential. Only if Bronson receives permission from the

trustees can he disclose the information to the alumnus.

7. c This question relates to Standard IV(B.2), Portfolio Investment Recommendations and Actions. In this case, Young must decide how to invest funds prior to discussing investment objectives with a client. Standard IV(B.2) requires that members make a reasonable inquiry into a client's financial situation, investment experience, and investment objectives prior to making any investment recommendation. To rely on outdated investment guidelines or firmwide strategies would be improper. Therefore, answers *a* and *b* are incorrect. For Young to make no decision and do nothing but hold the funds, answer *d*, would be equally inappropriate because doing so might violate a member's duty to safeguard the client's interest. The best course of action among the four choices is *c* because it adequately protects the client's interest until investment objectives are established.

8. a This question relates to a member's duty to inform his/her employer of the Code and Standards. The proper method to do so is in writing and through the member's direct supervisor.

9. c Under Standard III(E), Responsibilities of Supervisors, members may delegate supervisory duties to subordinates but such delegation does not relieve members of their supervisory responsibilities. As a result, answers *b* and *d* are incorrect. Moreover, whether or not Miller's subordinates are subject to AIMR's Code and Standards is irrelevant to her supervisory responsibilities. Therefore, answer *a* is incorrect.

10. d This question relates to Standard IV(A.1), Reasonable Basis and Representations. Willier's action in changing the recommendation based on the opinion of another financial analyst is not an adequate basis for the recommendation. Answer *a* is thus incorrect. So is answer *b* because, although it is true that members must distinguish between facts and opinions in recommendations, the question does not illustrate a violation of that nature. Answer *c* is incorrect; whether or not a member has to seek approval from the firm of a change in a recommendation is a matter of policy set by the firm; the Standards do not require that members seek such approval. If the opinion overheard by the member had sparked Willier to conduct additional research and investigation that justified a change of opinion, then a changed recommendation would be appropriate.

11. b This question relates to Standard II(C), Prohibition against Plagiarism, which states that members may use factual information published in recognized financial and statistical reporting services without attribution. Even if the information is communicated

verbally, members must use proper attribution of the material. Therefore, answer *c* is incorrect. Choices *a* and *d* are incorrect because whether or not plagiarized material is combined with a buy/sell recommendation or reported only to the member's employer or associates does not change the fact that the member is copying material without acknowledgment.

12. b Question 12 relates to Standard IV(A.3), Independence and Objectivity. When asked to change a recommendation on a company stock to gain business for the firm, the head of the brokerage unit must refuse in order to maintain his independence and objectivity in making the recommendation. He must not yield to pressure by the firm's investment banking department. To avoid the appearance of a conflict of interest, the firm should discontinue issuing recommendations about the company. Answer *a* is incorrect; changing the recommendation in any manner is a violation of a member's duty to maintain independence and objectivity. Answer *c* is incorrect because merely assigning a new analyst to decide if the stock deserves a higher rating will not address the conflict of interest. Answer *d* would actually exacerbate the conflict of interest.

13. a Standard II(A), Use of the Professional Designation, is the subject of this question. Albert, although still a candidate, uses the CFA designation with the word "candidate" as a modifier on her business card; Tye merely indicates in promotional material that he is participating in the CFA Program and has completed Levels I and II. Candidates may not use the designation in any form prior to actually obtaining their charter. Therefore, Albert has violated Standard II(A). Candidates may communicate that they are participating in the CFA Program, however, and may state the levels that they have completed. Therefore, Tye has not violated Standard II(A).

14. b Question 14 relates to Standard IV(A.2), Research Reports. Scott has issued a research report stating that he expects the price of Walkton Industries stock to rise by $8 a share "because the dividend will increase" by $1.50 per share. He makes this statement knowing that the dividend will increase only if Congress enacts certain legislation, an uncertain prospect. By stating that the dividend will increase, Scott failed to separate fact from opinion. Therefore, statement II is correct. The information regarding passage of legislation is not material inside information because it does not come from or pertain to company operations. Statement I is incorrect, as is statement III.

15. b Question 15, which relates to Standard IV(B.3), Fair Dealing, tests

knowledge of the procedures that will assist members to treat clients fairly when making investment recommendations. The steps listed in *a*, *c*, and *d* will all help ensure the fair treatment of clients. Answer *b*, distributing recommendations to institutional clients before distributing them to individual accounts, discriminates among clients based on size and class of assets and is a violation of Standard IV(B.3).

16. b This question deals with Standard V(A), Prohibition against Use of Material Nonpublic Information. The mosaic theory states that an analyst may use material public information or nonmaterial nonpublic information in creating a larger picture than shown by any individual piece of information and the conclusions the analyst reaches become material only after the pieces are assembled. Answers *a*, *c*, and *d* describe violations of the Code and Standards but are not the mosaic theory.

17. c Question 17 involves Standard III(D), Disclosure of Additional Compensation Arrangements. The arrangement described in the question, whereby Jurgens would be compensated, based on the account's performance, beyond that provided by her firm, is not a violation of the Standards so long as Jurgens discloses the arrangement in writing to her employer and obtains permission from her employer prior to entering into the arrangement. Answer *a* is incorrect; although the private compensation arrangement could conflict with the interests of other clients, members may enter into such agreements so long as they have disclosed the arrangements to their employer and obtained permission for the arrangement from their employer. Answer *d* is also incorrect. Answer *b* is incorrect because members are not required to receive permission from AIMR for such arrangements.

18. b Question 18 involves Standard IV(B.1), Fiduciary Duties—specifically, members' responsibilities for voting proxies and the use of client brokerage. According to the facts stated in the question, Farnsworth did not violate Standard IV(B.1). Although the company president asked Farnsworth to vote the shares of the Jones Corporation profit-sharing plan a certain way, Farnsworth investigated the issue and concluded, independently, the best way to vote. Therefore, even though his decision coincided with the wishes of the company president, Farnsworth is not in violation of his fiduciary duties. In this case, the participants and the beneficiaries of the profit-sharing plan are the clients, not the company's management. Had Farnsworth not investigated the issue or had he yielded to the president's wishes and voted for a slate of directors that he had determined was not in the best interest of the

company, Farnsworth would have violated his fiduciary duties to the beneficiaries of the plan.

In addition, because the brokerage firm provided the lowest commissions and best execution for securities transactions, Farnsworth has met his fiduciary duties to the client in using this brokerage firm. It does not matter that the brokerage firm also provides research information that is not useful for the account generating the commission, because Farnsworth is not paying extra money of the client's for that information. Farnsworth must, however, disclose that he receives research services from the broker.

19. a In this question, Brown is providing investment recommendations before making inquiries about the client's financial situation, investment experience, or investment objectives. Brown is thus violating Standard IV(B.2), Portfolio Investment Recommendations and Actions. As for answer *b*, why the client changed investment firms might be useful information, but it is not the only information the member needs to provide suitable investment recommendations, and Brown is under no obligation to notify AIMR of any violation of the Code and Standards other than her own. Answers *c* and *d* provide examples of information members should discuss with their clients at the outset of the relationship, but these answers do not constitute a complete list of those factors. Answer *a* is the best answer.

20. c Question 20 involves Standard IV(B.6), Prohibition against Misrepresentation. Statement I is a factual statement that discloses to clients and prospects accurate information about the terms of the investment instrument. Statement II, which guarantees a specific rate of return for a mutual fund, is an opinion stated as a fact and, therefore, violates Standard IV(B.6). If statement II were rephrased to include a qualifying statement, such as "in my opinion, investors may earn," it would not be in violation of the Standards.

21. d This question involves three Standards. Anderb, the portfolio manager, has been obtaining lower prices for her personal securities transactions than she gets for her clients, which is a breach of Standard IV(B.1), Fiduciary Duties. In addition, she violated Standard II(B), Professional Misconduct, by failing to adhere to company policy and hiding her personal transactions from her firm. Anderb's supervisor, Bates, violated Standard III(E), Responsibilities of Supervisors; although the company had requirements for reporting personal trading, Bates failed to adequately enforce those procedures. Therefore, statements I, II, and III are all correct.

22. a Question 22 relates to Standard I, Fundamental Responsibilities—specifically, international application of the Code and Standards. Members who practice in multiple jurisdictions may be subject to various securities laws and regulations. If applicable law is more strict than the requirements of the Code and Standards, members must adhere to applicable law; otherwise, members must adhere to the Code and Standards. Therefore, statement I is correct. Statement II is incorrect because members must adhere to the higher standard set by the Code and Standards if local applicable law is less strict. Statement III is incorrect because when no applicable law exists, members are required to adhere to the Code and Standards.

23. b The best course of action under Standard IV(A.3), Independence and Objectivity, is to avoid a conflict of interest whenever possible. Therefore, paying for all expenses is the correct answer. Answer *c* details a course of action in which the conflict would be disclosed, but the solution is not as appropriate as avoiding the conflict of interest. Answer *a* would not be the best course because it would not remove the appearance of a conflict of interest; even though the report would not be affected by the reimbursement of expenses, it could appear to be. Answer *d* is not appropriate because, by failing to take advantage of close inspection of the company, Ward would not be using all the information available in completing his report.

24. c Standard III(B), Duty to Employer, states that members may undertake independent practice that may result in compensation or other benefit in competition with their employer so long as they obtain written consent from both their employer and those for whom they undertake the independent practice. [Note that Standard III(D), Disclosure of Additional Compensation Arrangements, also requires that members disclose in writing all monetary compensation or other benefits they receive in addition to those paid by their employer.] Statements II and III are consistent with Standard III(B). Statement I is not correct because the Standards do not include a complete prohibition against undertaking independent practice. Statement IV is also incorrect because the Standards allow members to make arrangements or preparations to go into competitive business so long as those arrangements do not interfere with their duty to their current employer.

25. c Question 25 relates to AIMR's summary suspension powers as defined in the organization's Bylaws and discussed in "AIMR's Professional Conduct Program." Statements I, II, and III describe grounds for summary suspension of membership in AIMR and/or the right to hold and use the CFA designation.

26. c This question involves Standard IV(B.7), Disclosure of Conflicts to Clients and Prospects, and Standard III(C), Disclosure of Conflicts to Employer. Statements I, II, and III describe conflicts of interest for Smithers or her firm that would have to be disclosed. Statement I describes an employment relationship between the analyst and the company that is the subject of the recommendation. Statement II describes the beneficial interest of the analyst's employer in the company's stock, and statement III describes the analyst's own beneficial interest in the company stock. In statement IV, the relationship between the analyst and the company through a relative is so tangential that it does not create a conflict of interest necessitating disclosure.

27. d Question 27 relates to Standard IV(B.6), Prohibition against Misrepresentation. Although Michelieu's statement regarding the total return of his client's accounts on average may be technically true, it is misleading because the majority of the gain resulted from one client's large position taken against Michelieu's advice. Therefore, this statement misrepresents the investment performance the member is responsible for. He has not taken steps to present a fair, accurate, and complete presentation of performance. Answer *c* is thus incorrect. Answer *b* is incorrect because although Michelieu is not guaranteeing future results, his words are still a misrepresentation of performance. Answer *a* is incorrect because failing to disclose the risk preferences of clients does not make a statement misleading and is not a violation of the Standards in this context.

28. b The best policy to prevent violation of Standard V(A), Prohibition against Use of Material Nonpublic Information, is the establishment of "Fire Walls" within a firm to prevent exchange of insider information. The physical and informational barrier of a Fire Wall between the investment banking department and the brokerage operation prevents the investment banking department from providing information to analysts on the brokerage side who may be writing recommendations regarding a company stock. Prohibiting recommendations of the stock of companies that are clients of the investment banking department is an alternative, but answer *a* states that this prohibition would be permanent, which is not the best answer. Once an offering is complete and the material nonpublic information obtained by the investment banking department becomes public, resuming publishing recommendations on the stock is not a violation of the Code and Standards because the information of the investment banking department no longer gives the brokerage operation an advantage in writing the report.

Answer *c* is incorrect; whether or not a fiduciary duty is owed to clients does not override the prohibition against use of material nonpublic information. Therefore, allowing the sale of current holdings by clients based on information obtained from the investment brokerage department would violate Standard V(A). Answer *d* is incorrect because no exchange of information should be occurring between the investment banking department and the brokerage operation, so no monitoring of such exchanges should be occurring.

29. c Under Standard IV(B.1), Fiduciary Duties, members who manage a company's pension funds owe a fiduciary duty to the participants and benefits of the plan, not the management of the company or the company shareholders.

30. a Question 30 relates to Standard IV(B.8), Disclosure of Referral Fees. Statements I and II give the two primary reasons listed in the *Standards of Practice Handbook* for disclosing referral fees to clients. The purpose given in statement III is not a primary consideration.

APPENDIX
Association for Investment Management and Research

Rules of Procedure for Proceedings Related to Professional Conduct

As amended and restated February 6, 1998

Rule 1: Preamble

"Covered Person(s)," as defined in Article 2 of the Association for Investment Management and Research (AIMR) Restated Bylaws (herein *Bylaws*), are required to conduct their activities in accordance with the AIMR Code of Ethics and Standards of Professional Conduct (herein Code and Standards). This document, "Rules of Procedure for Proceedings Related to Professional Conduct" (herein Rules of Procedure or the rules), governs the procedures to which both AIMR and Covered Persons must adhere when a professional conduct matter is being investigated.[1]

Rule 2: Discipline

2.1 Authority of the Professional Standards and Policy Committee.

The Professional Standards and Policy Committee (PSPC), a committee of the AIMR Board (herein Board), or an officer or subcommittee designated by the PSPC shall conduct disciplinary investigations and impose disciplinary sanctions (herein Sanctions) upon Covered Persons in accordance with the *Bylaws* and the *Rules of Procedure*.

The PSPC may exercise its authority and duties through subcommittees, hearing panels, review panels, and as otherwise permitted in the *Bylaws*, with said positions to be filled by members of PSPC subcommittees and members of the AIMR Board of Governors under PSPC direction.

The Disciplinary Review Subcommittee (herein DRS), acting on behalf of the PSPC, is responsible for (a) enforcement of the Code and Standards; (b) reviewing and recommending amendments to the

[1]The Rules of Procedure are supplemental to and not in lieu of the Bylaws. If there is any conflict between the Rules of Procedure and the Bylaws, the Bylaws prevail.

Rules of Procedure; (c) reviewing and approving all stipulated disciplinary matters; (d) upon request of the Designated Officer, reviewing and approving "Summary Suspensions," as defined herein; and (e) such other matters as the PSPC shall request.

The Standards and Policy Subcommittee (SPS), acting on behalf of the PSPC, is responsible for (a) reviewing and revising the Code and Standards; (b) promoting the Code and Standards; (c) reviewing and revising AIMR's professional conduct handbook or similar publication; (d) reviewing and revising AIMR's self-administered standards of practice examination; (e) reviewing and revising AIMR's annual professional conduct statement; (f) assisting in professional conduct investigations, as deemed appropriate by the PSPC or its designees; and (g) such other matters as the PSPC shall request.

2.2 Grounds for Discipline.

Disciplinary action may be imposed upon Covered Persons for (a) violation of AIMR's Articles of Incorporation (*Articles*) and *Bylaws*, affiliate organizations' articles and bylaws, the Code and Standards, the Member's Agreement (as defined in Article 2 of the *Bylaws*), and/or the *Rules of Procedure* or other applicable rules; (b) the imposition of a disciplinary sanction or injunction by a governmental or judicial agency or by a public or private self-regulatory organization with jurisdiction over investment-related or similar activities, including securities, commodities, investment management, and financial analysis activities; (c) conviction for or guilty plea to a crime defined as a felony under the laws of the convicting jurisdiction, or if the laws of the convicting jurisdiction do not define felony, any crime punishable by more than one year in prison; (d) having been barred permanently, or for an indefinite period of time, from registration under the securities laws or similar laws relating to investments or from association or affiliation with a governmental or judicial agency or by a public or private self-regulatory organization with jurisdiction over investment-related or similar activities, including securities, commodities, investment management, and financial analysis activities; (e) failure to complete, sign, and return to AIMR, on an annual basis, the required annual professional conduct statement; (f) falsification of information, as applicable, on candidate or society membership applications; and/or (g) any "good cause," which shall include failure by Covered Person to cooperate with AIMR in its inquiry and investigation of the Covered Person's professional conduct.

2.3 Sanctions.

Sanctions include the following actions:

(a) *Private Censure.* The least severe sanction, private censure may be announced publicly, as defined in Rule 2.5, excluding Covered Person's name or other specifically identifying information.

(b) *Public Censure.* This sanction may be announced publicly as defined in Rule 2.5, including the Covered Person's name.

(c) *Timed Suspension of Membership.* Covered Person's membership in AIMR and its affiliate organizations and member societies is suspended for a specified period of time.

(d) *Timed Suspension of the Right to Use the CFA Designation* (hereafter Timed Suspension of Professional Designation). Covered Person's use of the CFA designation is suspended for a specified period of time.

(e) *Revocation of Membership.* A Covered Person's membership in AIMR and its affiliate organizations and member societies is permanently revoked.

(f) *Revocation of the Right to Use the CFA Designation* (hereafter Revocation of Professional Designation). A Covered Person's right to use the CFA designation is permanently revoked.

(g) *Summary Suspension.* This sanction automatically removes membership in AIMR and its affiliate organizations and member societies, the right to use the CFA designation, and/or the right to participate in the CFA Program.

(h) *Suspension or Revocation from Further Participation in the CFA Professional Designation Study and Examination Program* (hereafter Suspension/Revocation from Candidate Examination Program). Covered Person is automatically and/or permanently removed from participation in the Candidate Examination Program.

2.4 Notice of Disciplinary Action.

All Sanctions shall contain a "Notice of Disciplinary Action" that summarizes (a) the nature of the matter and disciplinary proceeding; (b) the applicable code, standard(s), and/or rule(s) that were violated; and (c) other appropriate information as determined by the PSPC, subject to the *Bylaws* and the rules.

2.5 Announcement of Sanctions.

Sanctions shall be announced in the manner determined by the PSPC pursuant to these rules.

All Sanctions shall be promptly communicated to the Covered Person. Public Sanctions, including Summary Suspension, shall be (a) announced in the *AIMR Exchange* or other AIMR publication(s) and may include information contained in the Notice of Disciplinary Action; (b) delivered to the Covered Person's regulator(s), along with information listed under Rule 11.2, "Exceptions to Confidentiality Policy"; and (c) announced to any member society of which the Covered Person is a member.

Private Censure and other private sanctions shall be announced in the *AIMR Exchange* or other AIMR publication(s) and may include information contained in the Notice of Disciplinary Action, with the exception of the Covered Person's name and other specifically identifying information.

2.6 Notice.

Documents sent to a Covered Person shall be deemed received by the Covered Person if such documents are mailed postage prepaid to the Covered Person at the last known preferred address shown in AIMR records.

It is the responsibility of the Covered Person to keep AIMR advised of his or her current mailing address, as stated in the Membership Agreement and annual Professional Conduct Statement.

Rule 3: Investigation

3.1 Designated Officer.

The Designated Officer, as defined in the *Bylaws*, may appoint designees, acting on his or her behalf, to assist in performing functions related to professional conduct inquiries.

3.2 Commencement.

The Designated Officer may conduct an investigation of any matter involving, or appearing to involve, the professional conduct of a Covered Person. The Designated Officer is authorized to (a) request assistance from the PSPC or a subcommittee thereof, (b) contact regulatory and other professional associations or advisors to assist in the investigation, and (c) contact any other party that may be able to provide assistance in the investigation.

3.3 Complaining Party.

Any person (hereafter referred to as the Complaining Party) who files a written complaint with AIMR concerning a Covered Person's professional conduct is requested to furnish the Designated Officer, or designees, with the following: (a) a statement of the circumstances underlying the complaint, and (b) copies of any supporting documentation that the Complaining Party believes will assist the Designated Officer in determining whether the Covered Person has failed to comply with the Code and Standards or other governing rules.

The identity of the Complaining Party will be made known to the Covered Person who is the subject of the complaint unless the Complaining Party specifically requests, in writing to the Designated Officer, that the source of the complaint remain anonymous. If anonymity is requested, the Designated Officer and other individuals involved in the investigation will make every reasonable effort to safeguard the identity of the Complaining Party, subject to the confidentiality provisions in these rules. Efforts to protect the anonymity of a Complaining Party may hamper AIMR's ability to investigate a given complaint, including AIMR's ability to establish that a violation has occurred.

3.4 Notice of Inquiry.

The Designated Officer shall furnish the Covered Person involved with a "Notice of Inquiry" and any other information that will reasonably assist the Covered Person in responding to the inquiry, including a copy of the *Rules of Procedure*, the *Articles* and *Bylaws*, the Code and Standards, and notice of the right to be represented by counsel.

The Covered Person shall respond in writing within thirty (30) days of receipt of the Notice of Inquiry.

Failure to respond to a Notice of Inquiry or any other request to submit information relating to the Covered Person's professional conduct shall constitute grounds for Summary Suspension for "failure to cooperate" as detailed in these rules.

3.5 Communications Regarding Inquiry.

All communications regarding the Notice of Inquiry and any subsequent investigation or proceeding, as detailed in these rules, must be directed to the Designated Officer or designee. Any communications on behalf of the Covered Person, regarding an inquiry or proceeding, to persons other than the Designated Officer or designee that may affect the integrity of an inquiry or proceeding shall result in the matter being automatically referred to the DRS or a subcommittee thereof. The DRS, or subcommittee thereof, will then assume the responsibility of the Designated Officer and resume the inquiry or proceeding.

3.6 Continuation of Proceeding after Resignation.

Disciplinary proceedings may continue and the Board, Designated Officer, or applicable subcommittee may impose disciplinary sanctions (notwithstanding a Covered Person's resignation from AIMR, from affiliate organizations, and/or as a holder of the CFA professional designation or status as a Postponed Candidate) if such disciplinary proceedings, as evidenced by the sending of a Notice of Inquiry, were commenced prior to such resignation or postponed status.

Rule 4: Action by the Designated Officer and the DRS

4.1 Termination of an Inquiry.

If the Designated Officer determines that there is not sufficient evidence to proceed with an inquiry, then he or she shall notify the Covered Person in writing and terminate the inquiry, except as otherwise provided herein. Termination of an inquiry shall not preclude the reopening of an inquiry at a future date involving the same allegations or conduct, based upon additional evidence.

4.2 Private Censure.

At the conclusion of an inquiry, if the Designated Officer determines that the Covered Person has committed a minor violation of the Code and Standards, the Designated Officer may impose a Private Censure on the Covered Person.

A Covered Person who receives a Notice of Private Censure shall have the right to reject the sanction by submitting to the Designated Officer a written rejection, accompanied by a written explanation, within thirty (30) days of the receipt of the notice. Failure to reject a Private Censure in writing shall constitute acceptance of the sanction.

The Private Censure shall not be imposed until (a) the Designated Officer has furnished the Covered Person with a Notice of Inquiry followed by a Notice of Private Censure and (b) the specified time has passed for the Covered Person to reject the Private Censure.

If the Covered Person rejects the Private Censure, the Designated Officer shall continue the inquiry or refer the matter to a "Hearing Panel," as described in Rule 5, "Request for Hearing."

If the Covered Person accepts the Private Censure, or fails to reject the Private Censure in writing within thirty (30) days of the receipt of the Notice of Private Censure, the determination of the Designated Officer and the imposition of the Private Censure shall be final and conclusive. In such event, the Covered Person shall be deemed to have admitted the violations, accepted the sanction, and waived all rights of appeal to the PSPC.

4.3 Stipulation Agreement.

At the conclusion of an inquiry, the Designated Officer may enter into a "Stipulation Agreement" with the Covered Person to terminate a professional conduct inquiry by (a) Public Censure; (b) Timed Suspension of Membership; (c) Timed Suspension of Professional Designation; (d) Revocation of Membership; (e) Revocation of Professional Designation; and/or (f) Suspension/Revocation from Candidate Examination Program.

Prior to entering into a Stipulation Agreement, the Covered Person shall be informed in writing that if the Stipulation Agreement is accepted, the Covered Person shall be deemed to have waived the right to further review by a Hearing Panel or the PSPC.

If the Covered Person does not consent to the Stipulation Agreement, he or she may request a Hearing before a Hearing Panel, as described in Rule 5, "Request for Hearing."

4.4 Covered Person Consents to Stipulation Agreement.

The Stipulation Agreement shall (a) be signed by the Covered Person and the Designated Officer, or designee; (b) contain a summary of the facts related to the alleged misconduct; and (c) state the sanction recommended by the Designated Officer and agreed to by the Covered Person.

The Stipulation Agreement shall be forwarded to the DRS, or a subcommittee thereof, which shall review the Stipulation Agreement and impose sanctions, if any. The DRS, or a subcommittee thereof, may (a) impose the same or lesser sanction; (b) dismiss the matter; or (c) refer the matter back to the Designated Officer or the DRS Chair for additional investigation and action.

Throughout the inquiry, every reasonable attempt will be made to negotiate a Stipulation Agreement with the Covered Person.

4.5 Covered Person Does Not Consent to Stipulation Agreement.

If the Covered Person does not explicitly accept or deny the proposed Stipulation Agreement within thirty (30) days after receipt by the Covered Person, then the Designated Officer will refer the matter to the PSPC Chair who shall designate a Hearing Panel. The Hearing Panel shall proceed pursuant to Rule 5, "Request for Hearing."

Rule 5: Request for Hearing

5.1 Notice of Hearing, Statement of Charges, and Designation of Hearing Panel.

Upon receipt of a "Statement of Charges" from the Designated Officer or the DRS, the PSPC Chair shall designate a Hearing Panel, consisting of three to five members, which shall hear the charges and render a decision. At least one of the members of the Hearing Panel shall be a member of the PSPC; however, the PSPC Chair shall not serve on the Hearing Panel. The remaining members may be appointed by the PSPC Chair from the Board of Governors or from the PSPC subcommittees. The PSPC Chair shall designate one member of the Hearing Panel to serve as Hearing Panel Chair. No member of the Hearing Panel who indicates a conflict of interest or who has been previously involved in the investigation of the matter shall serve on the Hearing Panel.

5.2 Pre-Hearing Procedures.

All Hearings will be held by telephone conference call unless an "In-Person Hearing" is requested by the Covered Person, in writing addressed to the Designated Officer.

The Designated Officer shall schedule a date and time (and place if the Covered Person requests an In-Person Hearing) promptly after receiving a request for Hearing by the Covered Person. If a mutually agreeable date and time is not provided by the Covered Person to the Designated Officer within thirty (30) days, the Hearing Panel Chair shall determine the date and time (and place if applicable) for the Hearing and give the Covered Person thirty (30) days notice thereof. The notice shall include the Statement of Charges and inform the Covered Person of the right (a) to have a reasonable opportunity to be heard in his or her own defense, (b) to be represented by counsel, (c) to present witnesses and evidence, and (d) to cross-examine any witness.

The Hearing shall be held within 120 days of the request for Hearing by the Covered Person. Once a Hearing has been scheduled, any requests by the Covered Person to reschedule the Hearing shall be submitted, in writing, to the Hearing Panel Chair. The Hearing Panel Chair shall have sole discretion to grant or deny the Covered Person's request to reschedule the Hearing.

The Covered Person may furnish to the Hearing Panel written information or demonstrative evidence on his or her behalf. Any written information or evidence not received by the Designated Officer at least fourteen (14) days prior to the Hearing shall not be considered by the Hearing Panel. The Covered Person shall provide eight (8) copies of such information or evidence to the Designated Officer, who shall provide the information to the Hearing Panel. At least fourteen (14) days prior to the Hearing, the Covered Person shall also provide the Designated Officer with a list of all witnesses that will testify at the Hearing on the Covered Person's behalf, including the name, address, and telephone number of the witness and a brief description of the expected testimony of each witness.

The Designated Officer may also submit written material to the Hearing Panel. Such submission shall be sent to the Hearing Panel, in conjunction with any material submitted by the Covered Person, no later than seven (7) days prior to the Hearing. The Covered Person shall receive a copy of the Designated Officer's submission to the Hearing Panel.

5.3 Hearing Procedures.

At the outset of the Hearing, the Hearing Panel Chair shall make a short statement detailing the nature and purpose of the Hearing and the procedures by which the Hearing shall be governed. The Hearing Panel Chair shall administer an oath to all witnesses, including the Covered Person, prior to their testimony.

The Designated Officer, designee, or if applicable, DRS member shall present evidence in support of the recommended sanction at the Hearing or may waive that right and rely upon its written submission. The Covered Person shall then present any written information and/ or demonstrative evidence in the Covered Person's defense. The Designated Officer, designee, or if applicable, DRS member shall have the opportunity to respond to the evidence and/or statement made by the Covered Person.

The Hearing Panel shall not be bound by the rules of evidence applicable in courts of law, and the Hearing Panel Chair may exclude matters that, in his or her judgment, are irrelevant. Any member of the Hearing Panel can ask questions or request further information at any time during the course of the Hearing.

At the conclusion of the Hearing, the Hearing Panel shall deliberate, outside the presence of the Covered Person and Designated Officer, designee, or if applicable, DRS member to make a determination regarding the appropriate sanction, if any. A finding of misconduct shall be established by a preponderance of the evidence.

A recording of the hearing shall be made. The cost of the recording shall be paid by AIMR.

5.4 Hearing Panel Report and Determination.

The Hearing Panel shall prepare a report of its findings and determination. The report shall include findings of fact related to the alleged misconduct of the Covered Person; findings as to the violations, if any, of the rules related to professional conduct; or other basis for the Sanction. The report and determination shall be delivered to the Covered Person and to the PSPC Chair within thirty (30) days after the Hearing. The Sanction, if any, recommended by the Hearing Panel shall be imposed unless the Covered Person requests a review by the PSPC as described below.

5.5 Review of Hearing Panel Determination.

If disciplinary action is imposed by the Hearing Panel as described above, the Covered Person may request a review of the Hearing Panel decision. The recommended Sanction shall be imposed unless the Review Panel determines that, because of exceptional or unusual circumstances, it would be inequitable to impose the sanction determined by the Hearing Panel.

The Covered Person must submit a written request for review of the Hearing Panel decision to the Designated Officer within thirty (30) days of the date of the Hearing Panel decision.

The PSPC Chair shall appoint a Review Panel to consider the Hearing Panel's determination. The Review Panel shall meet by telephone conference call. The Review Panel shall consist of three to five members, appointed by the PSPC Chair from the Board of Governors or from the PSPC. The Review Panel shall not include any of the members of the PSPC who indicate a conflict of interest or who may have been previously involved in the inquiry of the Covered Person's conduct or the Hearing Panel. Within thirty (30) days after the request for review of the Hearing Panel decision, the Covered Person may furnish written material or information pertaining to whether it would be inequitable to continue the sanction determined by the Hearing Panel because of exceptional or unusual circumstances.

The Review Panel shall request from the Covered Person, the Hearing Panel Chair, and/or the Designated Officer any additional information it reasonably believes necessary to reach a determination. The Hearing Panel Chair or designee shall present the matter to the Review Panel in support of the Hearing Panel's determination. Within thirty (30) days of its review, the Review Panel shall notify the Covered Person of its determination. The Review Panel's determination is final and conclusive.

Rule 6: Summary Suspension

6.1 Defined.

Summary Suspension constitutes removal (a) from membership in AIMR and its affiliate organizations, (b) from membership in Member Societies, (c) of the right to use the CFA designation, and/or (d) from participation in the CFA Program.

6.2 Grounds for Summary Suspension.

The Designated Officer or DRS shall impose a Summary Suspension upon a Covered Person if the Covered Person (a) is convicted, pleads guilty, or consents to a crime that is defined as a felony under the laws of the convicting jurisdiction or, if the laws of the convicting jurisdiction do not define felony, any crime punishable by more than one year in prison (herein category "A"); (b) is barred permanently, or for an indefinite period of time, from registration under the securities laws or similar laws relating to investments or from association or affiliation with a governmental or judicial agency or by a public or private self-regulatory organization with jurisdiction over investment-related or similar activities, including securities, commodities, investment management, and financial analysis activities (herein category "B"); (c) fails to cooperate with AIMR in its investigation of the member's conduct (herein category "C"); or (d) fails to complete, sign, and return to AIMR, on an annual basis, the required annual professional conduct statement in the form adopted by AIMR (herein category "D").

6.3 Summary Suspension for Conviction or Bar (Categories A and B).

If Summary Suspension is based on Categories A and B, the Designated Officer shall obtain a verified copy of the final ruling in the matter, after which, the Covered Person shall automatically receive a Summary Suspension. The Designated Officer shall notify the Covered Person of the automatic Summary Suspension and the Covered Person's right to petition for a review of the suspension before a "Summary Suspension Review Panel," as described in Rule 7, "Request for Review by Summary Suspension Review Panel."

If the Covered Person submits a written request for review of the Summary Suspension to the Designated Officer within thirty (30) days of notification of the Summary Suspension, the Designated Officer shall promptly deliver such request to the PSPC Chair, who shall proceed as described in Rule 7, "Request for Review by Summary Suspension Review Panel."

After the conclusion of the thirty (30) day period, if the Covered Person has not submitted a written request for review of the Summary Suspension, the Covered Person may not submit a request for review of the Summary Suspension until one (1) year has elapsed since the date of Summary Suspension. No additional request for review of a Summary Suspension shall be accepted within one (1) year of a denial by the Summary Suspension Review Panel of a previous request.

Summary Suspension shall be announced in the same or similar manner outlined under Rule 2.5, "Announcement of Sanctions."

A Summary Suspension shall automatically become a Revocation of Membership and/or CFA designation if the Covered Person does not petition for review of the Summary Suspension within five years from the date of Summary Suspension.

The Summary Suspension shall be terminated immediately upon filing with the Designated Officer a certificate demonstrating that the underlying criminal conviction or professional suspension has been reversed; however, the PSPC may continue its inquiry of the matter unabated.

If the Summary Suspension has been terminated, a notice thereof may, at the written request of the Covered Person, be announced in the same or similar manner as described in Rule 2.5, "Announcement of Sanctions."

6.4 Summary Suspension for Failure to Cooperate (Category C).

If Summary Suspension is based on category C, the suspension shall not be imposed until the Covered Person has been furnished with a Notice of Summary Suspension.

A Covered Person who has been issued a Notice of Summary Suspension shall have the right to object to the suspension by cooperating with the inquiry or by submitting to the Designated Officer a written objection and request for review of the Summary Suspension, accompanied by a written explanation within thirty (30) days of the receipt of the Notice. Failure to object to the Summary Suspension, within thirty (30) days of receipt of the Notice, in writing, shall constitute acceptance thereof.

If the Covered Person submits a written request for review of the Summary Suspension to the Designated Officer within thirty (30) days of notification of the Summary Suspension, the Designated Officer shall promptly deliver such request to the PSPC Chair who shall proceed as described in Rule 7, "Request for Review by Summary Suspension Review Panel."

After the conclusion of the thirty (30) day period, if the Covered Person has not submitted a written request for review of the Summary Suspension, the Covered Person may not submit a request for review of the Summary Suspension until one (1) year has elapsed since the date of Summary Suspension. No additional request for review of a Summary Suspension shall be accepted within one (1) year of a denial by the Summary Suspension Review Panel of a previous request.

Summary Suspension shall be announced in the same or similar manner outlined under Rule 2.5, "Announcement of Sanctions."

A Summary Suspension shall automatically become a Revocation of Membership and/or CFA designation if the Covered Person does not petition for review of the Summary Suspension within five years from the date of Summary Suspension.

If the Summary Suspension has been terminated, a notice thereof may, at the written request of the Covered Person, be announced in the same or similar manner as described in Rule 2.5, "Announcement of Sanctions."

6.5 Summary Suspension for Failure to File Annual Statement (Category D).

If Summary Suspension is based on category D, the suspension shall not be imposed until the Covered Person has been furnished with a Notice of Summary Suspension.

A Covered Person who has been issued a Notice of Summary Suspension shall have the right to object to the suspension by submitting to the Designated Officer a written objection and request for review of the Summary Suspension, accompanied by a written explanation within thirty (30) days of the receipt of the Notice. Failure to object to the Summary Suspension, within thirty (30) days of receipt of the Notice, in writing, shall constitute acceptance thereof.

If the Covered Person submits a written objection to the Notice of Summary Suspension to the Designated Officer and complies with his or her obligation to file professional conduct statements for the years that he or she was delinquent, as well as for any years subsequent to the suspension, then the Designated Officer shall promptly review the matter. The Designated Officer may require the Covered Person to demonstrate a fitness to practice financial analysis and professional competence and such other conditions as may be reasonably required by the Designated Officer, including the passing of a self-administered standards of practice examination.

Upon conclusion of the review, the Summary Suspension may be terminated by the Designated Officer. If the Summary Suspension is not terminated by the Designated Officer and if the Covered Person submits a written request to the Designated Officer for further review within thirty (30) days of notice that the Summary Suspension has not been terminated, the Designated Officer shall promptly deliver such request to the PSPC Chair, who shall proceed as described in Rule 7, "Request for Review by Summary Suspension Review Panel."

No additional request for review of a Summary Suspension shall be accepted within one (1) year of a denial by the Summary Suspension Review Panel of a previous request.

Summary Suspension shall be announced in the same or similar manner outlined under Rule 2.5, "Announcement of Sanctions."

A Summary Suspension shall automatically become a Revocation of Membership and/or CFA designation if the Covered Person does not request a review of the Summary Suspension within five (5) years from the date of Summary Suspension.

If the Summary Suspension has been terminated, a notice thereof may, at the written request of the Covered Person, be announced in the same or similar manner as described in Rule 2.5, "Announcement of Sanctions."

Rule 7: Request for Review by Summary Suspension Review Panel

7.1 Designation of Summary Suspension Review Panel.

Upon receipt of a request for review of the Summary Suspension from the Designated Officer, the PSPC Chair shall designate a Summary Suspension Review Panel, consisting of three to five members appointed from the PSPC, DRS, and/or SPS. The PSPC Chair shall not serve on the Summary Suspension Review Panel. The PSPC Chair shall designate one member of the Summary Suspension Review Panel to serve as Summary Suspension Review Panel Chair. No member who indicates a conflict of interest or who has been previously involved in the investigation of the matter shall serve on the Summary Suspension Review Panel.

7.2 Pre-Review Panel Procedures.

All proceedings of the Summary Suspension Review Panel shall be held by telephone conference call.

The Designated Officer shall schedule a date and time for the proceeding promptly after receiving a petition for review of the Summary Suspension by the Covered Person. If a mutually agreeable date and time is not provided by the Covered Person to the Designated Officer within thirty (30) days, the Summary Suspension Review Panel Chair shall determine the date and time for the Summary Suspension Review Panel. The Summary Suspension Review Panel Chair shall give the Covered Person thirty (30) days written notice thereof. The notice shall include the "Statement of Charges" and inform the Covered Person of the right (a) to have a reasonable opportunity to be heard in his or her own defense, (b) to be represented by counsel, (c) to present witnesses and evidence, and (d) to cross-examine any witness.

The Summary Suspension Review Panel shall be held within ninety (90) days of the written petition for review. Once a Summary

Suspension Review Panel has been scheduled, any requests by the Covered Person to reschedule the Summary Suspension Review Panel shall be submitted, in writing, to the Summary Suspension Review Panel Chair. The Summary Suspension Review Panel Chair shall have sole discretion to grant or deny the Covered Person's request to reschedule the Review Panel proceeding.

The Covered Person may furnish to the Summary Suspension Review Panel written information or demonstrative evidence on his or her behalf. Any written information or evidence not received by the Designated Officer at least fourteen (14) days prior to the proceeding shall not be considered by the Summary Suspension Review Panel. The Covered Person shall provide eight (8) copies of such information or evidence to the Designated Officer, who shall provide the information to the Summary Suspension Review Panel. At least fourteen (14) days prior to the proceeding, the Covered Person shall also provide the Designated Officer with a list of all witnesses who will testify at the proceeding on the Covered Person's behalf, including the name, address, telephone number, and a brief description of the expected testimony of each witness.

The Designated Officer may also submit written material to the Summary Suspension Review Panel. Such submission shall be sent to the Summary Suspension Review Panel, in conjunction with any material submitted by the Covered Person, no later than seven (7) days prior to the proceeding. The Covered Person shall receive a copy of the Designated Officer's submission to the Summary Suspension Review Panel.

7.3 Review Panel Procedures.

The Designated Officer, designee, or if applicable, DRS member shall present evidence in support of the Summary Suspension to the Summary Suspension Review Panel or may waive that right and rely upon his or her written submission. The Covered Person shall then present any written information and/or demonstrative evidence in the Covered Person's defense. The Designated Officer, designee, or if applicable, DRS member shall have the opportunity to respond to the evidence and/or statement made by the Covered Person.

The Summary Suspension Review Panel shall not be bound by the rules of evidence applicable in courts of law, and the Summary Suspension Review Panel Chair may exclude matters that, in his or her judgment, are irrelevant. Any member of the Summary Suspension Review Panel can ask questions or request further information at any time during the course of the proceeding.

At the conclusion of the Summary Suspension Review Panel proceeding, the Summary Suspension Review Panel shall deliberate, outside the presence of the Covered Person and Designated Officer, designee, or if applicable, DRS member. The Summary Suspension shall be terminated if the Summary Suspension Review Panel determines that, because of exceptional or unusual circumstances, continuing the Summary Suspension would be inequitable to the Covered Person.

7.4 Summary Suspension Review Panel Report and Determination.

The Summary Suspension Review Panel shall prepare a report of its findings and determination. If the Summary Suspension Review Panel determines not to terminate the Summary Suspension, such notification shall contain a statement of reasons for the decision. The report and determination shall be delivered to the Covered Person and to the PSPC Chair within thirty (30) days of the proceeding.

The Summary Suspension Review Panel's determination is final and conclusive.

The fact that a Covered Person has received a Summary Suspension shall not prevent continuation of the investigation or the imposition of other Sanctions pursuant to the *Bylaws* and these rules.

Rule 8: Reinstatement Following Timed Suspension

A Covered Person who has received a timed suspension, either through Stipulation Agreement or determination by Hearing Panel and/or Review Panel, shall be reinstated upon the expiration of the period of suspension, provided the Covered Person completes and files a professional conduct statement with AIMR confirming that he or she has not been the subject of any disciplinary action since the suspension became effective.

Rule 9: Reinstatement Following Revocation

9.1 Petition for Reinstatement Following Revocation.

A Covered Person whose membership and/or CFA designation has been revoked may seek reinstatement of the revoked privileges. To be eligible to seek an order of reinstatement, the Covered Person must (a) wait at least five (5) years after the effective date of the Revocation of Membership; (b) demonstrate to the PSPC's satisfaction fitness to practice financial analysis and professional competence, which shall include sufficient evidence demonstrating rehabilitation and full compliance with all disciplinary orders; and (c) adhere to such other conditions as may be reasonably required by the PSPC, including the completion and filing of a professional conduct statement and passage of a self-administered standards of practice examination.

9.2 Investigation.

Promptly upon receipt of a "Petition for Reinstatement," the Designated Officer shall conduct an investigation as may be necessary. The petitioner shall cooperate in any investigation. The Designated Officer, upon completion of the investigation, shall submit a report to the PSPC including the petitioner's past disciplinary record and any recommendation regarding reinstatement.

9.3 Successive Petitions.

No petition for reinstatement shall be accepted within two (2) years following a denial of a previous petition for reinstatement.

Rule 10: Waiver of All Rights and Proceedings

A Covered Person may—at any point in the proceedings prior to final action by the Designated Officer, DRS, Hearing Panel, Summary Suspension Review Panel, or PSPC—waive any or all procedures provided herein and tender a "conditional admission of misconduct," constituting grounds for discipline. The conditional admission shall be made in writing and in a form acceptable to the Designated Officer. The Designated Officer shall submit the Covered Person's conditional admission of misconduct to the PSPC, or a subcommittee thereof, for final review and approval.

Rule 11: Confidentiality of Proceedings

11.1 Confidentiality Policy.

Except as otherwise provided, all proceedings conducted pursuant to these rules shall be confidential and the records of proceedings shall remain confidential and shall not be made public.

11.2 Exceptions to Confidentiality Policy.

The pendency, subject matter, and status of proceedings conducted pursuant to these rules may be disclosed if the alleged violation is a clear violation of law or regulations or if it caused or has the potential to cause serious harm to the investment management profession, the financial analysis community, and/or the general public. Additional exceptions include (a) violation predicated on criminal conviction or bar as defined herein, (b) waiver of confidentiality by the Covered Person, or (c) disclosure as required by legal process of a court of law or other governmental body or agency having appropriate jurisdiction.

In addition, the PSPC or its designee may provide copies of the following information to the Covered Person's regulator(s): (a) the Stipulation Agreement; (b) the Notice of Disciplinary Action; (c) decisions of the Hearing Panel and/or Review Panel; (d) information determined by the Designated Officer to be publicly available; (e) information obtained by AIMR prior to the Covered Person's disclosure of such information to AIMR; (f) information that AIMR received from sources other than the Covered Person, so long as AIMR does not breach an obligation of confidentiality owed by AIMR; (g) information received by AIMR from the Covered Person without restrictions on its disclosure; and (h) such additional information of the type and scope that the receiving regulator is legally permitted to keep confidential (e.g., exempt from the Freedom of Information Act disclosure requirements).

The Designated Officer may seek confirmation from the PSPC, or its designated committee or subcommittee representative, as deemed necessary regarding the above noted exceptions.

Rule 12: Records

A record of all investigations, appeals, hearings, recommendations, determinations, and actions in all matters involving a Covered Person's conduct shall be preserved for six (6) years, two of which shall be in a readily accessible location.

A

B

C

E

F

L

M

O

P

Q

R

S

T

U

V

W